Web Services in Finance

DR. PAUL A. WATTERS

Apress®

Web Services in Finance

Copyright © 2005 by Dr. Paul A. Watters

Lead Editor: Jim Sumser
Technical Reviewers: Dr. Ian Krycer, Alex Ng
Editorial Board: Steve Anglin, Dan Appleman, Ewan Buckingham, Gary Cornell, Tony Davis, John Franklin, Jason Gilmore, Chris Mills, Dominic Shakeshaft, Jim Sumser
Project Manager: Kylie Johnston
Copy Edit Manager: Nicole LeClerc
Copy Editor: Scott Carter
Production Manager: Kari Brooks-Copony
Production Editor: Linda Marousek
Compositor: Gina Rexrode
Proofreader: Nancy Sixsmith
Indexer: Ann Rogers
Artist: Kinetic Publishing Services, LLC
Cover Designer: Kurt Krames
Manufacturing Manager: Tom Debolski

Library of Congress Cataloging-in-Publication Data

Watters, Paul A.

Web services in finance / Paul A. Watters.

p. cm.

Includes index.

ISBN 1-59059-435-5

1. Web services. 2. Finance--Data processing.   I. Title.

TK5105.88813.W38 2004

332.1'0285'4678--dc22

2004022217

Printed and bound in the United States of America 9 8 7 6 5 4 3 2 1

Trademarked names may appear in this book. Rather than use a trademark symbol with every occurrence of a trademarked name, we use the names only in an editorial fashion and to the benefit of the trademark owner, with no intention of infringement of the trademark.

Distributed to the book trade in the United States by Springer-Verlag New York, Inc., 233 Spring Street, 6th Floor, New York, NY 10013, and outside the United States by Springer-Verlag GmbH & Co. KG, Tiergartenstr. 17, 69112 Heidelberg, Germany.

In the United States: phone 1-800-SPRINGER, fax 201-348-4505, e-mail orders@springer-ny.com, or visit http://www.springer-ny.com. Outside the United States: fax +49 6221 345229, e-mail orders@springer.de, or visit http://www.springer.de.

For information on translations, please contact Apress directly at 2560 Ninth Street, Suite 219, Berkeley, CA 94710. Phone 510-549-5930, fax 510-549-5939, e-mail info@apress.com, or visit http://www.apress.com.

The information in this book is distributed on an "as is" basis, without warranty. Although every precaution has been taken in the preparation of this work, neither the author(s) nor Apress shall have any liability to any person or entity with respect to any loss or damage caused or alleged to be caused directly or indirectly by the information contained in this work.

This book is dedicated to my daughters, Arwen Ellen and Bounty Sóller.

Contents at a Glance

Contents

About the Author

DR. PAUL A. WATTERS is a Senior Lecturer in the Postgraduate Professional Development Program and Department of Computing at Macquarie University, Sydney, Australia. He has developed numerous commercial Web applications and services for clients that include the Universities Admissions Centre (UAC) and Reef Internetware. Dr. Watters has served on the Centre for Networking Technologies for the Information Economy (CeNTIE) information brokering panel, which explores future applications in finance, banking, and taxation at the Commonwealth Scientific and Industrial Research Organisation (CSIRO). Dr. Watters currently teaches "ITEC833 Web Server Technologies and Web Services." He is the author of Solaris 10: The Complete Reference (McGraw-Hill/Osborne, 2002), and coauthor of *Web Services Security* (McGraw-Hill/Osborne, 2003).

About the Technical Reviewers

DR. IAN KRYCER has a Master of Technology degree in Software Engineering from Macquarie University and a Ph.D. from the University of Sydney, Australia. He initially pursued an industrial career and became the IT Manager for two U.S. multinational companies operating subsidiaries in Sydney. Dr. Krycer managed numerous projects ranging from ERP implementation, Web-based B2B product configuration and ordering, and custom asset-tracking and billing applications. For the last four years, Dr. Krycer has worked as an adjunct IT lecturer at Macquarie University and as a consultant for small- and medium-sized enterprises. Dr. Krycer's research interests include Web services, application integration, change management, and mobile commerce.

ALEX NG holds a Bachelor of Science degree in Electronics/Computer Science from the Chinese University of Hong Kong and a Master of Technology degree in Software Engineering from Macquarie University, Australia. Through the past 15 years, Alex has worked in various positions, such as assembler coder for BSC3270/3780 protocols, as a consultant for communication systems, and in software development. He is now pursuing a Ph.D. in Computer Science at Macquarie University. Alex's research interest is in the performance issues of Web services and related communication protocols.

Acknowledgments

I would like to thank my Apress editor, Jim Sumser, for his insight and advice during the development of this book. Neil Salkind and the team at Studio B deserve great credit for their hard work in getting the project underway and on track. I would like to acknowledge the outstanding work done by Kylie Johnston and Scott Carter in copyediting and ensuring that production ran very smoothly. The two technical editors, Dr. Ian Krycer and Mr. Alex Ng, ensured that the gaps in my knowledge were quickly filled. Finally, I would like to thank my family for their patience during my many absent hours during the writing of this book.

Introduction

This book provides an introduction to XML Web Services, representing the current generation of distributed computing architectures. Web services provide a loosely coupled framework for exchanging messages that can represent remote procedure call requests and responses, using a standard data description and format language (XML). Web services have advantages over existing standards for distributed computing, such as CORBA, because exposure of existing services as Web services is essentially declarative, and doesn't require extensive source modification. Web services provide an easy route to systems integration, both internal and external, and are most useful when they can be deployed in real-time data processing.

More than any other vertical market, the finance industry has traditionally suffered from computer system integration problems. Because the buying and selling of securities requires reliable, real-time invocation of services and data exchange through brokers, exchanges, clearing houses, etc., it's critical that a secure, highly available architecture is available to support future business models.

While not all components of a complete Web services framework have yet been developed, significant progress in tackling the problems of reliable messaging, single sign-on authentication, and stateful conversations suggest that the finance industry has much to gain from adopting Web services as a future architecture for systems integration.

Who This Book Is For

This book is primarily for developers and their managers working in the finance industry. Material is presented at a high level, with simple examples acting as primers for more extensive and in-depth investigations of protocols, RFCs, standards, and specific APIs. The book aims to answer the important question of *why* we need Web services, and *how* they are currently implemented. Implementations will certainly change rapidly over the next few years, but the underlying ethos remains a constant theme in computing: how to meet consistently the ever-expanding range of nonfunctional requirements in distributed computing.

I attempt to provide, in ten chapters, a review of the core and mature Web services elements, such as XML, SOAP, and WSDL, before tackling some of the harder issues. Security, as a good example, is an area in which basic standards have provided important advances in interoperability of credentials and services (such as authentication), but where there is further scope for enhancement.

CHAPTER 1

■ ■ ■

Introduction to Web Services

Developers in the finance industry face two challenging tasks: to plan and develop tomorrow's applications today, and to integrate those applications with yesterday's technology. When developers sign up to work in finance, they may have a fairly rosy idea of what they'll be working on—electronic banking, portals, B2B exchanges—all of the sexy work that uses cutting-edge technology that they've learned at college. For example, most new enterprise applications will be written for the Java 2 Enterprise Edition (J2EE) or Microsoft .NET environment, so new employees will feel gratified that their education has equipped them for working in the brave new world of distributed, object-oriented systems that are highly available, reliable, and fun to work with.

Of course, after the first day on the job, they realize that in addition to working in these new, cool areas of application development, they'll also need to integrate their software with systems probably written before they were born, where code is often not documented, definitely not object-oriented, and anything but easy to work with. They'll no doubt be pulling out their hair in frustration at the seemingly unplanned nature of the enterprise data center, where projects and systems have a way of growing to encompass entire floors of buildings—and where teams of developers support very specific parts of an application written in COBOL, or if they're very lucky, in the C programming language. David Linthicum, in his book *Enterprise Application Integration*, refers to the reality of large-scale implementations that cross generations of developers and management as "enterprise chaos." Since the cost of rewriting applications every time a new language or platform is developed is far too costly for the enterprise, Enterprise Application Integration (EAI) "glue," in the form of middleware, must be used to connect and integrate brittle applications. Until recently, no widely adopted standards for developing middleware existed, although specific vertical industry standards have been developed for exchanging documents, including the popular Electronic Data Interchange (EDI) standard. However, EDI requires adherence to very specific definitions for document structure, and it cannot be readily customized to suit local conditions.

On the other hand, when developing new applications and services that are distributed, developers have had a set of tools available for many years. UNIX, for example, has had standard Remote Procedure Call (RPC) technology since System V was introduced, and Common Object Request Broker Architecture (CORBA) promised to deliver cross-platform, cross-language RPC for object-oriented systems. What both approaches had in common was the requirement that client/server interfaces were manually specified in an Interface Definition Language (IDL), or that a significant amount of code modification was required to "distribute" applications. Here's an example of an IDL specification:

```
module PhoneBanking
{
    interface account
    {
        string getBalance();
    };
};
```

In this example, a module called PhoneBanking contains a single interface called account, and has one method defined called getBalance(), which returns a string corresponding to a bank account balance. Multiple interfaces to PhoneBanking can be declared within a single IDL specification, and multiple methods with different return types and numbers of parameters can be specified on a per-interface basis.

The process for invoking a remote method by using CORBA is shown in Figure 1-1. An object reference is created in the CORBA client, which then invokes the remote method on the server by calling the client Object Request Broker (ORB) that connects to the server ORB, and exchanges data using the Internet InterORB Protocol (IIOP).

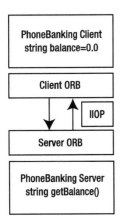

Figure 1-1. *Invoking a remote method using CORBA*

The server and client stubs and skeletons can be generated by an IDL-to-Java, IDL-to-C++, or IDL-to-whatever-language that is supported by vendors. This allows client and server systems to be implemented in completely different languages, which is clearly desirable for interoperability. Although the CORBA specification very clearly defines the operations required to support this cross-platform mapping, vendor ORBs encountered problems in communicating with each other, particularly across different versions of the CORBA specification as implemented in individual products. This approach led to many problems in finance, where changes in CORBA specifications or ORB implementations meant recoding IDL interfaces and/or source code each time a change was made. Since many systems in finance are distributed, many of these problems were commonly encountered when developing new systems or maintaining existing applications. Consequently, significant disillusionment has spread through the programming industry regarding remote method calling and cross-platform distributed computing in general, and especially in finance.

That's a pretty negative way to start a book—but good news is on the horizon. Web services have been promoted as standards for exchanging data, invoking remote services, and providing a generic platform for achieving interoperability. These characteristics are associated with a number of business, consumer, and technological drivers for change—including the huge cost of maintaining software in the enterprise. Web services are being developed around a set of core protocols and specifications for interoperability, which are now mature. These include eXtensible Markup Language (XML); Simple Object Access Protocol (SOAP); and Universal Description, Discovery, and Integration (UDDI). Currently, these protocols allow the building of simple applications that permit a range of services to be invoked by using standard data formats, and by allowing dynamic identification of service providers through a directory service. More complex standards for supporting transactions and reliable messaging are still being developed. The focus of this book is to explore and investigate the relevance of these protocols for the typical enterprise applications used in the finance industry.

From the developer's perspective, one neat aspect of Web services is that source code does not need to be modified to expose existing application and service interfaces as Web services—new development tools, such as IBM's WebSphere Studio Application Developer (WSAD), generate the necessary Web Services Description Language (WSDL) interfaces automatically, without developer intervention, as shown in Figure 1-2.

The advantage of the point-and-click approach to defining new Web services interfaces to existing applications is that the previously elusive promise of object reusability can be easily achieved, whether in J2EE or in .NET. The following Java class gives an example of the kind of existing systems easily enabled for Web services by using the technique shown in Figure 1-2:

```
public class Account
{
    // Account.java - allows a bank balance to be set or queried
```

```
private double accountBalance=100.00;

// Checks bank balance
public double getBalance()
{
    return accountBalance;
}

// Sets bank balance
public void setBalance(double balance)
{
    accountBalance=balance;
}
```

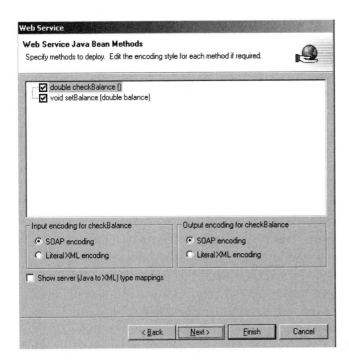

Figure 1-2. *Specifying WSDL interfaces by point-and-click with IBM's WebSphere Studio Application Developer*

Web services promise two things: an easy way to integrate existing applications with new ones, and a new way to interact with business partners in a highly connected world. Since EAI consumes a large slab of a typical IT budget, Web services allow more money to be devoted to developing new products that deliver services. Because finance is essentially a service-based industry, in which multiple entities are party to any one transaction, there is great potential for B2B e-commerce to succeed with a set of standard Web services, as opposed to the chaos that surrounded earlier attempts.

In almost every application that brings business partners together, money is involved. That fact alone makes Web services particularly relevant to finance. In addition, businesses within the finance industry represent the typical enterprise; they have systems, services, and applications deployed in production that were introduced and developed during different times. Thus, all the integration problems experienced by most enterprises are also experienced by organizations within finance. So, rather than writing a technology-focused book dealing with abstract, made-up organizations, I'll attempt to cover realistic scenarios in external and internal integration.

Web services cover two main areas in finance: EAI and dealing with yesterday's mistakes; and building new, integrated applications and providing new services with business partners in a dynamic, transient commercial world. Both areas are driven by consumer and business demands and by technological developments.

Business Drivers

The main business driver for engaging in EAI is to improve efficiency and lower costs. This is because software maintenance costs often comprise around 80 percent[1] of the total ownership cost—initial development costs are a meager 20 percent! Thus, any technology that can reduce the costs of integration in the enterprise will be welcomed. Lower costs can arise from improved efficiency, where more can be achieved for the same cost. For example, CORBA requires an ORB to be running on both the client and server sides, whereas Web services do not require an ORB-like entity to operate. In addition, lower overheads can emerge with Web services, because ORB products are not required, so their expensive license fees can be directly saved. This can reduce costs on a per-transaction basis, which is important in finance.

Although Web services integration is a great story, the great potential of the technology is in the area of improving collaboration with business partners. Although B2B e-commerce systems, such as on-line marketplaces, have met with limited success, there is a clear business need for a technology to make integration with business partners easy. For example, GE's Global eXchange Services (GXS) runs a B2B e-commerce system in 58 countries that engages 100,000 trading partners and has over 1 billion annual transactions totaling more than $1 trillion every year (http://www.gxs.com/). Since all participants in the exchange must use standard methods of communicating,

---

1. Robert Seacord, Daniel Plakosh, and Grace Lewis, *Modernizing Legacy Systems: Software Technologies, Engineering Processes, and Business Practices* (Boston, MA: Addison-Wesley, 2003).

they can all communicate with each other. Web services enables standards for data interchange to extend beyond any one exchange or point-to-point integration. For example, the Society for Worldwide Interbank Financial Telecommunications (SWIFT) supports payment processes among more than 7,000 financial institutions.

Using standards solves a number of existing problems associated with data integrity, such as the dual entry of data because one or more applications has a different interface but requires similar data to be entered. For example, a bank might process credit applications from farmers annually based on each farmer's chart of accounts, which could be submitted in a spreadsheet form, or by using any one of numerous accounting packages. No standard exists for formatting and presenting the data, so data entry operators must manually collate and re-enter the farmers' information into the bank's internal loan approval systems to process their credit request. Not only does this duplication waste the banks' and customers' valuable time, but it introduces the potential for transcription and semantic errors arising from the incorrect interpretation of nonstandard account entries. By taking advantage of the generic, platform-independent integration Web services protocols, the farmer could fill out a Web form, or integrate his accounting package with the bank's system, thereby avoiding the double entry of data.

The nature and pace of business collaboration makes it both dynamic and transient. Technologies for building tomorrow's finance applications must be able to cope with this. For example, when a customer goes to an on-line music store and buys a CD, several parties are involved:

- The customer, who places the order and eventually receives the CD

- The retailer, who takes the order, requests payment authorization from a bank, and arranges delivery from the warehouse

- The wholesaler, who supplies the CD to the retailer

- The bank, which provides the payment service

- The courier service, which delivers the CD

In real time, when the order is placed, the retailer must check with the warehouse to determine if the order is in stock, place an authorization request to the bank for the amount charged to the customer's credit card, and contact the courier service to arrange delivery. The workflow is summarized in Figure 1-3. This part of the process happens in a few seconds, and if an exception occurs on the process, such as a credit card being declined, then no physical processes needs to be reversed. However, the transaction itself can span several days from ordering to delivery, during which time something may go wrong, and the transaction will have to be rolled back. For example, the customer may return the CD because it is faulty and ask for a refund. So, the bank needs to reverse the debit made against the customer's credit card, the wholesaler must be contacted to claim a return on the faulty disc, the courier service still needs to be paid because it performed the delivery as requested, and so on. So, the integration must be able to cope with short-time and long-time aspects of a transaction within the same framework. A similar problem occurs with backorders, where only part of an order can be supplied. If the customer returns the CD, the bank will provide a credit rather than roll back the debit. If the CD is faulty the wholesaler would probably replace rather than credit. The courier might need to be paid twice, depending on the terms of trade, such as free returns for faulty goods. Remember, this is an e-tailer who may not have a shop front.

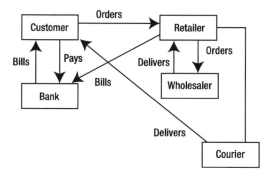

Figure 1-3. *Retail workflow showing the steps required to purchase an item from a retailer*

A potential new business opportunity arises with the coordination of services offered by different organizations presented as a single shop front to the consumer or to other businesses. The Internet economy in the business-to-consumer (B2C) space was initially driven by disintermediation—the idea of cutting out "the middleman" and dealing directly with wholesalers. The logical chain of consumer-retailer-wholesaler, however, drastically simplifies business processes, and completely ignores the "value add" that retailers can bring to bear. For example, traditional supermarkets build their entire business upon their capability of reliably sourcing thousands of grocery lines from individual wholesalers and manufacturers, which enables consumers to buy groceries at a single physical location. This is incredibly convenient; imagine having to visit every wholesaler or manufacturer's shop just to buy one or two products for your weekly shopping! In addition, wholesalers typically don't want to enter the retail game—they know exactly what business they are in, and it's not retail.

Existing retailers have great opportunities to act as intermediaries between consumers and multiple wholesalers and manufacturers by adding value to existing services. For example, Internet banking has grown tremendously in popularity, and it drastically reduces the cost per transaction to the bank compared to a face-to-face teller transaction. At present, most Internet banking services cover the typical range of transaction accounts: electronic transfer of cash between linked accounts; and paying bills, credit card debt, mortgages, etc. However, banks could offer new services that link with partners in insurance, mutual funds, foreign exchange, tax payments, investments, and all finance activities. Essentially, the intermediary best able to provide the largest number of most valuable services will be able to retain the greatest number (or perhaps the highest spending group) of customers.

Not only does this strategy improve opportunities for new businesses, but also it allows companies to offer new services that will drive customer demand. If customers find the new aggregated services to be useful, their loyalty will increase—if overall customer service and satisfaction can be enhanced. Being able to provide a "one-stop shop" can be a very successful strategy for improving customer service and increasing the number of hits containing a transaction for a specific site.

From an operational perspective, an important requirement for success is the identification of business intelligence. By increasing customers' interaction that can be logged and cross-checked with their other activities, it is possible to get a much more precise picture of who your customers are, what their real requirements are, and how you can best meet those requirements. For example, in an Internet banking application, the paths taken from the login screen can be used to identify the most commonly used services, and the sequences thereafter, to improve the design and layout of the site. For example, if your logs identify that 95 percent of users check their bank balances after conducting a share purchase transaction, then you need to be able to provide more integrated access to those functions. That requires integration with business partners, and hence the driver from the Web services perspective. The great feature of using the Web to interact with customers is that business intelligence is easily gathered from logs of services actually used, with very precise event-based activity. Also, by electronically trapping a customer's profile and buying habits into a data-mining application, it is possible to recognize patterns that can lead to new marketing opportunities.

As a technology implementer, it's important to understand the business drivers behind new types of technology like Web services, because ultimately technology choices must be justified in business terms. It's critical to keep abreast of changes in the business landscape, particularly in finance, to ensure that your company can stay ahead of its competitors, or so it can cooperate using standards when necessary and desirable.

Consumer Drivers

The main driver for change from the consumer's perspective is the perception of reduced personal time, which necessarily increases the value of that time. Consumers want more convenient and personal efficiency, and no longer want to perform mundane, boring tasks themselves. This either means employing someone else to do them—which has led to a boom in the "personal services" industry—or it means automating some tasks that they currently perform manually. The sense that modern life has somehow sped up has been well covered in the literature—James Gleick's *Faster: The Acceleration of Just About Everything* covers the changes in behavior associated with the changes in speed at which we can do even the most complex things. Living "on Internet time" has increased the customer service expectations of consumers, along with a concurrent desire to reduce the total amount of time spent on mundane tasks.

Although technology has certainly assisted in this area, consumers are demanding even further integration. For example, every bank, insurance company, and investment house offers a range of on-line services, from banking to investment to brokering. However, many consumers have relationships with a number of different institutions. This may be because they want to diversify financial risk in dealing with multiple parties, or it could just be an accrual of relationships developed over years of working for different employers, getting married, inheriting money, and so on. Remembering ten different user names and passwords to access ten different sites is challenging for any consumer; this is why some organizations, like the Commonwealth Bank in Australia, have integrated access to multiple sites, from many different organizations, into a single, customizable interface known as "my online summary." Bank customers can now consolidate multiple views on different accounts and services into a single log-in, which reduces the inconvenience of remembering lots of different passwords. It also means that the bank is effectively channeling its customers through its own site whenever they access the services of the bank's competitor, thereby reinforcing customer loyalty.

Because so many services offered by multiple organizations can be channeled into a service like "my online summary," standards for formatting and exchanging data are clearly required; otherwise, the "enterprise chaos" mentioned earlier will extend from within each enterprise to all of that enterprise's trading and business partners.

Apart from providing faster service and being able to bind many existing services together into a single offering, there is also a demand for more personalized value-added services. For example, mom-and-pop investors have fueled the growth in equity markets over recent years. Rather than naively trading their way out of a fruitful retirement, many investors are looking for personalized services that provide advice in the areas of budgeting, payments, credit, and taxation. While an intermediary may be able to provide some of these services, many cases require new services, and the funding to create them. If consumers demand them, then it's up to technologists to deliver them in a secure, speedy manner.

Technology Developments

A key issue regarding the provision of services over the network, rather than a local client/server model, is that network bandwidth is increasing at a rate far exceeding the growth rate of CPU speeds. Technological advances in hardware bring about continuous improvements in speed and bandwidth. Several laws have been formulated to predict these changes, and these have generally proven true. For example, Moore's Law, formulated in the 1970s by Gordon Moore of Intel, predicts that CPU speeds will double every 18 months. In the networking world, Gilder's Law predicts that bandwidth triples every 12 months. The resulting trends are shown in Figure 1-4, with the current and future years plotted against the CPU speed (MHz) and network bandwidth (Mbps), assuming a nominal starting point of 1 GHz and 1 Gbps on a logarithmic scale. Note the rapid divergence of network bandwidth from CPU speed. While this difference may motivate CPU manufacturers to strive to outdo Moore's Law, in all likelihood, Moore's Law will hold.

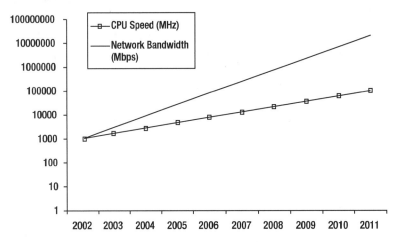

Figure 1-4. *Relationship of Moore's Law (CPU) and Gilder's Law (network bandwidth) speed increases*

This leaves software developers with the task of developing applications that use relatively less CPU time and relatively more network bandwidth; otherwise, the network will lay idle for most of the time. For example, if a task takes 10 minutes to compute 1 Gb of data, but then takes only 1 second to transmit, then the network is being used for only 1 second out of 600. This represents only 0.16 percent of its total capacity. Idleness of 99.84 percent is not effective resource utilization. Technology is subject to the law of supply and demand—if there is no demand for increased bandwidth because applications cannot make use of it, then supply will have to be cut, and the implications for the network hardware industry could be quite serious. The key requirement for increasing demand for high bandwidth networking is to effectively close the gap between CPU speed and network bandwidth by developing applications that make better use of network bandwidth and hardware.

Networks are experiencing rapid changes in their structure and mode of operation while simultaneously massively increasing their capacity to carry traffic. Gigabit wireless network interface cards and switches are now available, allowing the development of high-speed wireless LANs. The mobility of network connections is coupled with improvements in networking protocols to guarantee specific levels of bandwidth for a specific connection and for a specific latency. For example, Multiprotocol Label Switching (MPLS) allows the labeling of individual packets so that routers and other traffic carriers can achieve specific performance levels (see `http://www.ietf.org/rfc/rfc3031.txt` for definitions of the different labels).

Currently, there are 46 million broadband subscribers worldwide.[2] This is likely to increase in the near future, and in the finance world, most financial institutions will have their own private networks in addition to being connected to the Internet. This future in connectivity will allow customers to interact with financial institutions, allow these institutions to connect with each other, and also allow peer-to-peer connections between customers. Connectivity is not limited to devices—cellular and mobile phones, in combination with personal digital assistants, allow client applications to be executed in a networked environment. These technology developments may change the way banks exchange data and the way customers do business with each other. For example, mobile phone users may be able to simply point their phones at each other to exchange tokens representing electronic cash debits and credits, which are then communicated to each participant's respective banks. Currently, only businesses can perform this kind of transaction by being a credit card merchant. In the future, technological developments will allow these scenarios to be extended into the consumer arena.

Changes in computing have created large increases in the amount of computing power and storage available to the ordinary consumer. This technology needs to be used for something, or consumer demand will dry up. There are potentially large, unexplored areas in fat-client technology, for example, to enhance the user experience. Although Java applet technology did not achieve the desktop revolution that many had hoped for, the lessons learned from that experiment may lead to improved user experiences in the future. For example, users currently interact with the Web by essentially using a set of forms and brochures. This request/response model, where the page viewed by the user must be refreshed after every action, is incredibly clunky, particularly for complex, multipage applications. While HTML is certainly a standard for presenting data on the Internet, it is certainly not the same as using a normal desktop application.

Technology Problems

So far, we've examined the business, consumer, and technical drivers behind the demand for Web services—and basically, it boils down to being able to exchange data and execute remote services in standard ways. And the focus here is definitely on services in the

---

2. See "Worldwide Broadband Trends" at `http://cyberatlas.internet.com/markets/broadband/article/0,,10099_1435681,00.html`.

broader sense—services for consumers and business, and the implementation of services. This focus can be crystallized by the term *Service Oriented Architecture* (SOA),[3] which describes the platform for developing, deploying, managing, and monitoring services that can be discovered and bound to at run time. This dynamic and transient environment is quite different to the brittle, monolithic application architectures of previous generations. In the new environment, where global systems are connected by reliable, broadband networks, applications will be composed dynamically from services offered by many different businesses, and these constituent parts may change or be modified at run time.

Within an organization, this dynamic is trivial, because you are implementing and deploying services in a secure environment. But when you effectively open your firewall to allow access to external clients, you need to be able to authenticate them and authorize their actions inside your firewall. Although security is being addressed by standards such as WS-Security and Security Assertion Markup Language (SAML), trust is often considered one of the largest inhibitors to the growth and adoption of Web services.

A larger problem exists with the requirement to connect the two platforms used to design and implement the current batch of enterprise applications. In addition, these platforms must integrate with each other and with previous generations of enterprise systems affectionately known as "legacy" applications. The Y2K problem highlighted just how many of these back-end systems were still in use many years after their initial implementation!

On an application level, many enterprise applications are being used across the finance enterprise, and there is a consistent need to reliably integrate these systems. For example, financial applications must be connected to HR applications. In addition, operating system interoperability is a consistent headache for system and network administrators, as they need to connect UNIX, Windows, and mainframe systems. Traditional integration involves moving data between applications, composing new services from multiple applications, and/or centralizing integration through a business process specification of some kind. Data and process ideally need to be moved between systems and applications without having to change existing infrastructure or applications. In the virtual enterprise, or in any B2B integration scenario, one partner may not allow the other partner to specify platforms or applications. Ultimately, partners should be able to agree on interface definitions and standards for exchanging security data, and should provide an agreed service level.

At the integration level, existing technology comes in the form of application servers, integration brokers, and virtually any technology that can sit between applications and data (thus, some database servers actually play a middleware role as well). Application

---

3. See "The Tao of e-business services: The evolution of Web applications into service-oriented components with Web services" by Steve Burbeck (http://www-106.ibm.com/developerworks/webservices/library/ws-tao/?dwzone=webservices) for more information.

servers are platforms for building component-based applications from sets of encapsulated components, by using modern object-oriented techniques. Application servers support multitier application designs, distribution of components across multiple servers, tools for integrating components and other application layers, and they provide a critical separation of business and presentation logic. In reality, it is rarely possible to achieve this separation for any specific application; a Java Server Page (JSP) can contain Java code, and an Active Server Page (ASP) can contain Visual Basic scripts, for example. The major players in the application server market are Microsoft, with .NET and COM+, and Sun, with J2EE. Although CORBA played a historical role, most CORBA vendors are focused on integrating their products with J2EE or .NET.

The J2EE approach to development involves writing new components (Enterprise Java Beans) that are written in a single language, and that are executed through a single Java Virtual Machine (JVM). This is a very "pure" approach from an object-oriented perspective. Until recently, J2EE did not have any standards for connecting new applications to existing applications, but the Java Connector Architecture (JCA) has rectified this missing link to some extent. However, given the large number of legacy applications for which connectors must be written, J2EE developers may not easily find a way to connect multiple legacy applications to new applications by using JCA.

In contrast, .NET appears to be targeted more at the pragmatic side of integration, since a single Common Language Runtime (CLR) executes components and applications written in multiple languages. Combining Visual Basic code with C#, the new object-oriented player on the block may horrify some developers, but this is exactly the kind of task that must be undertaken for successful system integration. Most importantly, from a Web services perspective, SOAP is actually the native remoting protocol for .NET, so no additional toolkits are required to implement Web services when using the .NET framework. J2EE does support Web services, but each vendor has released its own implementations and APIs, making it sometimes, but not always, difficult to standardize application interfaces across different application servers. These incompatibilities typically result from the object serialization or the use of xsi:type attributes.

Integration brokers have a hub-and-spoke architecture that defines input/output mapping, message translation and data conversion, flow control through intelligent routing that reflects business processes, and some degree of programmability through rule-based processing. Although integration brokers have allowed a movement away from point-to-point integration solutions, they introduce complexity into system operations, because a change in one spoke can affect the rest of the system, perhaps requiring changes to many different system components. In addition, external suppliers and partners cannot be easily integrated into the system because they may use their own brokering technology that is not compatible with the local system. This is one reason why integration broker vendors such as webMethods have been keen to support standards like Web services for external integration.

Future Business for Finance

Given these advances in distributed system technology and their related problems, what sort of services will be offered in the finance industry, and what are the implications for using that technology? Without crystal-ball gazing too far into the future, we can cautiously say that there will be an increase in collaboration and partnership between finance organizations. Collaborations will occur between finance businesses, certainly, but more than likely, finance businesses will become the cornerstone of e-commerce activity because of their central role in processing payments and managing finance. The need to integrate payments and finance systems from finance businesses to external parties has already caused significant problems in data exchange. Since most businesses maintain firewalls to prevent unauthorized access to locally deployed services, the prospect of allowing external users to invoke those services remotely, and in real time, gives network and system administrators nightmares! However, to maintain a competitive edge in the future, this kind of collaboration will be both necessary and desirable.

Providing payment services for external customers is one thing; these parties are already merchants, partners, or customers who do not compete in the core business areas of finance business. For example, if a bank provides payment services to a retailer, then the retailer is not competing with the bank (although it's interesting to note that large retailers now have the ability to operate as financial institutions by offering credit facilities of their own). However, if financial institutions need to collaborate, then their service offerings will be available to their competitors! How can the traditional security barriers be maintained to prevent competitors from obtaining information that might give them a competitive advantage?

On a technical level, there is a requirement for secure group communications protocols that can be used to add and remove partners from electronic transactions in a planned way, so that they do not obtain "open slather" access to their competitor's systems. Many businesses have overlapping needs that can be centralized with responsibility shared between institutions. For example, in Australia, the BPay bill payment-clearing house (http://www.bpay.com.au/) is supported by all the major banks, because bill payments are generic, and there is no clear advantage for any bank to compete in this space. This also has great advantages for merchants, since only one API is required to process bill payments for any local bank. For businesses to cooperate in an untrusted environment, they must have secure access to a shared document repository, where fine-grained access control can be granted to principals outside the local authentication domain. To further integrate with partners and even potential competitors, finance organizations will need to participate in dynamic and transient virtual enterprises. The term *virtual enterprise* generically refers to business that operate in the virtual world of e-commerce, where *virtual* means "created, simulated, or carried on by means of a computer or computer network."[4] Thus, any enterprise that operates by means of a computer and uses a computer network may be considered a virtual enterprise. Examples of this kind of virtual enterprise include B2B and B2C e-commerce systems, which use computer networks exclusively to conduct business transactions that have traditionally been conducted by physical enterprises. By becoming virtual enterprises, firms can take advantage of selling goods and services to a global audience, and reduce operational costs by centralizing commercial operations around a single portal. If recent history is any judge, these benefits have yet to be realized, particularly where physical delivery of a product is involved, since they can be largely mimicked by physical enterprises. For example, a mail-order company can distribute catalogues by post or newspaper insert, or through an Internet site. Any kind of print advertising with associated distribution costs is expensive. However, maintaining an enterprise level e-commerce system is also expensive. Common costs for both physical and virtual enterprises include warehousing, distribution, and procurement. So while virtual enterprises are new, it's not always clear that they have a clear advantage over physical enterprises. The exception is in the area of services, especially digital services such as finance.

Technologies for providing services over the Internet are only now maturing with the adoption of standards by members of the Web Services Interoperability Organization (WS-I). Web services have the potential, through integration and cooperation between a number of different enterprises, to enable virtual enterprises to deliver something different from what physical enterprises can. This sense of *virtual* relates more to the root *virtuall*,[5] from Middle English, meaning "to be effective." So virtual enterprises should be defined to mean "enterprises that operate more effectively than physical enterprises by means of a computer and computer network."

Systemwide Integration in Finance

One reality that must be faced, particularly in the finance context, is that private networks will eventually be removed in favor of the public Internet. This will not happen tomorrow, but inevitably, the high cost of maintaining point-to-point links will ensure that they are closed as soon as reliable broadband is deployed between all finance businesses and their partners. System-wide integration will encompass not just divisions within a particular business, but also external business partners. Supply chains will become more adaptive and integrated to remove current inefficiencies and single points of failure. Real-time selection of trusted business partners is essential for the continuity of production. A good example of where this technology is urgently required is in the

---

4. *American Heritage Dictionary*, Fourth Edition. (Boston, MA: Houghton Mifflin, 2000).
5. Ibid.

automotive industry in Australia; a strike by workers at an exhaust system manufacturing facility bought the entire industry (including multiple car manufacturers) to a complete standstill because of a single point of failure. Supply chains are so brittle that a problem at one small company was able to stop the entire industry. If the supply chain was more adaptive, then new suppliers could have been immediately identified, and the process of even arranging for the importation of exhaust systems could have been arranged in real time. This approach would prevent the kind of expensive downtime witnessed during that dispute, and would also lead to greater efficiencies by allowing a more market-driven system to be implemented.

The truly frightening aspect of finance industry interaction with customers is the amazing amount of paperwork that is still processed. The paperless office couldn't be any further from reality. The Web has improved many of these processes by allowing simple form-based input to be recorded electronically by banks and other institutions. Ultimately, this will reduce the amount of paper handling and dual entry of data into enterprise systems. The secure sharing of electronic data between businesses is also important—not just from an efficiency perspective, but also from a privacy perspective. For example, a bank may need to share data with the IRS. For the sake of the customer's privacy, the bank must ensure that the IRS can have access to only specific types of data. It's important to note that giving the IRS electronic access to the bank's data is not as simple as creating a user name "irs" in the local domain and sending the local agents the password; every principal from the IRS will need to be authenticated, which means that the IRS must supply the bank with some kind of authentication and authorization data. This kind of secure but transient access is a key requirement for improved collaboration, particularly where financial credentials are involved. If you don't have standards for exchanging this data, then you will need to develop an API for every partner or customer that you deal with. Another great motivator for embracing Web services!

The Australian Taxation Office (ATO) developed an e-tax return, where taxpayers are authenticated against their previous year's tax return serial number. The ATO sends you a digital signature (once only), and then you sign the return using their interactive application, which self-calculates and guides you with questions, and then sends the responses over HTTP.

Web Services Technology Requirements

We've looked at technology drivers for the adoption of Web services, and the potential problems with its integration. The common theme emerging from these discussions is that standards are required—for delivering flexible integration within the enterprise and with external business partners, and for building new applications to realize new opportunities. Otherwise, every time you need to interact with an external or internal service, you will have to create a different API. It's no wonder that 35 percent of development time is estimated by Gartner Inc. and Forrester Research Inc. to be spent on developing point-to-point interfaces![6] Standards are required for the following areas:

- Data exchange

- Remote services invocation

- Directory access

- Transactions

- Security

This list is not meant to be exhaustive, but it contains the most important elements for developing a complete (and open) distributed computing platform.[7] At the same time, many of the technological developments mentioned earlier will need to be realized. These include

- Widespread adoption of personal digital assistants

- Agreement on how to balance privacy. security, and productivity issues

- How to give users control over their own data

- Implementation of pervasive networking with guaranteed service levels

- Integration of wireless technologies with business-grade public networks

- Adoption of common integration technologies

What benefits we will gain from the adoption of Web services, as they exist today, include

- Vendor neutrality (avoids vendor lock-in to a proprietary solution)

- Platform independence that allows changing deployment platform without rewriting interfaces

---

6. See Michael J. Schroeck's article on this phenomenon at http://www.dmreview.com/article_sub.cfm?articleId=1951.

7. A complete list is available at http://www.w3.org/TR/2002/WD-wsa-reqs-20020429#N1011D.

- Language independence that allows back-end code to be modified without changing interfaces

- Freedom to choose your platform (and change it at any time)

- Freedom of platform choice for partners, allowing interaction with a wider range of associates

- Ability to select the best platform, with the most productive language(s), without being restricted to a vendor or partner

- Adoption of a service-oriented architecture

- "Web service" enablement without source modification, unlike competing standards-based distributed computing platforms such as CORBA

Currently, many design patterns are supported by Web services, including but not limited to

- Static, with a simple three-tier client/server architecture

- Dynamic, with client/server architecture in which services are discovered through a registry lookup

- Composition, allowing multiple services to be bound on request from a single client

- Invocation and dynamic invocation

- Static binding and dynamic binding

With respect to the technologies for supporting a service-oriented architecture through Web services, what specifications are currently available? Well, as a reality check, Figure 1-5 shows the layering of the Web services "stack," and which parts are mature (light gray), maturing (white), or still to be determined (dark gray).

The role of developing standards for Web services has been undertaken by organizations like WS-I, Internet Engineering Task Force (IETF), Organization for the Advancement of Structured Information Standards (OASIS) e-business standards organization, and the World Wide Web Consortium (W3C). It is critical that all players in the Web services space continue to work toward common integration goals in the areas of competition and cooperation, and in interoperability between vendor platforms.

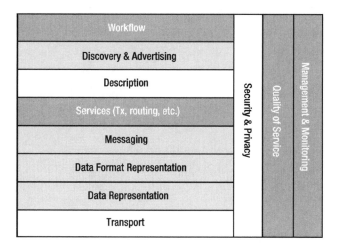

Figure 1-5. *Web services technology stack showing mature (light gray), maturing (white), or still to be determined (dark gray) technologies*

Mature Standards

I'd briefly like to cover some of the core Web services specifications before moving on to discuss emerging standards. Although each chapter examines one specification in detail, an overview may help you navigate through the Web services maze.

Simple Object Access Protocol (SOAP)

SOAP is basically a platform-independent way of exchanging data and requesting services. It is mostly used as a cross-platform request/response RPC mechanism (SOAP-RPC), although the protocol is much more general. SOAP data is formatted using XML, and generally uses HTTP as its transport mechanism, which itself runs over TCP. This transport has been used historically because it is ubiquitous on the Internet, and because SOAP requests can be embedded within normal HTTP traffic, thereby bypassing the normal firewall blocking on remote RPC calls. Of course, a new industry has now emerged with XML firewalls, where products aim to block access to Web services from the outside. However, a number of alternative and potentially more useful transport protocols can be utilized, including SMTP (for one-way messaging), WebSphere MQ (for reliable delivery—formerly called MQSeries), and TCP (for speed). Most implementations still use HTTP, but this may change in the future; Direct Internet Message Encapsulation (DIME), (Blocks Extensible Exchange Protocol (BEEP), Representational State Transfer (REST), and Abstract Syntax Notation 1—XML Encoding Rules (ASN.1 XER) are the emerging transport protocols in this area.

Every SOAP message contains three elements: the envelope, which marks the boundary of a message; the header, which encloses message meta-data; and the message, which comprises the actual message data. A typical SOAP request looks like this:

```
POST /BankAccount HTTP/1.1
Host: www.somebank.com
Content-Type: text/xml
Content-Length: 1024
SOAPMethodName: Account-Namespace-URI#GetBalance
<SOAP:Envelope xmlns:SOAP="urn:schemas-xmlsoap-org:soap.v1">
    <SOAP:Body>
        <m:GetBalance
            xmlns:m="Account-Namespace-URI">
                <AccountNumber>5551234322</AccountNumber>
        </m:GetBalance>
    </SOAP:Body>
</SOAP:Envelope>
```

Here, an HTTP POST for the application /BankAccount on www.somebank.com is made using the SOAP method GetBalance, which is defined by the Account-Namespace-URI. The SOAP body passes an AccountNumber data element to the GetBalance method. Let's have a look at the response to this request.

```
HTTP/1.1 200 OK
Content-Type: text/xml
Content-Length: 1232
<SOAP:Envelope xmlns:SOAP="urn:schemas-xmlsoap-org:soap.v1">
    <SOAP:Body>
        <m:GetBalanceResponse xmlns:m="Account-Namespace-URI">
            <Balance>1000000</Balance>
        </m:GetBalanceResponse>
    </SOAP:Body>
</SOAP:Envelope>
```

Here, an account balance of $1,000,000 is returned. Like the request, the response also has a SOAP envelope.

Web Services Description Language (WSDL)

WSDL is an IDL that allows client/server interfaces to be specified, similar to CORBA IDL. The difference is that WSDL is defined by using XML, and it specifies the remote object members (methods and data) that can be accessed by using SOAP. WSDL supports several different types of operations, including request/response, one-way, solicit/response, and notification. The different elements within WSDL define protocols and data formats, message content, specific operations for specific services, port numbers and types, service definitions, and data types. Typically, two files are generated for each service supported: a service definition file and a bindings file.

A service definition file (such as Account-service.wsdl) looks like this:

```
<?xml version="1.0" encoding="UTF-8"?>
<definitions name="AccountService"
  targetNamespace="http://localhost:8080/Applications/wsdl/Account-service.wsdl"
  xmlns="http://schemas.xmlsoap.org/wsdl/"
  xmlns:tns="http://localhost:8080/Applications/wsdl/Account-service.wsdl"
  xmlns:binding="http://www.account.com/definitions/AccountRemoteInterface"
  xmlns:soap="http://schemas.x mlsoap.org/wsdl/soap/">
  <import namespace="http://www.account.com/definitions/AccountRemoteInterface"
    location="http://localhost:8080/Applications/wsdl/Account-binding.wsdl"/>
  <service name="AccountService">
    <port name="AccountPort" binding="binding:AccountBinding">
      <soap:address
    location="http://localhost:8080/Applications/servlet/rpcrouter"/>
    </port>
  </service>
</definitions>
```

The preceding sample shows the various namespace, service, and port definitions for a service. This file sets key parameters for the Account class, including the target name - space (http://localhost:8080/Applications/wsdl/Account-service.wsdl), XML schema type (http://schemas.xmlsoap.org/wsdl/), SOAP schema (http://schemas.xmlsoap.org/wsdl/soap/), and the service binding details (http://www.account.com/definitions/AccountRemoteInterface). In addition, the transport-neutral RPC router is defined for the local server. The service defined within <service> is contained within the AccountBinding.wsdl file.

```
<?xml version="1.0" encoding="UTF-8"?>
<definitions name="AccountRemoteInterface"
targetNamespace=http://www.account.com/definitions/AccountRemoteInterface
 xmlns=http://schemas.xmlsoap.org/wsdl/
 xmlns:tns=http://www.account.com/definitions/AccountRemoteInterface
 xmlns:xsd=http://www.w3.org/2001/XMLSchema
 xmlns:soap="http://schemas.xmlsoap.org/wsdl/soap/">
  <message name="getBalance">
    <part name="result" type="xsd:double"/>
  </message>
  <message name="setBalance">
```

```
      <part name="balance" type="xsd:double"/>
   </message>
   <portType name="AccountJavaPortType">
     <operation name="getBalance">
       <output name="getBalance" message="tns:checkBalance"/>
     </operation>
     <operation name="setBalance">
       <input name="setBalance" message="tns:setBalance"/>
     </operation>
   </portType>
   <binding name="AccountBinding" type="tns:AccountJavaPortType">
     <soap:binding style="rpc" transport="http://schemas.xmlsoap.org/soap/http"/>
     <operation name="getBalance">
       <soap:operation soapAction="" style="rpc"/>
       <output name="getBalance">
         <soap:body use="encoded"
encodingStyle=http://schemas.xmlsoap.org/soap/encoding/
namespace="http://tempuri.org/Account"/>
       </output>
     </operation>
     <operation name="setBalance">
       <soap:operation soapAction="" style="rpc"/>
       <input name="setBalance">
         <soap:body use="encoded"
encodingStyle=http://schemas.xmlsoap.org/soap/encoding/
namespace="http://tempuri.org/Account"/>
       </input>
     </operation>
   </binding>
</definitions>
```

Recall that the two public methods defined within the `Account` class were `setBalance` and `getBalance`—the service definition contains elements that define `messages`, `portTypes`, `operations` for each method, including return value data types, and the SOAP-RPC operations being performed. A key benefit of WSDL is that it generally does not require manual coding; development tools take care of this for you.

Universal Description, Discovery, and Integration (UDDI) Registry

UDDI provides a registry service containing White, Yellow, and Green Pages that lists company details and specifications for the services that they provide. This allows dynamic binding at run time between different service providers to deliver applications composed of those services. UDDI providers work together to provide a coherent and highly available service for clients to discover services. White Pages contain business details listed like a normal phone book, and Yellow Pages contain the same contact information, but sorted into categories, just like the *Yellow Pages* phone book. The main difference between a phone book and a UDDI registry is that service definitions are published as Green Pages, allowing the dynamic discovery of business partners and their definitions. Sets of tModels in the Green Pages contain meta-data for service definitions. More details of the recent changes to UDDI vis-à-vis the merging of private and public registries are discussed in the UDDI chapter.

Immature Standards

The core Web services specifications have been around for several years now in various immature forms. In a similar way, many proposals still under development deal with more complex issues, and these may even be dropped in the future. This is caused by the fairly Darwinian process of optimal selection that occurs when a critical mass of users, vendors, and businesses begin to adopt one standard over another. However, some vendors are attempting to provide "roadmaps" of the various outcomes that the protocol sets are geared to achieving. For example, IBM and Microsoft have devised the Global XML Web Services Architecture[8] that defines the architectural principles underlying Web services: modularity, generic nature, federation, and standards. Supporting these principles are new standards, such as WS-Security, WS-License, WS-Routing and WS-Referral (Chapter 8 describes WS-Security at length).

This section reviews some of the more promising standards required to build a reliable service-oriented architecture for finance using Web services. To find out more about each protocol, you'll need to read the relevant chapter in the book.

Security

WS-Security defines a SOAP extension that provides protection for the integrity and confidentiality of messages, based on the existing XML Signature and XML Encryption standards. It provides message authentication, but it does not mandate specific encryption algorithms or security models to be used, nor does it cover key exchange or trust issues. It forms the basis for several advanced security protocols yet to be developed.

---

8.   See `http://www.gotdotnet.com/team/XMLwebservices/gxa_overview.aspx` for details.

Reliable Messaging

One of the first attempts to deliver guaranteed and assured delivery for Web services was Reliable HTTP (HTTPR) from IBM, which worked only with MQSeries. HTTPR aimed to provide reliable message delivery for Web services, providing a "send and forget" facility through a guaranteed messaging model. It provided guaranteed delivery because it automatically retried requests if a link or a server was down. However, OASIS WS-Reliability (`http://www.oasis-open.org/committees/tc_home.php?wg_abbrev=wsrm`) and WS-ReliableMessaging proposed by IBM, BEA, TIBCO, and Microsoft (and submitted to W3C) are the new competing protocols for reliable messaging.

Routing

Efforts are being made to move SOAP away from relying on transport protocols and toward defining a path between two endpoints for a one-way message exchange. WS-Routing was the original specification that allowed routing information to be specified within the SOAP envelope without relying on routing provided by the transport, since the transport was decoupled from the messaging protocol. Because most Web services currently are deployed over HTTP, IP routing provides a very transport-specific routing protocol. WS-Addressing is the new standard in this area (`http://www.theserverside.net/news/thread.tss?thread_id=25545`).

Orchestration and Workflow

Current workflow engines that allow the specification of complex business logic operations are largely not interoperable. This in turn hinders the creation of dynamic virtual enterprises where business partners can integrate and change workflows in real time. Business Process Execution Language (BPEL) is one standard that allows the specification of complex business processes; it links disparate activities based on services and data, with the underlying integration performed by Web services. It also provides sophisticated error handling and exception management, and nesting. Other standards in the area include the Business Process Modeling Language (BPML) and the Process Definition Markup Language (XPDL).

Activity Coordination

WS-Coordination is one protocol that coordinates the activities of distributed applications composed entirely of services. It underlies transactional consistency wherever data is shared, and provides a context for activity propagation between services using message correlation. The coordinator provides activation, registration, and associated protocols. Again, other protocols support activity orchestration, including the Web

Service Choreography Interface (WSCI) and the Web Service Choreography Definition Language (WS-CDL).

Distributed Transactions

WS-Transaction provides one framework and protocols for transactions in distributed applications, such as two-phase commit. It defines two coordination types: Atomic Transactions, which are short Atomic, Consistent, Isolation, and Durable (ACID) transactions, and a Business Activity, which is a long-running transaction. WS-Transaction also manages failure and prevents corruption of shared data (this may also be prevented by using WS-Attachment). OASIS Business Transaction Protocol (BTP) provides a set of activities that can also support distributed transactions, albeit through a relaxation of some ACID properties.

Summary

In this chapter, I have described the future of enterprise systems in the finance industries, covering the business and consumer demands for cost reduction and new services respectively. We examined the technological drivers and barriers to the introduction of Web services as the enablers of service-oriented architecture. In the chapters that follow, I examine finance scenarios to explore the Web services standards (both mature and immature) in the context of developing new applications and services today. After reading this chapter, you may feel that Web services are really quite easy to develop and deploy, but as always, the devil is in the details, and it's important to understand the capacities and limitations of each technology as it is described in the subsequent chapters.

CHAPTER 2

■ ■ ■

Enterprise Systems

In Chapter 1, I discussed Web services in the context of business and technical problems for which they attempt to provide a cross-platform, interoperable solution, and I introduced the major types of infrastructure and communication protocols. However, before I jump in to examine each new protocol more closely, it's worthwhile to look at the current state of enterprise systems.[1] This is not meant to be a history lesson, but the whole rationale of Web services is derived entirely from the failure of enterprise systems to solve what scientist Stephen Grossberg calls the "stability-plasticity" dilemma—that is, enterprise systems have been deliberately designed for brittleness, inflexibility, and the inability to adapt to change.

There are certainly justifiable reasons for this stoicism; enterprise systems are designed to deliver certainty in high-availability environments, and flexibility always introduces an aspect of uncertainty. For example, the Apache Web server provides a large number of configuration options that affect its dynamic behavior with respect to serving client requests for HTML pages or invoking CGI applications. Small changes in these parameters can have dramatic effects on the system's ability to service requests; for example, client request timeouts can be set to anything from 10 seconds to 10 minutes, depending on the average speed of client response times. Keeping connections alive for long periods uses up valuable server RAM and CPU resources. Coupling a large timeout with an unlimited number of spawned child processes can quickly bring a Web server to its knees during periods of high demand. In this case, the plasticity or the flexibility on configuring the system can have a net result not unlike the "butterfly effect" of chaos theory; small perturbations can lead to chaos in the long term dynamic behavior of the system.

The concern for stability in enterprise systems has often been coupled with vendors' failure to adopt standards produced by external industry bodies. Indeed, even the notion of an external application programming interface (API) is relatively new, since packaged software systems are typically developed to take care of all aspects of an enterprise operation, even where those activities include the integration of vertical applications. For

---

1. For more information on enterprise architectures, see http://www.pera.net/Pera/ faq_More_Types_of _Architecture.html.

example, packaged applications, like enterprise resource planning (ERP) systems, attempt to create a single logical enterprise application that can be centrally administered, or at least managed on a modular basis. However, many packaged applications still provide only a proprietary API because there was no generally accepted method for specifying these interfaces, unless one adopted a particular framework (such as CORBA) to expose all interfaces as distributed objects. This was clearly unacceptable to many vendors and end users, even though CORBA was driven by a standards body. The major challenge for Web services in providing cross-platform, interoperable standards for APIs exposed over the Internet is to overcome some of the objections to CORBA that were raised during its heyday.

In this chapter, I review the different types of enterprise systems and the sorts of software generally required to support such systems in production. Clearly, a prerequisite for modern enterprise systems is that they run and execute on a networked operating system, such as one of the UNIX variants or Microsoft Windows. Indeed, some enterprise applications are now included as a standard part of the operating environment supplied with the operating system distributions. For example, Sun Microsystems' Solaris 10 contains directory and application servers, and Windows contains Microsoft Message Queuing (MSMQ) software. While reviewing all of the types of subsystems that compose "an enterprise system," keep in mind the Web services standards discussed in Chapter 1, and how they might improve the scenarios described here. For example, although UDDI is the new Web services directory standard, most current implementations simply use UDDI as a standard interface to the Lightweight Directory Access Protocol (LDAP). Most enterprise systems require some type of directory system, but not all use LDAP, so UDDI is the next-level abstraction that allows all directory servers to communicate with a common language.

Monoliths

Many enterprise applications can be characterized as monolithic, which sounds nasty, but from an administrative perspective, should allow easy management. This is true if an enterprise has to maintain only a single monolith, but most enterprises end up with several monoliths running, and most do not share any common infrastructure. For example, sales and customer relationship management (CRM) systems tend to be different from human resources (HR) applications, which are in turn quite different from finance applications. The rise of the tightly coupled vertical application has been a major limiting factor in achieving enterprise integration. The irony is that many of the records found in a CRM system would also appear in a finance application; debtors, creditors, and the other entities a firm deals with would all require access to the same underlying data. Unfortunately, if the CRM and finance applications do not have externally accessible and standards-compliant APIs, the chances of getting other applications to integrate with them are quite difficult. This lack of integration then leads to major business headaches; records are being stored in multiple databases, so a call center operator could be examining customer records from the CRM and finance applications that simply don't agree. How can data consistency be assured when multiple copies of the same record exist, and there is no mechanism for global integrity checking and data element validation?

A number of vertical application vendors have attempted to rectify the problem. Oracle, for example, sells many vertical applications, which in turn make use of its database server as a common persistence layer. This allows some level of database integration and, coupled with Oracle's J2EE application server, a high level of interoperability within and between Oracle applications.

However, most enterprises use the products of multiple vendors to minimize vendor risk. While avoiding vendor lock-in is a necessary risk-management strategy from a business perspective, it introduces a high degree of complexity from a technical perspective. In the case of Oracle applications, choosing a different J2EE application server (such as BEA's WebLogic or IBM's WebSphere), and a different database connectivity layer vendor (such as Caribou Lake), and perhaps an object-relational mapping tool (such as TopLink) can make integration with vertical applications a grand challenge. In theory, all of these products meet J2EE standards, but when there is a run-time failure, it can be quite difficult to identify the component or layer causing the problem, particularly when multiple vendors are involved.

Monolithic applications are sometimes developed with little thought about possible future expansion or modification that may be required, particularly with prototypes that end up being moved into production because of cost or time limitations. Cost-cutting in the current economic environment may bring new meaning to the term *reuse* as restrictions are placed on software engineering processes. Rather than reinventing the wheel, how can reuse be easily achieved for enterprise applications?

Middleware

So, what's the solution to successfully integrate these vertical applications to achieve system efficiency and data consistency? The answer has often been touted as middleware, or the software "glue" that can bind multiple applications. Early middleware systems received a bad rap because they did not adhere to any standards, so integration would be possible only with a small number of products. Alternatively, some middleware products were limited to point-to-point integration, limiting the ability to customize or bundle applications. Given that complexity theory says that the sum of the parts is always greater than the whole, the sorts of tasks that multiple systems can achieve in concert is usually much greater than can be achieved alone. So, it's important that middleware can be used to develop new applications that build on top of multiple items of existing infrastructure, without changing the underlying code of those items. For example, as a developer, if I want to integrate the Oracle database into my system, I shouldn't have to modify the source code of the database server—but I should be able to write custom code that can wrap any calls to the database server. The promise of Web services is that this kind of integration can be achieved by using standards across platforms to deliver a new generation of systems that can share data and business objects with few, if any, restrictions.

Certainly, Web services is not the first attempt to solve the integration problem in this way, and it may well be useful to take a step back and analyze the failures of the most immediate predecessor to Web services in cross-platform integration: CORBA. In some ways, CORBA has been very successful, laying the foundation for later distributed-object systems, such as Enterprise JavaBeans (EJB), that form the component layer for J2EE. CORBA systems have proven to be very reliable over a number of years. CORBA ORBs were developed by members of the CORBA steering group, the Object Management Group (OMG).

CORBA experienced two major problems: standards creep and tight coupling. Small differences in vendor implementations limited the extent to which ORBs from different vendors could interoperate, because many of the core standards were not agreed to until very late in the standards process. For example, the BOA (Basic Object Adapter) and POA (Portable Object Adapter) standards only appeared after several iterations, and were never fully implemented by some ORBs. Since the object adaptors were responsible for interpreting objects references to invoke remote methods, this was a serious failure. Lack of vendor agreement is also a risk for Web services.

However, there is a major architectural difference in coupling between Web services and CORBA that limits the impact of this problem: The Web services SOAP is based on loosely coupled messaging, while CORBA was based around tightly coupled direct method invocation. Clearly, if the mechanisms for portable method invocation were not standardized in CORBA, this would cause more problems than for SOAP, where a message is passed and interpreted asynchronously. Getting agreement on the format of the interface for interpreting messages—WSDL—was clearly a priority, and both SOAP and WSDL are now considered mature.

CORBA

CORBA was based on an RPC architecture with a twist; instead of replicating Distributed Computing Environment (DCE) and other standard RPC systems, the remote procedures were always object methods. These objects could provide event-based transactional access to back-end relational or object-oriented databases in a secure environment. The OMG provided standards for many enterprise application layers, but in areas such as threading, directory access, load balancing, and the like, there was considerable scope for vendors to implement their own solutions. In a Web services world, the back-end implementation is encapsulated, so differences in operating systems and platforms matter less than they did with CORBA implementations.

Since CORBA is object-oriented, it was an excellent platform for developers to use, because objects instantiated on servers could be invoked by using standard method call syntax, in any supported language, and these objects were stateful. The architecture was based on a stub and skeleton that would be distributed to the client and server, respectively, based on an agreed interface definition specified in the CORBA IDL. CORBA was supported by a wide variety of languages such as Java, C, C++, and Ada. So, a CORBA client built with C would be able to access a much richer set of features by invoking a CORBA server built with C++ or Java. And, because many legacy systems do not support modern object-oriented languages, CORBA provided an excellent solution for developing interfaces in e-commerce applications. For example, while a CORBA client might handle front-end page generation, the back-end processing could be performed on a mainframe running a CORBA server. A simple request/response cycle could be initiated based on HTTP sequencing.

Let's examine a sample CORBA application, written for Borland's VisiBroker, which demonstrates some of the features and problems of CORBA. This system is based on a phone-banking scenario, where a user can dial into a Voice Response System (VRS), enter their account number and PIN, and hear the account balance over the phone. The following interface, specified using IDL, defines an interface phone for the module bank.cassowary.net, with a single method: checkAccountBalance(). This method has two in parameters—the accountNumber and PIN (both short integers)—and the out parameter is the account balance (floating point). Note that CORBA methods have return values (in this case, a string), but can also return multiple values using the out parameter syntax from a single method. This approach is quite attractive to clients that are not object-oriented, since all returned parameters do not need to be wrapped by a single large object—although this approach certainly frightened many object-oriented designers! A module can contain multiple interfaces, and each interface can specify multiple methods, so the system is quite flexible. The source for phone.bank.cassowary.net is shown here:

```
module net
{
    module cassowary
    {
        module bank
        {
            interface phone
            {
                string checkAccountBalance
                (
                    in short accountNumber,
                    in short PIN,
                    out float balance
                );
            };
        };
    };
};
```

Two implementations now need to be developed: a server and a client implementation. The server provides an implementation of the modules, interfaces, and methods specified by the IDL, through an ORB. Firstly, an ORB object is created, and the appropriate object adapter is initialized through a series of different stages, all of which depend on the underlying ORB implementation. Finally, the run method on the ORB is called when the object adapters have been created, as shown here:

```java
import org.omg.PortableServer.*;
import java.sql.*;
import java.io.*;
import java.util.*;

public class Server
{
    public static void main(String[] args)
    {
        try
        {
            org.omg.CORBA.ORB orb = org.omg.CORBA.ORB.init(args,null);
            POA rootPOA = POAHelper.narrow(orb.resolve_initial_references
                ("RootPOA"));
            org.omg.CORBA.Policy[] policies =
            {
                rootPOA.create_lifespan_policy(LifespanPolicyValue.PERSISTENT)
            };
            POA myPOA = rootPOA.create_POA("phone_agent_poa",
                rootPOA.the_POAManager(), policies );
            PhoneImpl phoneServant = new PhoneImpl();
            byte[] phoneId = "Phone".getBytes();
            myPOA.activate_object_with_id(phoneId, phoneServant);
            rootPOA.the_POAManager().activate();
            System.out.println(myPOA.servant_to_reference(phoneServant)
                + " is ready.");
            orb.run();
        }
        catch (Exception e)
        {
            e.printStackTrace();
        }
    }
}
```

For each method and interface defined for each module, a method implementation is required. In this example, the class PhoneImpl would contain a definition for the method checkAccountBalance(). A sample checkAccountBalance() method is shown here:

```
public String checkAccountBalance(short accountNumber, short PIN,
 org.omg.CORBA.IntHolder accountBalance)
{
 // Method implementation
}
```

The use of the org.omg.CORBA.IntHolder allows parameter values to be returned outside a return type of a wrapper object. The method implementation might invoke a local Java Database Connectivity (JDBC) API request to a database holding the account records, or it might invoke a method on a stateless session bean, providing a wrapper for an entity bean, which in turn provides access to the back-end database. The level of abstraction required depends on many factors, including the complexity of the application, the degree of sharing of data persistence objects between different applications, and whether the server is J2EE-compliant.

On the client side, the remote object must be bound by using the POA before any remote methods can be invoked. Local variables should be initialized with the parameter-passed values, except for the case of the special out parameter, whose value is set by checkAccountBalance() after invocation. Once the balance is returned to the client, another method can be invoked to speak the result through the telephone by using text-to-speech conversion. Sample client code is shown here:

```
public class Client
{
    public static void main(String[] args)
    {
        short accountNumber=55528751;
        short PIN=9999;
        org.omg.CORBA.IntHolder accountBalance=new org.omg.CORBA.IntHolder();
        try
        {
            org.omg.CORBA.ORB orb = org.omg.CORBA.ORB.init(args,null);
            byte[] phoneId = "Phone".getBytes();
            net.cassowary.bank.Phone p =
                net.cassowary.bank.PhoneHelper.bind(orb, "/phone_agent_poa",
                phoneId);
            speakResult(p.checkAccountBalance(accountNumber, PIN,
                accountBalance);
        }
```

```
        catch (Exception e)
        {
            System.err.println(e);
        }
    }

    private void speakResult(String accountBalance)
    {
        // Method implementation
    }
}
```

Rather than focusing on the details of the CORBA implementation, the basic approach should be clear; CORBA relied heavily on RPC-style invocation of remote methods, essentially requiring tight coupling. Web services, on the other hand, rely on loose coupling of client and server interfaces, where connectivity is only required asynchronously. Some Web services might require guaranteed delivery, while others would not. Messaging systems are asynchronous and can provide either guaranteed or nonguaranteed delivery, and therefore make an ideal platform for building Web services.

Messaging

Messaging comes as a shock to many developers who are used to invoking a remote method and having the client application wait until a response is received, as with CORBA. This type of synchronous method calling is the idealized norm often taught in undergraduate college courses. However, messaging is more commonly found in enterprise systems, where continuous connectivity in "loosely coupled" systems cannot be guaranteed, so asynchronous messaging is used instead. This approach allows a more general client/server method of communication, since both asynchronous and synchronous applications can be supported. Messaging also underlies SOAP, which supports both synchronous and asynchronous messaging patterns.

Asynchronous applications are very error-tolerant, because they can deal with network or systems failures very gracefully. Once a client writes a message to a queue, it then considers the operation a success and does not wait for a response. Indeed, in many scenarios a response other than an acknowledgment is not required—and with the right infrastructure, an acknowledgment is not always required. For example, think of print-queuing technology; in some single-user operating systems, when you submit a print job to the printer, the client application waits until the printer returns an acknowledgment that printing has succeeded before it allows any other operations to be performed. This synchronous sequence is shown in Figure 2-1. This is a very common scenario in finance, where contract notes are printed by batch every evening to be posted to investors and traders.

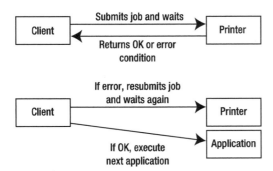

Figure 2-1. *Synchronous processing of printer jobs*

The rationale is that the user must be notified of any error conditions. This is clearly unnecessary, especially if the success or failure of printing can be judged by checking the printer physically, or, if an error occurs, the (modern Ethernet-connected) printer can simply e-mail an error message to the user. A worse situation would occur if all user applications on all terminals were held up because other users had submitted jobs that were still printing. Clearly, the best approach is asynchronous, and most modern printer queues operate on this principle.

Another important feature of messaging is demonstrated by the printing example; the user does not need to invoke a method executing on the printer directly. On UNIX systems, the printer daemon typically queues messages on the server side, and then passes them across to the printer for execution when it signals that it is ready to print the next job. Indeed, some printers also have a queue on the printer itself, and modern printers have a large amount of RAM available for holding jobs in the queue before executing a print program on them. This asynchronous sequence is shown in Figure 2-2.

From a security perspective, messaging is also superior because direct access to remote method calls is not permitted; rather, a request for processing is made, with the data encapsulated in a message, which is then processed by the printer on its own time, and not when the client demands it. This may be useful in preventing denial-of-service attacks, where a remote method is continuously and mischievously executed by a rogue external user, since the application can simply defer processing of malicious requests. However, since many messaging products broadcast their contents "in the clear," security of the transport layer is a key issue in subscriber-based services.

Like the print queue, some messaging systems are based on FIFO queuing, however, MSMQ and IBM WebSphere MQ (MQ Series) allow triggers, priorities, and selection filters to specify handling of different messages using the same queue. Once a message has been written to the queue by a client application, the client considers the operation successful. Some messaging systems also feature transactions; these ensure that message writing can be part of an atomic sequence of operations that can be rolled back if at least one of the operations fails. Transactions typically can be executed on either the client or server, or both. However, it's important to note that atomicity is not preserved across the queue; a transaction committed on the client is unaffected by a transaction rollback on the server.

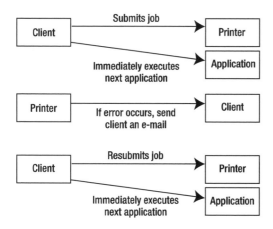

Figure 2-2. *Asynchronous processing of printer jobs*

Generally, message queues are set up to support either IP unicast or IP multicast transmission—that is, single-client/single-server or single-server/multiple-client operations. The unicast (1–1) model is primarily provided by IBM's MQ Series and Microsoft's MSMQ, while the multicast (1–many) model is implemented in TIBCO's Rendezvous product. However, the lines between different products are now somewhat blurred, because some versions of MQ Series now support publishing, and TIBCO supports 1–1 publishing where there is only one publisher and one subscriber.

Figure 2-3 shows a simple unicast message writing operation, where a client simply writes a message using a send operation, while the server processes a message using the receive operation.

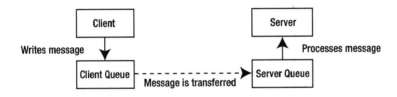

Figure 2-3. *Reading and writing a message using a unicast messaging system*

In contrast, Figure 2-4 shows a more complex message writing operation, where a server broadcasts a message using a "publish" operation on one channel, while all clients that subscribe to that channel process the message using the "subscribe" operation. This is the foundation for so-called "publish-and-subscribe systems." Typically, subscribers are set up to listen for specific topics or subjects being broadcast, with subjects often being set up in a hierarchy. For example, a publisher of news stories might broadcast messages with the subjects /Breaking, /World, /National, /Sports, /Technology, /Business, etc. A subscriber, in this example, may be an application server that dynamically generates pages for a sports magazine Web site; so, only the /Sports messages would be listened for and converted to HTML as required for display on the Web site. A more specific fishing Web site might only listen for messages belonging to /Sports/ Fishing, and so on. Subscribers might choose to listen for multiple subjects; clearly, it just depends on end-user requirements.

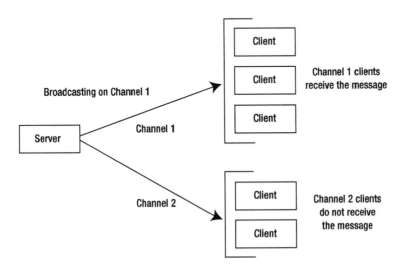

Figure 2-4. *Publishing a message and subscribing to a channel using a multicast messaging system*

In a classical publish-and-subscribe system, the publisher simply broadcasts its messages without regard to who the subscribers are, just like a broadcast TV station. However, for "premium" content, cable-TV subscribers pay a subscription fee each month for continued access to the service. This presents a number of issues related to the subscription architecture. One possible architecture is to encrypt all messages so that only an authenticated and authorized subscriber can interpret the messages. This approach can be easily implemented by using public key cryptography infrastructure (PKI). However, as the number of subscribers increases, the burden of having to encrypt messages for each subscriber quickly becomes impossible because of poor perform-ance—after all, broadcasting is all about sending once to be received by many. So, a variant of PKI is used, whereby each subscriber receives a group private key that enables content decryption, requiring the publisher broadcast and encrypt the message only once.

However, a subscriber who has a copy of the group key can simply keep viewing the encrypted content without having to keep paying the subscription fee. So, the group key must be continuously reissued to only current subscribers; this ensures backward and forward confidentiality. Unfortunately, these rekeying operations can be very expensive, so many open issues still exist relating to the performance of publish-and-subscribe systems where a high level of security is required.

Another quirky use of asynchronous messaging is to use it to emulate synchronous method invocation; thus, a message is sent as a method request from the client to the server, the method is executed on the server, which then returns a message to the client. This could be a method to support transactions with three phases: 1) server sends and commits, 2) client receives and commits, 3) client confirms back to server. If the server does not receive a confirmation within a given time, it rolls back. Why use this round-about way of achieving what CORBA can do? Adopting the "loosely coupled" architecture for all RPC-type operations means that your systems can tolerate failure much more easily because they are not dependent on a remote server being available immediately to answer a request. For example, if the response from a remote method to be invoked does not have to be received by the client within a couple of seconds, then using asynchro-nous messaging reduces the potential for failure resulting from extended latencies induced by system or network failure.

Enterprise Architectures

We've looked at the CORBA experiment in the context of its role as middleware, but what of the more modern enterprise architectures, such as Microsoft's .NET and Sun's J2EE, which revolve around component architectures rather than service architectures? How do these ensure interoperability? The basis for both these architectures is the partitioning of application functionality and the layering of individual partitions, with components encapsulating business logic at the back-end. For example, in a retail sales operation, functionality can often be divided along service lines; one service is required for each of the following business operations:

- Accepting customer orders and supplier invoices

- Managing warehouse inventory

- Authorizing credit card debits

- Managing the shipping process

While all of these services could be provided technically by one system, in practice, different businesses generally operate these quite separately, so integration must be performed between partitioned systems, as shown in Figure 2-5.

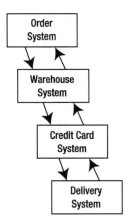

Figure 2-5. *Partitioning systems by functionality*

Each partitioned system is then responsible for providing four individual layers, again separating functionality. These layers are

- Presentation layer

- Business logic layer

- Data access layer

- Data persistence layer

Both J2EE and .NET have this basic architecture. In addition, at the business logic layer, integration is typically possible between these systems (and packaged applications like ERP systems). Both architectures incorporate synchronous and asynchronous method invocation and messaging; for example, J2EE provides access to EJB using a message-driven or a method-driven interface.

What are the major drivers for adopting an enterprise architecture? There are certainly benefits in meeting functional requirements—in providing the best solution to business problems. But perhaps the kind of distributed architectures typically implemented using J2EE and .NET can support the following nonfunctional requirements:

- Ensuring consistent performance across multiple systems, platforms, and operating systems

- Guaranteeing scalable performance across multiple systems with minimal operating cost

- Increasing failure resistance and fault tolerance where redundancy is built in to components and systems

- Implementing policies for security and secure communications

- Providing facilities for integrated exception handling and operational management

- Optimizing team development by providing logical chunks for teams and individuals to work on

The interaction between the different layers in enterprise architectures is shown in Figure 2-6.

Enterprise architectures also provide vertical layers that bind various horizontal layers in the model. For example, common services like security, management and monitoring, directory access, messaging, transactional policies, and network communications infrastructure are provided where required across the different layers; J2EE can provide the Java Transaction Service (JTS), Java Naming and Directory Interface (JNDI), Java Messaging Service (JMS), and Java Connector Architecture (JCA) APIs.

Modern enterprise systems are based on component systems being implemented in the business logic layer. So, J2EE has EJB components, while .NET has COM+ components. How compatible are component-based models with service-based models? In theory, a service is any piece of software that services requests by way of responses being sent through an external interface. Services encapsulate data and their own internal implementations, so it is not essential that they be implemented as components. However, given the many advantages of component-based systems—such as making distributed computing operate like local method invocation—it is likely that most newly developed service-based systems will be component-based. However, the value of Web services is that these component systems can be easily integrated with existing noncomponent systems. Hence, SOAs can be seen as extensions of component architectures.

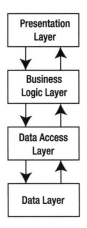

Figure 2-6. *Enterprise system layering*

J2EE and WWW

The emergence of the J2EE platform can be traced to the failure of the first-generation Web applications based on fat client Java applet technology, which was intended as a replacement for dynamic applications hosted on the server side, made accessible through the CGI. Indeed, predating the introduction of CGI was the widespread acceptance of WWW as the standard for networked hypertext. Its ascendancy was not guaranteed, since HTTP was designed as a simple request/response protocol to allow scientists to exchange papers and cross-reference each other's work using hypertext links. While FTP already did file transfer, and some platforms already had hypertext (e.g., Mac OS HyperCard), HTTP combined generic transport and hypertext with all accessible content defined by a URL. But it competed strongly with alternative technologies like Gopher, which also combined transport and hypertext and was in widespread use in the early 1990s, and Wide Area Information Service (WAIS), which focused on providing search and indexing services for hypertext documents.

It's commonly believed that WWW won out because it supported pictures and Gopher didn't (the early Mosaic browser supported text, images, and other multimedia, while Gopher and friends retained the hypertext focus). Today, only the WWW survives, retaining the emphasis on thin clients and lightweight protocols. HTML allows for the marking up of data for display using standard tags such as <h1> for headings, and has many structural elements, such as <head> and <body>. On the pragmatic side, HTML also has some display directives such <i> and <b> for italics and bold, respectively.

Early versions of HTML were compatible with all browsers, but incompatibilities in the interpretation of HTML across browsers caused numerous headaches, even with the introduction of Cascading Style Sheets. In recent years, there has been a move toward using XML to define both data and metadata, although many Web sites still use static HTML to present data.

Pure HTML has the greatest cross-platform compatibility, but is very limited in its programmability, even with the support of scripting languages like JavaScript, which is an object-oriented, interpreted programming language running in the client browser. JavaScript has some similarities to Java, and is very useful for validating form input. Unfortunately, it is very messy to work with, and is notoriously hard to debug off-line. Like HTML, its behavior is different across browsers, and being interpreted, has limited scope for doing real programming. However, it is efficient in the sense that it can generate menus, populate drop-down boxes, etc., without making new connections to the server.

CGI was intended to allow complex, compiled applications to be executed on the server side, with scripting support provided by JavaScript on the client side. CGI provided easy access to server-side databases, was useful for form processing, and supported a large number of languages, such as C, C++, Fortran, and even Java, as well as scripting languages like Perl, PHP, and Tcl. CGI made it easy for Web users to access existing legacy applications because simple wrappers could be provided to these applications, and it was easy to administer because no dedicated application server was required.

However, CGI was very inefficient and not scalable, since each new client would spawn a new process, and if the CGI application was interpreted (such as a Perl script), one instance of the interpreter also needed to be loaded into memory at run time. Security vulnerabilities were rampant, with buffer overflows occurring when bounds were not checked on input streams, leading to the stack space being overwritten.

Java applets were seen as one replacement for CGI scripts, because more application logic could be shifted to the client side. In this model, applets could replace the clunky request-response cycles of HTTP, and dynamic, sandboxed applications could be downloaded to local client over the Internet. A connection to the downloading server could be made using Java Remote Method Invocation (RMI), and a JVM would execute inside the client browser, enabling execution of Write Once, Run Anywhere (WORA) Java bytecodes. However, in practice, the sandboxing proved too restrictive for many applications (e.g., files could not be read from or written to the local hard drive), and there were many incompatibilities with different browsers. In retrospect, applets were a cute technology, but enterprises wanted to deploy real apps over the WWW.

At this point, the focus switched to server-side Java as a replacement for CGI, with Java servlets providing the original solution, ultimately growing to include the entire J2EE architecture. Servlets were designed as small, encapsulated applications that gave access to Java's enormous non-GUI libraries, including security, networking, threading, and database connectivity. An example servlet is shown here:

```java
public class SimpleServlet extends HttpServlet
{
    public void doGet (HttpServletRequest req,
        HttpServletResponse res) throws ServletException, IOException
    {
        ServletOutputStream out = res.getOutputStream();
        res.setContentType("text/html");
        out.println("<HEAD><TITLE>Hello World</TITLE></HEAD>");
        out.println("<BODY>");
        out.println("<h1>Hello World!</h1>");
        out.println("<P>A very simple servlet…");
        out.println("</BODY>");
        out.close();
    }
}
```

As you can see, the actual code required to print an HTML document dynamically is very small, and is executed through a servlet "runner" inside a single JVM process. Servlets generate HTML pages dynamically inside a Java source in a way similar to CGI, with one instance of each servlet class loaded into memory after the first request. Servlets have service methods corresponding to HTTP, GET, and POST, with variables inside methods protected. Access to members outside service methods require synchronized access, which can create bottlenecks as users increase, unless the SingleThreadModel is used, giving one instance per user just like CGI.

Servlets have a number of benefits; they can be used to deploy platform-independent enterprise applications, run through a standard Web interface, and allow object reuse, because components can be bundled as "beans." Servlets execute on servers with different operating systems and hardware, and can be easily replaced with newer systems, with no concerns for application stability when porting. Faster performance can be gained by using "Just-In-Time" (JIT) compilers for specific platforms, with process and memory overhead reduced by threading and caching. Session tracking is available for supporting multipage applications, allowing stateful interactions, while connection pooling is available for efficiently accessing databases.

Servlets have a number of important limitations, which is why they need support from various J2EE architecture components to provide a basis for enterprise WWW applications. They are inflexible, since to change the embedded HTML, the Java source must be modified and recompiled. All associated code must be written in Java, so it is difficult to integrate servlets with legacy apps. Some important Java libraries cannot be accessed, such as the Java 2D/3D libraries, and many servlet libraries have already been deprecated, so .class files may not execute with future JVMs without revision and recompilation. Servlets are also potentially dangerous, as an unhandled exception in one servlet could affect others running in the same runner process, and synchronization problems in multithreaded applications can become deadlocked. On the human side, HTML developers can get access to Java code, since there is no separation between business logic and the user interface implementation.

To ameliorate these deficiencies, J2EE was developed as an enterprise platform, providing a multitiered application architecture that can support load balancing, dynamic failover, EAI, transactions, clustering, logging and auditing, management, middleware, and security. J2EE consists of a number of existing technologies, such as RMI, servlets, JDBC, and directory services, and adds EJB components and JSPs for the user interface. Interfaces to existing distributed computing architectures like CORBA are also supported.

J2EE is a tiered architecture that separates presentation logic from application and business logic, and supports essential nonfunctional requirements for enterprise applications, such as scalability, availability, and robustness. In many cases, single points of failure can be eliminated, but state management quickly becomes an issue wherever it needs to be replicated in real time.

At the presentation tier, applets and HTML/JavaScript pages are supported by a separate client tier, comprising JSPs, servlets, and JavaBeans. In the business logic tier, EJBs provide a component model for encapsulating business logic, which connects to a data tier, with access to databases provided by JDBC. Binding these horizontal tiers is a set of vertical integration services, such as security and directory services, provided by the container in which enterprise applications run. The container provides a common framework for security, transactions, components, and database access. The embedded component models provide state management, business logic encapsulation, and object-relational access to RDBMS or message queues. There is the capacity to integrate with legacy applications in the back-end by using JCA.

The most important part of J2EE as an architecture is the central role played by EJB components. EJBs are encapsulated components with well-defined interfaces, and multiple components can be pipelined to perform complex operations. Both stateful and stateless component models are supported, and as with CORBA, building distributed systems based on J2EE can be done as easily with remote components as it can with local components. However, the underlying issues that make messaging preferable—such as latency and failure semantics—are the same as for CORBA.

The J2EE model has these component types:

- **Session beans (stateless and stateful)**: Encapsulate business processes

- **Entity beans**: Provide an object view of business data stored in an RDBMS, using either bean-managed or container-managed persistence, and support transactions

- **Message-driven beans**: Provide message queue access using the JMS API

In many applications, session beans provide a "wrapping" for entity beans, giving an overall more complex than .NET, which has no entity bean equivalent (see the following section on .NET). Even though early Java application servers did not always support J2EE, most now do so.

EJB components reside inside the J2EE container, which provides a standard way of assembling and deploying them, along with a common framework for transactions, state management, resource sharing, threading, and security. The container is a piece of implicit middleware, with a focus on implementing business logic and not the supporting environment. For example, by pooling bean instances, scale-up can be available as required, and the reuse of objects provides efficiency. In terms of security, common authentication and access control mechanisms are available, as is support for different transaction isolation levels to ensure sequential processing (high isolation) or improve performance (low isolation). Location transparency of components and containers is provided by the JNDI naming service, and remote components can be invoked as if they were local by using RMI.

EJB components provide the natural building blocks for supporting both existing and new stateful and stateless Web services.

One of the great features of J2EE is its inherent flexibility; the multitiered architecture can comprise products supplied by numerous vendors, allowing you to pick and choose the best vendors for each tier. This flexibility comes at a cost, however, especially when trying to debug an application supported by multiple vendors. While J2EE avoids vendor lock-in, it also provides a great opportunity for vendor hand-washing of sticky problems. It's worth noting that C# and CLI are now ECMA/ISO standards (`http://msdn.microsoft.com/net/ecma/`), while Java is not a standard.

.NET and WWW

Tight integration is one major advantage of Microsoft .NET over J2EE; while it is certainly possible to use different vendors' products on Windows, .NET provides a level of integration between services that makes development really easy to develop and deploy on Windows. Windows already contains many of the "add-on" services that J2EE mandates, such as directory, security, and messaging systems. At the core of .NET is the CLR, which supports more than 20 languages (the Java VM works only with Java). The .NET Framework has a common Class Library and a shared common type system, and also allows side-by-side execution of different assembly versions.

.NET applications written in C# .NET or Visual Basic .NET can be executed as managed code; that is, they are compiled to an intermediate language, much like Java bytecodes, and packaged as an assembly that contains associated metadata and other attributes. JIT compilation and CLR execution on a specific target system ensures that classes are only compiled natively as required in real time, increasing application performance. All other applications execute as unmanaged code in the .NET environment.

The native .NET remoting protocol is SOAP, making it easy to integrate with XML Web services. Support is provided for both Web-based applications and desktop clients, and integrated tools and server support make it easier to develop with .NET rather than tools from multiple J2EE vendors. .NET provides many innovations in diverse areas, such as workflow tools, administration, failover, and fault-tolerance, while focusing on scale-out rather than scale-up. Implementations of .NET are available for Windows (using Microsoft or Borland development tools), and even deployment on Linux, including the Rotor and Ximian Mono Projects!

Support for Windows Web applications has come a long way since the introduction of the Internet Information Server (IIS), which provided CGI-like application plug-ins, and the invention of compiled ASP pages, well before the equivalent of JSP in J2EE. ASP provides a separation between business logic and user interface implementation.

Like the JVM and the J2EE container, the CLR manages all code execution issues relating to security, threading, exception handling, and dynamic binding. However, .NET also provides a common set of class libraries that can be called from any language, leading to consistent design patterns across languages. Base classes are provided for text processing, networking, multithreading, and user interfaces. ADO.NET provides data access functionality with XML support, and ASP.NET supports Web-based applications.

While ASP.NET is very easy to use, the original ASP succeeded several attempts to support dynamic Web pages on Windows (including ADC and HTX). ASP is now a very mature technology, with VBScript code embedded using code blocks (`<%@ Language=VBScript %>`) and database support. However, ASP had a number of significant problems; for example, run-time typing was problematic, since only the variable type was assigned during interpretation. This reduced performance, but more importantly, it made debugging difficult because casting problems could not be identified during development. One solution was to move business logic into components (e.g., ActiveX DLLs), where strong typing was supported. ASP allowed HTML developers to get access to source code, and session management across pooled servers was difficult. It should be noted that JSP suffers from many of these problems as well.

While ASP.NET retains some similarities to ASP, it has many significant improvements. ASP.NET compiles pages using JIT, and access to all common class libraries is available. All ASP.NET pages inherit from System.Web.UI.Page, giving access to a standard set of data and methods. All services are available from the CLR, ensuring type safety, good debugging, and high performance. Code and HTML are now completely separated, while safer state management can be provided across clusters. From the developer's perspective, Web pages are now developed just as if they were normal applications, rather than requiring hand-coding of HTML sections, for example.

With respect to Web services, ADO.NET components build on the very mature COM/COM+/DCOM component models and provide excellent candidates for deployment as Web services. While J2EE is a very pure object-oriented environment, with a single-language VM, .NET has an integration focus on providing a standard run time and libraries for many different languages.

Enterprise Operating Systems

Some of the most significant interoperability and system integration issues don't arise at the application level, but at the operating system level. This is because operating systems provide the basic platform for applications to be developed and, most importantly, to be deployed. For example, modern operating systems provide threading to implement lightweight processes that are very efficient, since threads belonging to an application can be reused, rather than created from scratch. On an enterprise system designed with an uptime of say 99.9 percent, this creates great savings over a lifetime. If a server was multiprocess but single-thread, how would this affect multithreaded clients?

This example only affects efficiency and performance, but in some cases, it's simply not possible to translate the operations of one part of an operating system to another. Any protocol-based services are generally difficult to map between operating systems, except where there is an isomorphism between complementary operations. For example, UNIX systems generally use the Network File System (NFS) protocol to share files, while Microsoft Windows systems are built around the Server Message Block (SMB) protocol. Currently, it's not possible to map the operations of the two onto each other directly. So, many UNIX systems now run both NFS and Samba (a UNIX SMB implementation)—a clearly wasteful situation, since two systems need to be independently administered on the same server to perform exactly the same function.

Sometimes these differences arise from hardware variations; given sufficient levels of abstraction, however, it should be possible for most modern operating systems to interoperate, if they all support networking, have a similar process model, support virtual memory, etc.

What are the key obstacles to integration at the operating system level? Differences in the following areas cause typical frustrations:

- User and group models

- File permissions

- Role-based access control

- Process and threading models

- File system structures

- Scripting

- Printer sharing

- Networking, including routing

- File sharing

- Directory services

- Security

However, some areas where interoperability is broadly possible include e-mail. Perhaps it's no surprise that e-mail, unlike file sharing, is asynchronous. Unfortunately, mail protocols like SMTP do not guarantee delivery; while failure notification is provided by the local SMTP server if it cannot deliver a message because of a network outage, the remote SMTP server may discard a message where the recipient doesn't exist, has a full mailbox, or is not obliged to notify the sender. There has been much interest in utilizing SMTP as a transport protocol for SOAP because it supports both one-way and two-way communications by way of messaging, and because most servers also run a mail server. But realistically, SMTP is far too slow for this type of application.

ERP Systems

What about the more sophisticated approaches to interoperability, such as packaged applications, or removing the need for interoperability through ERP systems? One view is that Web services wouldn't be necessary if ERP systems had succeeded in integrating all departments and applications within a single organization under a single monolithic application. In many respects, the modular design of ERP systems and their attempts to unify and integrate data management have been very successful. There is great potential to save money by not rewriting existing applications, automating manual processes, and tying them into a coherent architecture.

ERP system vendors appear to be among the greatest supporters of Web services because they have been criticized in the past for providing only proprietary interfaces to their applications. Thus, developers were unable to access individual components or modules without using an ERP interface. There are clearly good reasons for this—the same reasons that object-oriented developers design classes explicitly with public and private methods! Because there have been no standards for exposing proprietary interfaces in a consistent way, Web services standards provide ERP vendors with an excellent means to achieve this goal.

Summary

In this chapter, I have examined the current state of enterprise systems, and how the various platforms and architectures being used to develop new applications and services can be integrated with existing by systems using Web services. Although each topic covered—such as ERP systems and operating systems—are quite complex in themselves, the common theme running through each is how to use a service-oriented architecture provided by Web services to integrate new and existing applications effectively. Other integration strategies—like the Enterprise Service Bus—extend and combine the concepts of messaging and Web services interfaces, but it's not clear how compatible these approaches are with messaging-based Web services protocols, such as WS-ReliableMessaging.

CHAPTER 3

■■■

Data Representation

A cornerstone of Web services is the standard data representation format known as XML. Although the idea of markup languages is not new (SGML has been around for many years), the widespread adoption of standards for exchanging data in combination with standards for defining interfaces is new. HTML has been widely used in the past ten years as the standard for the WWW. Some commentators have emphasized the links between XML and HTML, but in the enterprise world, they relate mainly be being subsets of SGML, rather than XML being a replacement for HTML.[1] The true advantage of XML for the finance industry is not in designing more flexible user interfaces; it lies in the ability to structure information in a way that is recognized and used by all businesses in specific vertical industries.

While HTML has a strict schema (HTML 4.0 has a limited number of tags that the browser can interpret, for example), XML has no such fixed-tag schema. This has resulted in numerous proposals for data formatting, such as commerce XML (cXML), electronic business XML (ebXML), and RosettaNet. While Web services avoids the need to define tag names, significant semantic issues between trading partners can still exist, and these will need to be resolved before integration is possible.

Imagine a world where all data exchanged between institutions in the finance industry was structured using a common data format—a transaction history from one bank could be used directly by another institution, or a deposit transaction record could be used by a number of different entities (banks, accounting packages, Internal Revenue Service, etc.) to record the transaction.

Data Standardization

Why is the standardization of data important? Many businesses find that the dual entry of data costs millions of dollars each year in duplicated effort and error corrections. Worse still, a significant number of errors are never detected at all. In finance, that means

---

1. In terms of designing user interfaces using markup languages, XML provides a greater level of flexibility than HTML, especially in the sense that presentation is not mandated by the tags themselves in XML, as it is in HTML.

that real dollars are often miscredited between accounts, orders for stocks one magnitude greater than what customers bid for are incorrectly purchased, and credit applications are routinely rejected because applicant data falls below a threshold although the client's true financial state is satisfactory. Conversely, applicants with a poor credit history may be receiving lines of credit from institutions because their data has been keyed incorrectly. In signal-detection terms, this means that a lot of false positives and false negatives are being potentially allowed through the financial systems currently used.

The major reasons that dual entry of data persists in the digital age are these:

- Lack of agreement among businesses about data structure

- Lack of standards adopted by software vendors to ensure interoperability

- No incentive to move from paper-based systems to computer systems across the board because data cannot be interpreted by partners and customers

The lack of agreement among businesses about data structure means that every business's dealings with their customers and partners involves a different data format, which may be binary, ASCII, and typically proprietary. How these formats are maintained and developed over the years are either a matter of luck and guesswork, or require constant attention from committees that must ensure compatibility with future applications while preserving existing services' functionality. The structure problem also relates to other problems within industries. For example, although generally accepted accounting principles are adopted by most countries, significant scope allows companies to customize their own accounting systems. This means that companies, their accountants, corporate regulators, and the IRS must all be able to decipher these accounts to perform the most basic of tasks, such as calculating earnings per share in a comparable way. The fact that the IRS does not receive electronic copies of all accounting documents from all entities registered for taxation costs that body millions of dollars each year is duplicated effort.

Before specific industries can agree upon standards for formatting data for exchange within themselves, it makes sense that every industry should speak the same language, because many businesses across industry boundaries have links. For example, banks, as the cornerstone of the economy, have relationships with every other type of industry. So, rather than developing a common language for banks to communicate with each other, banks should be able to communicate with all of their customers by using a common language. That language is XML, and the commonly agreed structures of data are known as schemas.

XML Files and Relational Data

Every data element drawn from a relational database should be capable of being described using XML and a schema. This is very important for enterprises, as they store most of their data in relational databases. For example, the following data definition can be used to describe the elements of a customer account:

```
create table customer
(
custno varchar(10) primary key,
firstname varchar(25),
lastname varchar(25)
);
```

This would create a table called customer which has three fields: custno (the primary key), firstname, and lastname. A record from the table customer would be formatted in the following way:

```
<customer>
<custno>98487556</custno>
<firstname>Charles</firstname>
<lastname>Dickens</lastname>
</customer>
```

The <customer> root element and its associated schema can be associated with a specific namespace that defines its elements, and this can be published for all users within an industry to follow. For example, if a finance industry body had the domain fincouncil.com, then the following namespace could be used:

```
<customer xmlns="http://www.fincouncil.com/xml/namespace/BFI-v5">
<custno>98487556</custno>
<firstname>Charles</firstname>
<lastname>Dickens</lastname>
</customer>
```

In this case, version 5 of the schema would be stored at http://www.fincouncil.com/xml/namespace/BFI-v5. For backward compatibility, different versions of the schema could also be stored at the same site. One of the nice features of XML is that data structures selected from multiple database tables (perhaps using a join) can be formatted into a single XML document, because elements can be nested according to the schema. For example, a query for every bank account belonging to Charles Dickens could be returned within a single document in the following way:

```
<customer xmlns="http://www.fincouncil.com/xml/namespace/BFI-v5">
<custno>98487556</custno>
<firstname>Charles</firstname>
<lastname>Dickens</lastname>
<accounts>
          <account number=75756865>Super Saver</account>
          <account number=75754545>Term Deposit</account>
</accounts>
</customer>
```

Here we can see that Charles Dickens has two <accounts>; both are identified by <account> elements, which are nested within the definition of <customer>. Within each <account> element, the number is specified as an attribute. The extent to which you generalize this process of normalizing data into the appropriate structures depends largely on business requirements for grosser or more fine-grained results from queries. A standard called XQuery allows XML documents to be queried directly—just like a relational database. However, because of performance reasons, few serious proposals exist to modify the internal structure of databases to store data natively in XML format.

XML DTD

A document type definition (DTD) is a specification for an XML document. The declared elements within a DTD determine which elements in an XML file can legally appear in all sections of the document. By creating a standard for document structures, clients, and servers—indeed, all users of the XML files created according to the specification—can be sure they are reading and writing the correct data. XML parsers can also verify that a specific XML file meets its DTD specification. Thus, any overflow errors or illegal entries can be detected before being committed to a database. For example, it is possible to specify how many times a specific element can occur within a file. Thus, if the element <deposit> could occur only ten times within a file (according to the relevant DTD), a file with eleven <deposit> entries would be rejected.

Let's examine a DTD for the <customer> namespace I declared earlier.

```
<!ELEMENT customer(custno, firstname, lastname, accounts)>
<!ELEMENT custno(#PCDATA)>
<!ELEMENT firstname(#PCDATA)>
<!ELEMENT lastname(#PCDATA)>
<!ELEMENT accounts(account*)(#PCDATA)>
<!ELEMENT account(#PCDATA)>
```

In this example, #PCDATA indicates normal text data, while a set of tokens enclosed in brackets following the root element declaration specifies the number of other elements that can appear. A * appearing after an element declaration indicates that it can appear zero or more times in a file, while a ? indicates that only one or zero elements can appear in a file.

As you can see in the preceding example, the relationship between a root element and its descendents is a hierarchical relationship: subordinate elements could be defined by "is-a" relations, or by any other verb for that matter. For example, I have shown that an <account> belongs to a set of <accounts> that is owned by a <customer>. This hierarchy is shown in Figure 3-1. This approach to structuring data allows semantic relations to be inferred from the structure. For example, <customers> are not owned by <accounts>; only the converse is true. This makes logical evaluation of data files presented to a parser more consistent than other types of data file.

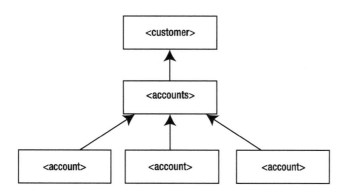

Figure 3-1. *Semantic hierarchy of elements defined within an XML file*

DTD Elements

Elements defined within a DTD can be of four different types:

- Data elements: These elements contain data items, which are always strings. XML does not contain any standards for defining specific data types, although the XML Schema standard does (see the XML Schemas section further on).

- Container elements: These elements group other types of elements, but don't contain data themselves.

- Empty elements: These elements don't contain data and are not containers.

- Composite elements: These elements contain both containers and data.

A number of general rules and requirements apply to all XML documents, including these:

- There must be one root element.

- Empty elements do not have data or containers.

- Other element types must contain the appropriate type of content.

If a XML file is validated, you can assume that it has met the set of validation rules required for a "well-formed" XML document.

XML Metadata

So far, we have examined data and container elements and how they can be used to structure the kinds of data stored within relational database tables. However, one of XML's great features is its ability to integrate data with metadata, which is something generally missing from database tables. At run time, however, metadata typically guides the correct deployment and execution of applications and the associated XML-encoded data. In XML documents, metadata can be specified by using attributes. Attributes can have both a case-sensitive name and a value, and each XML element can have multiple attributes associated with it.

The following XML document example shows how a payment transaction could utilize metadata at run time:

```
<payment HOSTNAME="payments.somebank.com" TIMESTAMP="20021201085602">
    <source>some.merchant.com</source>
    <creditcard TYPE="visa">4500998877665544</creditcard>
    <amount CURR="usd">50.00</amount>
</payment>
```

Here, the `<payment>` root element has two attributes associated with it: HOSTNAME, being the destination hostname of the payment transaction, and TIMESTAMP, being the date and time recorded when the transaction was received. The `<source>` element has no metadata, being the merchant's hostname that originated the transaction, while `<creditcard>` has a TYPE of visa, and the `<amount>` of $50.00 is expressed in U.S. dollars (usd). Note the convention of using lowercase for element tag names and uppercase for attribute names.

Attribute Rules

An important aspect of governing data contained in XML documents specified by DTDs is the inclusion of specific rules for attributes. This allows for validation of correctly formed attributes for applications that process XML documents. For the preceding payment example, the following rules might be defined within a DTD:

```
<!ATTLIST payment
HOSTNAME    (payments.somebank.com | payments1.somebank.com) #REQUIRED
TIMESTAMP  CDATA  #REQUIRED>
<!ATTLIST creditcard
TYPE    (visa | mastercard | diners) #REQUIRED>
<!ATTLIST amount
CURR    (usd | yen | aud) #REQUIRED>
```

In this example, you can see that all four attributes are REQUIRED; alternatively, they could be IMPLIED or directly specified with a default value. The payment element has two attributes—HOSTNAME and TIMESTAMP—with the restrictions that the transactions must be destined for payments.somebank.com and payments1.somebank.com, and normal text data, respectively. The TYPE attribute for the creditcard element can be visa, mastercard, or diners, and the CURR attribute for the amount element can be usd, yen, or aud, respectively.

XML Schemas

A number of standards are now emerging for XML, making it even more extensible, and potentially allowing it to be applied across the enterprise. These standards include

- XML namespace: Allows correct identification of documents and owners by declaring and defining unique namespaces

- XML Linking Language (Xlink): Allows XML documents to be associated with each other in a flexible way

- eXtensible Stylesheet Language (XSL): Mainly used to standardize presentation of XML data in Web browsers

- XSL Transformation (XSLT): Allows ready translation of XML documents in different formats

Although XML documents and their associated DTDs allow for data and metadata to be conveniently packaged in a standard way, they have a number of shortcomings evident from a programming perspective. These are especially apparent in the domain of schema definition using DTDs. For example, data field types cannot be defined by using a DTD as easily as they can in a variable declaration in a programming language, or in a field definition in a relational database table. In addition, DTDs are not really in XML format; although certainly XML-like, they really should follow the same syntax rules as XML documents for consistency, and allow the same parsers to read XML schema files as normal XML files. This means that a more advanced method of defining XML schemas is required, and it is found in the relatively new XML Schema standard (note the capital S!). XML Schema provides for strong typing of elements, just like variables, rather than emphasizing their tag names.

Namespace Definitions

An XML Schema starts with an XML Namespace definition, which allows tags with the same name to be distinguished and logically isolated by using different basenames to define each different tag. For example, imagine that in any accounting system, the tag <amount> might occur fairly regularly in different contexts; it might be a credit amount in the trade debtors column, a debit amount in the tax payable, or the value of total current assets. Since these amounts must ultimately appear in the same balance sheet, how could a parser reliably identify each amount as belonging to a specific item? The answer lies in the ability of namespaces to prevent tag name collisions by associating all elements and attributes within a document with a specific namespace, just like a Java or C# program. The following XML namespace implementation shows that the balance sheet application can reconcile the "amounts" from the trade debtors and current assets applications or functions:

```
<trade:debtor xmlns:trade="http://www.somebank.com/names/trade-REV3">
    <trade:name>Cassowary Computing Pty Ltd</trade:name>
    <trade:id>46356832</trade:id>
    <trade:amount>875.00</trade:amount>
</trade:debtor>
<assets:debtor xmlns:assets="http://www.somebank.com/names/assets-REV4">
    <assets:register>New York Asset Register 1</assets:register>
    <assets:currency>USD</assets:currency >
    <assets:amount>44000500.00</assets:amount>
    <assets:lastValuation>20021010</assets:lastValuation >
</assets:debtor>
```

In this example, the trade namespace has the element's name, id, and amount defined, and the assets namespace has the elements register, currency, amount, and lastValuation defined. The two amounts clearly do not collide, since they are discriminated by the prefixes trade and assets, which represent their respective namespaces for the data derived from the trade debtors and current assets applications. The location of the namespace definitions are specified by using the appropriate URI.

Schemas and DTDs

XML Schemas are associated with two individual documents: the schema document and the instance document. The schema document defines all information about the types of elements and attributes that can be defined in an XML document adhering to the schema, and the instance document describes a specific instance of the schema. The following example schema shows many similarities to a DTD definition, but the differences are important:

```
<?xml version="1.0" encoding="utf-8"?>
<xs:schema xmlns:xs="http://www.w3.org/2001/XMLSchema">
  <xs:element name="deposit">
    <xs:complexType>
      <xs:sequence>
        <xs:element name="customer" type="xs:string"/>
        <xs:element name="swiftID" type="xs:string"/>
        <xs:element name="payment" minOccurs="1" maxOccurs="1">
          <xs:complexType>
            <xs:sequence>
              <xs:element name="currency" type="xs:string"/>
              <xs:element name="date" type="xs:date"/>
              <xs:element name="amount" type="xs:double"/>
            </xs:sequence>
          </xs:complexType>
        </xs:element>
      </xs:sequence>
    </xs:complexType>
  </xs:element>
</xs:schema>
```

Here, you can see that the document is formatted using standard XML, with a namespace of xs. This allows elements and attribute names from the schema definition to be distinguished from instantiations of elements and attributes in specific documents. For example, while <xs:element name="deposit"> defines the element deposit, the same element is referred to (in an XML document that conforms to the deposit schema) as deposit:element, where *element* would be customer, swiftID, or payment. The definition for a deposit record requires the following data to be present in a valid deposit XML document:

- A customer name of simple type string.

- A swiftID of simple type string.

- A complex type called payment, which must occur once only in the XML document.

- Subelements of payment include currency (of simple type string), date (of type date), and amount (of type double).

The complex type of payment is enclosed by the tags <xs:complexType>, and the actual elements of deposit comprise a complex type, so the entire definition is also enclosed by <xs:complexType>. A complex type generally includes an <xs:sequence> element, because a complex type is just a collection of simple types.

Simple Types

The simple types listed in Figure 3-2 are supported by XML Schema, and for the most part reflect their counterparts in programming languages like Java.

binary	language	recurringDay
boolean	long	recurringDuration
byte	month	short
century	Name	string
date	NCName	time
decimal	negativeInteger	timeDuration
double	NMTOKEN	timeInstant
ENTITIES	NMTOKENS	timePeriod
ENTITY	nonNegativeInteger	unsignedByte
float	nonPositiveInteger	unsignedInt
ID	NOTATION	unsignedLong
IDREF	positiveInteger	unsignedShort
IDREFS	QName	uriReference
int	recurringDate	year

Figure 3-2. *Simple types supported by XML Schema*

Clearly, the large number of supported simple types exceeds those provided in most programming languages, and the ability to group simple types into aggregates reflects the basic structures found in languages such as C++. The fact that specific legal definitions exist for time-based elements such as dates, months, centuries, and years makes it very easy to validate the kinds of data generally existing in XML documents.

Separating Simple and Complex Types

As with a programming language, it is possible to separate the definitions of simple type elements and attributes from the definitions of complex types, including the actual definition of the root element. This approach makes it very clear which elements are simple and complex, as shown in the following example:

```xml
<?xml version="1.0" encoding="UTF-8"?>
<xs:schema xmlns:xs="http://www.w3.org/2001/XMLSchema">
  <!-- simple type definitions  -->
  <xs:element name="customer" type="xs:string"/>
  <xs:element name="swiftID" type="xs:string"/>
  <xs:element name="currency" type="xs:string"/>
  <xs:element name="date" type="xs:date"/>
  <xs:element name="amount" type="xs:double"/>
  <!-- complex type definitions -->
  <xs:element name="payment">
    <xs:complexType>
      <xs:sequence>
        <xs:element ref="currency" minOccurs="1" maxOccurs="1"/>
        <xs:element ref="date"/>
        <xs:element ref="amount"/>
      </xs:sequence>
    </xs:complexType>
  </xs:element>
  <!-- root element definition -->
  <xs:element name="deposit">
    <xs:complexType>
      <xs:sequence>
        <xs:element ref="customer"/>
        <xs:element ref="swiftID"/>
        <xs:element ref="payment" minOccurs="1" maxOccurs="1"/>
      </xs:sequence>
    </xs:complexType>
  </xs:element>
</xs:schema>
```

Creating New Types

A further enhancement is provided by the ability to define more precisely the characteristics of each simple and complex element type, by literally declaring each as its own
type. Thus, instead of just declaring a swift code as a string, it could be declared as a
string that must consist of 10 characters or fewer. Similarly, a customer's account number
may need to be fewer than 50 characters. In this way, illegal values contained in various
elements can be detected early in the application's logic, and discarded appropriately, as
shown in the following example:

```xml
<?xml version="1.0" encoding="UTF-8"?>
<xs:schema xmlns:xs="http://www.w3.org/2001/XMLSchema">
  <!-- simple type definitions  -->
  <xs:simpleType name="customerType">
    <xs:restriction base="xs:string">
      <xs:maxLength value="50"/>
    </xs:restriction>
  </xs:simpleType>
  <xs:simpleType name="swiftIDType">
    <xs:restriction base="xs:string"/>
      <xs:maxLength value="10"/>
    </xs:restriction>
  </xs:simpleType>
  <xs:simpleType name="currencyType">
    <xs:restriction base="xs:string"/>
  </xs:simpleType>
  <xs:simpleType name="dateType">
    <xs:restriction base="xs:date"/>
  </xs:simpleType>
  <xs:simpleType name="amountType">
    <xs:restriction base="xs:double"/>
  </xs:simpleType>
  <!-- complex type definitions  -->
  <xs:complexType name="paymentType">
    <xs:sequence>
      <xs:element name="currency" type="currencyType"/>
      <xs:element name="date" type="dateType"/>
      <xs:element name="amount" type="amountType"/>
    </xs:sequence>
  </xs:complexType>
  <xs:complexType name="paymentType">
    <xs:sequence>
```

```
        <xs:element name="customer" type="customerType"/>
        <xs:element name="swiftID" type="swiftIDType"/>
        <xs:element name="payment" type="paymentType" minOccurs="1"
maxOccurs="1"/>
      </xs:sequence>
    </xs:complexType>
    <!-- root element definition -->
    <xs:element name="payment" type="paymentType"/>
</xs:schema>
```

Groups

Further abstractions are available for creating aggregations of elements and attributes into structurelike entities. These entities are known as *groups*. The following example shows one group for elements (customerElements) and one group for attributes (customerAttributes). The customerElements group consists of a set of elements defining a customer's basic contact details, including the lastName and firstName (of type nameType), lines 1 and 2 of the address (of type addressType), and so on. The customerAttributes group consists of two attributes: the date the customer opened her first account (dateJoined), and her current primary account identifier (currentPrimaryAccount).

```
<!-- element group -->
  <xs:group name="customerElements">
    <xs:sequence>
      <xs:element name="lastName" type="nameType"/>
      <xs:element name="firstName" type="nameType"/>
      <xs:element name="address1" type="addressType"/>
      <xs:element name="address2" type="addressType"/>
      <xs:element name="city" type="cityType"/>
      <xs:element name="state" type="stateType"/>
      <xs:element name="zip" type="zipType"/>
      <xs:element name="country" type="countryType"/>
    </xs:sequence>
  </xs:group>
  <!-- attribute group -->
  <xs:attributeGroup name="customerAttributes">
    <xs:attribute name="dateJoined" type="dateType" use="required"/>
    <xs:attribute name="currentPrimaryAccount" type="xs:string"/>
  </xs:attributeGroup>
```

Both of these groups could be used to construct a complex type definition, as shown here:

```
<xs:complexType name="customerAccount">
    <xs:sequence>
      <xs:group ref="customerElements"/>
      <xs:element name="customer" type="customerType"
            minOccurs="1" maxOccurs="unbounded"/>
    </xs:sequence>
    <xs:attributeGroup ref="customerAttributes"/>
  </xs:complexType>
```

Generating Objects Using XML

One area in which application developers have the most difficulty working with XML is (unlike binary data or serialized object structures) the requirement for specialized parsers to extract data elements from their XML wrappings. In turn, these must be related to an underlying native data format, such as class members and relational database schema definitions.

Fortunately, you don't have to write your own parser! XML developers have used the Simple API for XML (SAX) and the Document Object Model (DOM) interfaces for Java to read, operate on, and navigate XML documents. W3C developed and endorsed DOM as a standard, and the XML developer community has been using SAX for several years. The major difference between SAX and DOM is that the former focuses on converting XML data into native object data, while DOM retains the XML tree format in memory after it has been processed.

As suggested by its name, SAX has a very simple, stack-based approach to parsing XML documents: a SAX parser reads the document serially, and when it encounters certain tags (like the start of a document or element) that have a matched callback function, it invokes that function. When an element is encountered, a corresponding object is pushed onto the stack, and when the parsing of the element has been completed, it is popped off accordingly. For very large documents, this process can be inefficient— particularly if searching for a single element buried deep within a document.

DOM provides random access to elements, just like a hierarchical file system provides efficient access to files. A DOM parser represents all elements as nodes within a tree, which can be more efficiently traversed compared to serial parsing, given the hierarchical nature of XML document structures. DOM is designed for reading and writing XML documents, while SAX was originally designed only to read XML.

A good discussion of when to use SAX and when to use DOM can be found at `http://developerlife.com/saxvsdom/default.htm`.

SAX

SAX defines the several interfaces to process XML documents, including XMLFilter, XML-Reader, and ContentHandler. The ContentHandler interface forms the main application developer API. The following methods are provided for:

- Finding the start of an element (`startElement`)

- Finding the end of an element (`endElement`)

- Finding the start of a namespace (`startPrefix`)

- Finding the end of a namespace (`endPrefix`)

- Identifying text data (`characters`)

- Identifying white space (`ignorableWhitespace`)

- Identifying processing instructions (`processingInstruction`)

- Identifying a skipped entity (`skippedEntity`)

- Identifying the document locator (`setDocumentLocator`)

Using these SAX interfaces (and DOM interfaces) directly requires the developer to perform a significant amount of manual coding. Higher level tools are required to realistically integrate large XML schemas into existing Java applications, although the Apache Jakarta Commons project has greatly assisted in this area (`http://jakarta.apache.org/commons/`).

Generating Schema Code

One tool that makes it easy to provide access to XML schema data elements programmatically is the Breeze Factor's XML Schema Binder. This system takes an XML schema and generates a Java bean that allows applications to operate on XML data elements as objects. Schema Binder works with both XML schema files and DTD files, meaning it can be used with newer and existing codebases, respectively.

Let's look at an example. The `payment.xsd` file defines a "payment transfer" schema for a bank, defining four entities (`accountFrom`, `bankFrom`, `accountTo`, `bankTo`) that represent the bank and account number for a payment of a specific amount to be made, and an account and bank number for the payment's destination account. A transaction number (`transNum`) is also recorded, as shown in the following schema file:

```
<?xml version="1.0" encoding="UTF-8"?>
<xsd:schema xmlns:xsd="http://www.w3.org/2001/XMLSchema" binding:schema-
source="file:/C:/schema.xsd">
    <xsd:element name="payment">
        <xsd:complexType>
            <xsd:sequence>
                <xsd:element name="accountFrom" type="xs:string" />
                <xsd:element name="bankFrom" type="xs:string" />
                <xsd:element name="accountTo" type="xs:string" />
                <xsd:element name="bankTo" type="xs:string" />
            </xsd:sequence>
            <xsd:attribute name="amount" type="xs:string" />
            <xsd:attribute name="transNum" type="xs:string" />
        </xsd:complexType>
    </xsd:element>
</xsd:schema>
```

Schema Binder generates Java code automatically based on this schema definition, as shown in the following example. Firstly, a set of constants is declared for each node name:

```
public static final String $PAYMENT = "payment";
public static final String $TRANS_NUM = "transNum";
public static final String $AMOUNT = "amount";
public static final String $BANK_TO = "bankTo";
public static final String $BANK_FROM = "bankFrom";
public static final String $ACCOUNT_TO = "accountTo";
public static final String $ACCOUNT_FROM = "accountFrom";
```

The rule for naming constants is clear: a dollar sign and capitalization of the element name. Next, a set of XML fields is declared:

```
protected String _AccountFrom = null;
protected String _BankFrom = null;
protected String _AccountTo = null;
protected String _BankTo = null;
protected String _Amount = null;
protected String _TransNum = null;
```

Again, the rule for naming fields is an underscore character prefixed to each element name. A series of get, set, has, and delete methods is then defined for each XML field

member, adhering to the object-oriented component model, as shown here for
_AccountFrom:

```
public String getAccountFrom ()
     {
   return (_AccountFrom);
}

public void setAccountFrom (String newValue)
     {
   _AccountFrom = newValue;
}

 public boolean hasAccountFrom ()
     {
   return (_AccountFrom != null);
}

 public void deleteAccountFrom ()
     {
   _AccountFrom = null;
}
```

In each case, the current value of the XML fields is either returned, modified,
checked for existence, or deleted. Next, a set of validators is created for each element,
as shown for _AccountFrom:

```
transient protected static XmlStringValidator;
_AccountFrom_validator_ = null;
_AccountFrom_validator_ = new XmlStringValidator
     (
   "Payment.AccountFrom", "Element",
   "payment/accountFrom", -1, -1, 1, 1
);
```

This code defined a validator element, which then passes the specific criteria for the
field to the XML validation routines, stored in the XmlStringValidator class. Errors are
also collected during navigation.

```
XmlValidationError e;
          e = _AccountFrom_validator_.validate(_AccountFrom);
          if (e != null)
```

```
            {
                            errors.addElement(e);
        if (return_on_error)
                                {
            return (errors);
        }
    }
}
```

Here, an XmlValidationError object is created and the validate method is called on the field name. If an error is returned, then it is added to a vector of errors, which is returned if the vector is nonempty after all validations have been completed.

Sample Application

Auxiliary methods are also supplied to populate objects with parsed XML values, and to physically read and write the XML streams. You can use the following generated sample application to begin building a real application that uses the XML schema:

```
/*
 * This sample application was generated for you by the
 * Breeze Studio Export Wizard.
 *
 * To run this sample application:
 *
 *    1) Ensure your CLASSPATH is set correctly to access this class and
 *        the generated JavaBean classes in addition to the breezetk.jar
 *         and xerces.jar.
 *    2) Move this file to the desired directory
 *    3) Compile this file and the generated JavaBean Java files.
 *    4) Write (or find) a XML file that adheres to your XML schema.
 *    5) Run the sample application:
 *        java SampleApp xml-filename
 *
 * This sample app will simply create an XML object from the supplied XML file
 * and then dump that XML object as XML to the console.
 */

import bank.transact.*;
import com.tbf.xml.*;

public class SampleApp
{
```

```
public static void main(String[] args)
    {
    /*
     * Make sure a filename was specified on the command line
     */
    if (args.length < 1)
                    {
        System.err.println("usage: java SampleApp xml-filename");
        System.exit(1);
    }
    /*
     * Create a XML object from the provided file. We use an instance
     * of the ObjectFactory to parse the file and create an instance
     * of the appropriate generated class.
     */
    String filename = args[0];
    ObjectFactory factory = ObjectFactory.getInstance();
    XmlObject obj = factory.getInstance(filename);
    if (obj == null)
                    {
        System.err.println("Error creating object: " +
            factory.getLastError());
        System.exit(1);
    }
    /*
     * Dump (marshal) the object to the console (System.out) as formatted
     * XML. To dump as un-formatted XML replace FormattedOutputStream
     * with RawOutputStream. See the Breeze Toolkit documentation in
     * <Breeze_install_dir>/docs/toolkit for more information.
     */
    FormattedOutputStream out = new FormattedOutputStream(System.out);
    obj.marshal(out);
    }
}
```

So, if you wish to display an XML file such as the payment example shown in the preceding example, after being parsed and validated by the sample application, the following command would be used:

```
$ java SampleApp payments.xml
<payment HOSTNAME="payments.somebank.com" TIMESTAMP="20021201085602">
    <source>some.merchant.com</source>
```

```
    <creditcard TYPE="visa">4500998877665544</creditcard>
    <amount CURR="usd">50.00</amount>
</payment>
```

Project

Take a simple document that you currently use to exchange data between applications, and walk through the following steps:

1. Decompose the data into elements and attributes.

2. Create an instance of an XML file containing these elements and attributes for a representative item of data.

3. Create a DTD for the XML file.

4. Do you want to place any complex data types or restrictions on validation? If so, create an XML Schema for the DTD with those restrictions defined.

5. Use SAX to create an interface to read your document.

6. If this takes too long and you give up in desperation, use Schema Binder to generate the interfaces automatically, and a sample application that you can use as the basis for a more complete application.

Advanced Protocols/Languages

To make the most of XML in Web services, you will almost certainly need to make use of a number of advanced protocols or languages in the area. XSLT and XPath (the XML Path language) provide the ability to convert data written in XML between different vocabularies. XSLT provides a front end to the conversions provided by XPath, which maps data locations within XML documents. For example, the XPath expression

```
stocks="SUNW"
```

articulates all descendants named "SUNW" of the stocks element. Similarly, logical expressions like

```
stocks="SUNW|MSFT"
```

can be created by using logical and set operators (like the union here). However, while XPath can be used to identify matching data locations within a document, it is not a full query language. XPointer is related to XPath, because it can be used to address individual sections of an XML document by using XPath addresses. XLink provides the ability to create hyperlinks from elements within XML documents.

An alternative approach for matching data within documents is provided by RELAX NG, which is a schema language for XML. For example, consider an XML document containing stock codes and prices for high-tech companies:

```
<stockDetails>
  <name>SUNW</name>
  <price>5.00</price>
</stockDetails>
<stockDetails>
  <name>MSFT</name>
  <price>30.00</price>
</stockDetails>
</stockPrices>
```

A RELAX NG schema for matching such documents could be specified easily as:

```
<element name="stockPrices" xmlns="http://relaxng.org/ns/structure/1.0">
  <zeroOrMore>
    <element name="stockDetails">
      <element name="name">
        <text/>
      </element>
      <element name="price">
        <text/>
      </element>
    </element>
  </zeroOrMore>
</element>
```

RELAX NG has the advantages of being easy to use, and it supports different levels of granularity in its pattern matching.

Summary

In this chapter, we've examined how to standardize data representations using XML, and how to generate and bind specifications to data format by using XML schema. Both of these technologies provide a core platform for standardized data processing within Web services.

■■■

## CHAPTER 4

Messaging

The core technology behind Web services is SOAP, which is designed to provide a common XML-based messaging framework that facilitates interoperability while minimizing the constraints imposed on the data-exchange process. For example, SOAP does not specify the transport type that must be used to exchange data, nor does it specify whether message passing is synchronous or asynchronous. The default message model is one-way; two messages must be combined to implement a request/response pattern, and more sophisticated messaging patterns like multicast may also be implemented. This flexibility is what makes SOAP so appealing for interoperability; integration of heterogeneous systems requires loose coupling and flexibility, and that's exactly what SOAP provides.

SOAP 1.2 is the current revision of the protocol, but many existing services use SOAP 1.1. I'll point out differences where it's useful to consider what changes might occur to SOAP in the future, and the protocols that are built on top of SOAP.

Simple Example

Before delving into the complexities of SOAP, let's take a quick look at how it is actually used in a typical RPC operation. After all, emulating RPC through messaging is what SOAP is most commonly used for. The SOAP message structure consists of three elements:

- The envelope, which defines a message's boundary and encapsulates it

- The header, which contains meta-data related to the message

- The body, which contains the actual message data

Figure 4-1 shows the conceptual relationship between these three SOAP elements.

Envelope (Mandatory):
Marks the start and end of a
message

Header (Optional):
General information about
message (e.g., authentication)

Body (Mandatory):
Data for the actual message
or document being sent

Figure 4-1. *Structure of a SOAP message*

SOAP RPC simulates a request-response cycle of method invocation by using
messaging: passing one message from the client to the server as a request, and back
from server to client (as a response). Here is a typical SOAP message for a method called
OrderItem:

```
POST /RetailManager HTTP/1.1
Host: www.some-retailer.com
Content-Type: text/xml
Content-Length: 1024
SOAPMethodName: Retail-Namespace-URI#OrderItem
<SOAP:Envelope xmlns:SOAP="urn:schemas-xmlsoap-org:soap.v1">
    <SOAP:Body>
        <m:OrderItem
            xmlns:m="Retail-Namespace-URI">
                <ItemName>Laptop Computer</ItemName>
        </m:OrderItem>
    </SOAP:Body>
</SOAP:Envelope>
```

In this example, an HTTP POST message is passed to the application /RetailManager
running at www.some-retailer.com, calling the SOAP method OrderItem defined within
the Retail-Namespace. The actual call on the OrderItem method is defined in the SOAP

body, passing "Laptop Computer" as the value for the parameter ItemName. This SOAP envelope and its enclosed body is sent from the client to the server, picked up by the Web server, and turned into a method call. The server runs the method's code and replies by sending back the SOAP message shown here:

```
HTTP/1.1 200 OK
Content-Type: text/xml
Content-Length: 1024
<SOAP:Envelope xmlns:SOAP="urn:schemas-xmlsoap-org:soap.v1">
    <SOAP:Body>
        <m:OrderItemResponse xmlns:m="Retail-Namespace-URI">
            <InStock>Yes</InStock>
        </m:OrderItemResponse>
    </SOAP:Body>
</SOAP:Envelope>
```

This response begins with an HTTP 200 OK code and follows this with the SOAP response message itself. The <InStock> element in the SOAP body defines the return value from the OrderItem method, in this case indicating whether the item requested is in stock. The full SOAP headers have been stripped from both these examples because they are quite verbose and don't add anything to our explanation.

The actual process of sending and receiving SOAP messages is similar to using the normal postal service, with some important distinctions. The basic message path is shown in Figure 4-2: A sender prepares a message contained within the SOAP envelope, which is then transmitted using some endpoint and is encoded according to some specification. Once the recipient receives the message, she can use the encoding description to "read" the contents of the message. The technologies that allow transmission, coding, and decoding are HTTP, XML, and XML Schema. XML is always used to code SOAP messages.

Just like the number of intermediate post offices between a sender and a recipient in a standard postal service, there can be a large number of intermediaries between a SOAP message sender and a recipient. Processing of various kinds can be performed at these intermediaries. Once the intended recipient has received a message, a number of actions must be performed before the message contents are interpreted, and, as an example, an object method is invoked. These actions include confirming that all message parts received are internally valid and externally consistent with other parts of the message; otherwise, an exception should be thrown and the message rejected.

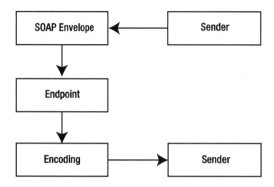

Figure 4-2. *Posting a SOAP message*

SOAP Overview

The simple example shown in Figure 4-2 demonstrates the most commonly implemented flavor of SOAP: synchronous-style SOAP messaging that emulates RPC using HTTP as the transport protocol. However, the binding to HTTP is entirely optional and dependent on the requirements of the application (synchronous or asynchronous); the transport protocol is pluggable, and it is possible to use other transports such as the SMTP for a one-way messaging system, or potentially as a message queue for reliable delivery. This design feature makes SOAP superior to distributed RPC systems like CORBA, discussed in Chapter 2.

One of the most important aspects of SOAP is that it decouples a method invocation request from its actual invocation on a server and the corresponding response operation. This means that it is very suitable for implementing a wide range of enterprise applications (described in Chapter 2) where it is not possible to guarantee connectivity between a number of different applications. For example, not all bank teller machines can be connected to a single database concurrently because of record-locking and performance constraints; a loosely coupled, decentralized model is required. This means that remote terminals (like ATMs) only need to put a message on queue rather than having direct access to a database table. This reduces contention and also reduces the time a customer might have to wait to receive an actual confirmation of a transaction. Historically, these are performed by batch during the dark hours; the customer might be waiting a long time!

Another key characteristic of SOAP is that remote method implementation is completely encapsulated by the remote interface; thus, the client has no idea of what programming language, application platform, or operating system the remote server is running when a method is remotely invoked. This means that the underlying implementation has been sufficiently abstracted to ensure that it does not depend on some common platform between the client and server—except that both must be able to send and/or receive SOAP messages across a common transport layer. Given that most systems today support HTTP running over TCP/IP, the simplicity of the interface makes SOAP fairly ubiquitous.

SOAP messages have four individual sections that need to be handled by each application passing SOAP packets: the header, envelope, body, and (possibly) the fault. XML is the basis of data and meta-data utilized by SOAP; XML, XML Schema, and XML Namespaces were covered in Chapter 3. The envelope `<SOAP-ENV:Envelope>` provides a wrapper for the SOAP message and specifies attributes like reference declarations, but does not provide addressing information. This is provided by the header `<SOAP-ENV:Header>`, which also provides details such as transaction IDs if required. Finally, the body `<SOAP-ENV:Body>` can contain messages, RPC calls or faults `<SOAP-ENV:Fault>`, if an error is encountered.

Message Envelope

The envelope specifies a general skeleton for the message and its ultimate interpretation by describing what a message contains, how it is encoded, and for whom it is ultimately intended for processing. All SOAP messages must have an envelope, and it may contain namespace definitions that must be defined. An envelope typically contains a number of namespace definitions, such as the SOAP namespace (`xmlns:SOAP-ENV="http:// schemas.xmlsoap.org/soap/envelope/)`, the XML Schema namespace (`xmlns:xsd= "http://www.w3.org/1999/XMLSchema`), and the instance namespace (`xmlns:xsi="http:// www.w3.org/1999/XMLSchema-instance`).

Given that even now there are multiple SOAP versions available and implemented in a wide variety of products, how does the recipient know what version of SOAP is being used? The SOAP namespace fills this role; if a different namespace is specified, then a mismatch is declared and an exception is thrown.

By using the `encodingStyle` attribute, remote applications can determine how to process the incoming message in terms of serialization. This allows the customization of data structures that can be exchanged over the wire—a very powerful facility when moving beyond the exchange of simple data types, especially since these additional items do not need to be negotiated between parties prior to exchanging messages. Note that if the namespace is wrong or the `encodingStyle` is not supported, then obviously the message will not be processed.

Message Header

SOAP headers specify how the receiver should deal with a message. This means that recipients can process the header before unwrapping the message, which allows the remote application to prepare to execute the operations specified in the message. Of course, if the server could not process the request in the message, this problem could be identified before the entire message was processed. The SOAP header provides an optional mechanism to broaden the scope of the protocol to support customized, application-specific features.

The SOAP header is not mandatory, and some early SOAP implementations made no use of it. However, it is very useful and is used extensively by advanced protocols such as WS-Security, WS-Policy, and WS-ReliableMessaging. Attributes such as encodingStyle and mustUnderstand can be used to ensure that a recipient is qualified to decode and process the message.

Header elements can also be used for intermediaries along the way. Once an intermediary accepts a SOAP header, it must not pass it along; such a mechanism could be used to propagate a message n times to a specific group, where n is decremented every time it is received by a recipient. The original header is never passed along; in this case a modified header containing $n-1$ is sent at each stage of propagation. The SOAP role (or SOAP actor in SOAP 1.1) attribute specifies the intended recipient of a message. If it is not specified, then the first recipient is considered to be the ultimate recipient.

Attributes can be either mandatory or optional. The mustUnderstand attribute is used to set this value for each header item. If mustUnderstand=1, then the recipient must be able to process the item in question.

Message Body

The body of the SOAP message is where marshaled RPC calls are contained, along with any other application data. Method calls are usually contained within a <Body> element, and must follow the declaration of the header if present, or the envelope if a header is not included. XML is used for defining all elements within the body. SOAP provides a standard set of conventions for defining and specifying RPC mechanisms that follow a standard request-response pattern. Identical elements within the SOAP body and header are generally considered equivalent.

All SOAP messages must contain a compulsory body element, even if it is empty. Each body item is uniquely identified by a combination of namespace URI and a restricted local name. The only predefined item in the body is the message Fault, described next.

Message Fault

A fault is generated whenever an exception is encountered, although only one can be contained within each body. Debugging distributed systems can be difficult, so the fact that SOAP supports a context-specific error reporting system is very useful. For example, errors can be generated by a SOAP version mismatch, if header entries were uninterpretable, if a message was incorrectly generated according to the specification, or if the server was unable to process the message.

Three elements can be defined within a fault message: the `<faultcode>` specifies the origin of the fault, the `<faultstring>` contains a plaintext description of the error, and `<faultfactor>` specifies the service that generated the error. Any extra information relating to the fault is contained within the `<detail>` element.

Here is an example fault for a sample service:

```
<SOAP-ENV:Fault>
    <faultcode>SOAP-ENV:Server</faultcode>
    <faultstring>Null pointer exception</faultstring>
    <faultactor> /jaxm-simple/receiver</faultactor>
</SOAP-ENV:Fault>
```

In this example, the Server `faultcode` is reported, but other possible values include `VersionMismatch`, `MustUnderstand`, and `Client`.

SOAP Encoding

SOAP messages are encoded using XML, where variable types are specified by using the XML schema instance (`xsi:type`) convention. This approach is very similar to any programming language or data definition system. Variables can be defined as either simple types or can be combined together to form compound types, which are similar to objects. Although XML is used for defining the encoding rules, those used for SOAP are really a subset of what is available.

These values are recognized as valid for SOAP encoding:

- Simple variables, such as particular strings, integers, floating point numbers, etc.

- Compound variables, which contain a group of simple variables

- Array variables, which are ordinal sets of compound variables

- Struct variables, which have unique handles among members

Corresponding types are associated with every variable described in the message. The most commonly used simple types include

- Positive integers (int)

- Floating point numbers (float)

- Negative integers (negativeInteger)

- Strings (string)

Here is an example of how these variables may be expressed within a schema:

```
<element name="interestRate" type="float"/>
<element name="totalSharesIssued" type="int"/>
<element name="marketDepth" type="negativeInteger"/>
<element name="sponsoredBroker">
  <simpleType base="xsd:string">
    <enumeration value="Small Jones and Co"/>
    <enumeration value="Bounty and Son"/>
    <enumeration value="Great Southern Stocks"/>
  </simpleType>
</element>
```

Their corresponding instantiations may appear as follows:

```
<interestRate>8.7</interestRate>
<totalSharesIssued>1000000</totalSharesIssued>
<marketDepth>-3254</marketDepth>
<sponsoredBroker>Bounty and Son</sponsoredBroker>
```

Handles

These data types have some features unique to XML Schema. For example, it is possible to define a handle on individual string elements. The following example shows a string defined as #CurrentStock, which can then be referred to by its handle:

```
<buystock id="CurrentStock">ORCL</buystock>
<sellstock href="#CurrentStock"/>
```

These two elements would be encoded with the same string in the message:

```
<buystock>ORCL</buystock>
<sellstock>ORCL</sellstock>
```

Structs

As I've just shown, enumerated types can be useful to specify values for nonnumeric types, i.e., valid values cannot be directly specified on a nominal, ordinal, interval, or ratio scale. Often, it is possible to specify related values on a scale—colors could be specified by their wavelength, for example—but asking users to select wavelengths rather than color names might not be too successful!

Structs can be very useful when tying together related pieces of data—just like an object without methods. For example, if a customer accessing an ATM withdrew $100, then the variables concerned should be atomic; they should not be serialized individually. So, a transaction record might look like this:

```
<e:ATMTransaction>
    <customer>5552673</customer>
    <operation>withdrawal</operation>
    <amount>100.00</amount>
</e:ATMTransaction>
```

The relevant XML Schema would look like this:

```
<element name="Book">
    <complexType>
        <element name="customer" type="xsd:int"/>
        <element name="operation">
            <simpleType base="xsd:string">
                <enumeration value="deposit"/>
                <enumeration value="withdrawal"/>
            </simpleType>
        </element>
        <element name="amount" type="xsd:float"/>
    </complexType>
</element>
```

Struct references can also extend beyond locally defined variables to URLs. For example, if a more precise definition were required, the references to transaction types in the operation enumeration could be defined by using URLs rather than simple names:

```
<e:ATMTransaction>
    <customer>5552673</customer>
    <operation href="http://www.somebank.com/definitions/withdrawal/"/>
    <amount>100.00</amount>
</e:ATMTransaction>
```

Compound Variables

The following example shows how a number of parameters can be defined and passed in a message that forms part of an RPC request. The name of the method to be invoked is buyStocks and the namespace is called trading, which is specified by a Universal Resource Name (URN). A URN is used because it is not location-specific like a URL, but both are forms of URIs.

```
<?xml version='1.0' encoding='UTF-8'?>
<SOAP-ENV:Envelope
    xmlns:SOAP-ENV="http://schemas.xmlsoap.org/soap/envelope/"
    xmlns:xsi="http://www.w3.org/1999/XMLSchema-instance"
    xmlns:xsd="http://www.w3.org/1999/XMLSchema">
    <SOAP-ENV:Body>
        <bank:buyStocks xmlns:bank="urn:trading"
            SOAP-ENV:encodingStyle="http://xml.apache.org/xml-soap/literalxml">
        <stockName xsi:type="xsd:string"
            SOAP-ENV:encodingStyle=
            "http://schemas.xmlsoap.org/soap/encoding/">SUNW</stockName>
        <buyPrice xsi:type="xsd:float"
            SOAP-ENV:encodingStyle=
            "http://schemas.xmlsoap.org/soap/encoding/">3.50</buyPrice>
        </bank:buyStocks>
    </SOAP-ENV:Body>
</SOAP-ENV:Envelope>
```

The two parameter types specified here, xsd:string and xsd:float, correspond to those defined by XML Schema, as described in Chapter 3.

In this example, you can see that two parameters, stockName and buyPrice, are passed to the buyStocks remote method. Alternatively, instead of passing these parameters as simple variables, you could create a compound value by linking two, as shown in the following example:

```
<stock xsi:type="complex">
        <stockName xsi:type="xsd:string">SUNW</stockName>
        <buyPrice xsi:type="xsd:float">3.50</buyPrice>
</stock>
```

This is not quite an object, but it's getting close. To make it an object, you'd define a separate namespace that corresponded to the name of the class (e.g., `stockMarket`), as shown in the following example:

```
<stock
    xmlns:bank="urn:trading"
    xsi:type="ns3:stockMarket">
        <stockName xsi:type="xsd:string">SUNW</stockName>
        <buyPrice xsi:type="xsd:float">3.50</buyPrice>
</stock>
```

Note that it is not possible to serialize object code in the same way that CORBA provides remote object references. Remember, SOAP is really only emulating RPC; it does not implement RPC directly. So, remote method invocation is provided as part of a service interface. You never get direct remote object access with SOAP.

Arrays

Data types other than simple data types can be represented and used. For example, byte arrays could be used to represent binary image data in a text format using Base-64 encoding. The following example shows a `<picture>` element defined by its corresponding XML Schema type:

```
<picture xsi:type="SOAP-ENC:base64">6gfhjhf6k8gh87jh8kjh98jhjj==
...
</picture>
```

Compound types, such as structs and arrays, are also very useful. I've already looked at structs, but arrays are quite different and in some ways more flexible than enumerations, for example. Arrays have the type `SOAP-ENC:Array`, and in turn they can contain values of any type. They can be limited to particular variables of specific XML Schema types, such as `xsd:float` or `xsd:int`, or any user-defined types.

The following example shows a transaction number history for a particular bank customer:

```
<element name="txList"
        type="SOAP-ENC:Array"/>

<txList
  SOAP-ENC:arrayType="xsd:int[3]">
    <txid>5746</txid>
    <txid>4433</txid>
    <txid>4453</txid>
</txList>
```

Here, we can see that the array is declared as type xsd:int with three elements representing individual transaction identifiers. Arrays can also be created with a mixture of different types. The following example shows an array using types xsd:int, xsd:decimal, xsd:string, and xsd:uriReference to define an entry for a purchase order:

```
<SOAP-ENC:Array SOAP-ENC:arrayType="xsd:ur-type[4]">
    <cat xsi:type="xsd:int">4635654</cat>
    <cat xsi:type="xsd:decimal">24.50</cat>
    <cat xsi:type="xsd:string">
       Web Services development software package.
    </cat>
    <cat xsi:type="xsd:uriReference">
       http://www.somecompany.com
    </cat>
</SOAP-ENC:Array>
```

A catalog number, price, description, and URL to the company's details all can be contained within a single array. It might actually make more sense to create arrays of structs rather than one array of all the data elements used in a single transaction. For example, if you defined a struct called cassowary:Purchase, you could wrap multiple struct elements into a single array:

```
<SOAP-ENC:Array SOAP-ENC:arrayType="cassowary:Purchase[3]">
    <Purchase>
        <catalogID>4635654</catalogID>
        <price>24.50</price>
        <description>Web Services development software package</description>
        <url>http://www.somecompany.com</url>
    </Purchase>
    <Purchase>
        <catalogID>4635655</catalogID>
        <price>58.50</price>
        <description>Java development software package</description>
```

```
        <url>http://www.somej2eecompany.com</url>
    </Purchase>
    <Purchase>
        <catalogID>4635658</catalogID>
        <price>123.50</price>
        <description>Java development magazine subscription</description>
        <url>http://www.somemagcompany.com</url>
    </Purchase>
</SOAP-ENC:Array>
```

For more complex operations, it may well be necessary to define an array that itself contains a number of different arrays. For example, in an auditing application, one array of critical incidents may be logged, while a separate log of errors is maintained. The following example shows how this could be implemented:

```
<SOAP-ENC:Array SOAP-ENC:arrayType="xsd:string[][2]">
    <item href="#critical"/>
    <item href="#errors"/>
</SOAP-ENC:Array>
<SOAP-ENC:Array id="critical" SOAP-ENC:arrayType="xsd:string[3]">
    <eventID>7654-agdh</eventID>
    <eventID>7332-fggd</eventID>
    <eventID>9785-fgfh</eventID>
</SOAP-ENC:Array>
<SOAP-ENC:Array id="errors" SOAP-ENC:arrayType="xsd:string[3]">
    <eventID>8876-jjhg</eventID>
    <eventID>7658-gghf</eventID>
    <eventID>4544-gghf</eventID>
</SOAP-ENC:Array>
```

Better still, SOAP supports multidimensional arrays, so related values can be matched. So, to create a version of the preceding 2×3 array, the following could be defined:

```
<SOAP-ENC:Array SOAP-ENC:arrayType="xsd:string[2,3]">
    <eventID>7654-agdh</eventID>
    <eventID>7332-fggd</eventID>
    <eventID>9785-fgfh</eventID>
    <eventID>8876-jjhg</eventID>
    <eventID>7658-gghf</eventID>
    <eventID>4544-gghf</eventID>
</SOAP-ENC:Array>
```

Since XML is verbose, and SOAP is a text-based protocol unlike CORBA's binary IIOP protocol, verbosity of data can become an issue. While it is possible to compress on the sending end and decompress on the receiving end, a better approach is to send only data elements that are actually required. Fortunately, arrays transmitted by SOAP can be selected by indicating the starting record to transmit. Unfortunately, all records from that point must be transmitted, so the saving may well be minimal. The following example shows a six-element array having all records transmitted after record three (counting from zero):

```
<SOAP-ENC:Array SOAP-ENC:arrayType="xsd:string[6]" SOAP-ENC:offset="[3]">
    <transID>5</transID>
    <transID>6</transID>
</SOAP-ENC:Array>
```

Document/Literal Encoding

There are two types of encoding that must be specified within the SOAP message: method formatting and parameter formatting. Method formatting specifies the method request within the body (using either the document or rpc encoding styles). Parameter formatting determines how the input and output parameters are formatted (using either the literal or encoded encoding styles). While rpc/encoded is the SOAP standard, it is also possible to use document/literal, which is the .NET method.

Using the rpc/encoded style, parameters are encapsulated within one element after the Web method, whereas document/literal uses an XML schema for the service mapping.

SOAP with Attachments

Once you've started working with SOAP for a while, you will realize a fundamental limitation in the sorts of data that can be transferred between clients and servers. If your data isn't easily expressible as a set of primitive types or simple objects like arrays, your ability to use SOAP in a distributed application may be limited. For example, you may want to retrieve a multimedia slide presentation from a service, but this binary file format cannot be converted into the sorts of data types readily supported by SOAP and XML Schema.

This is where SOAP with attachments comes into play. The messages exchanged between clients and servers can be viewed as messages that can contain embedded documents and normal object-style data. These documents can be encoded using MIME, which is more traditionally used to support e-mail attachments. However, it is also possible to use more modern binary document encapsulation techniques like DIME.

HTTP Binding

Most people use SOAP as a cross-platform RPC system using HTTP as the transport protocol, so let's look at the binding of SOAP to HTTP. HTTP has two very different methods for making requests on a server: the GET and POST methods. In practice, both methods can be used to send a list of parameters along with a URL to an HTTP server to request a Web page, CGI script invocation, etc. The difference in methods is that GET encodes these parameters and their values inside the URL, but POST encodes these parameters inside the body of the HTML page being sent. It's important to note that SOAP 1.1 supports only POST requests, but that SOAP 1.2 supports both GET and POST. Also note that many, better performing, alternatives to HTTP are being actively developed, including BEEP, which is based on TCP and supports streaming and asynchronous communication.

You can use several headers with SOAP to provide a context for the message being received. For example, the SOAPAction HTTP header provides a mechanism to define a subject, similar to the publish-and-subscribe scheme described in Chapter 2. Most commonly, the SOAPAction header takes the form of a URI, which might describe the method name to be invoked. However, the method name should also be specified within the SOAP message body, so it may be redundant to specify the method name in both places. Other possible uses for the SOAPAction header include client identification and routing. One problem with relying on SOAPAction is that it's not a part of the HTTP protocol, and XML firewalls may well use it to filter out SOAP requests.

HTTP defines a large number of status codes that may need to be implemented partially or completely, depending on application requirements. These codes define request success, request, or server errors. If an HTTP request is successful, then one of the codes in Table 4-1 is returned.

Table 4-1. *Successful HTTP Request Codes*

Code	Definition
200	Request OK
201	Created
202	Accepted
203	Nonauthoritative information
204	No content
205	Reset content
206	Partial content

Most requests receive a 200, but it may also be possible to use other codes in acknowledging a message, such as 202. If the request fails, then one of the codes in Table 4-2 is returned.

Table 4-2. *Unsuccessful HTTP Request Codes*

Code	Definition
400	Bad request
401	Unauthorized
402	Payment required
403	Forbidden
404	Not found
405	Method not allowed
406	Not acceptable
407	Proxy authentication required
408	Request timeout
409	Conflict
410	Gone
411	Length required
412	Precondition failed
413	Request entity too large
414	Request-URI too long
415	Unsupported media type
416	Expectation failed

A number of these codes may be returned by an enterprise application. For example, if the service being accessed is pay-per-view or subscription-based, then 402 would be returned if payment had not been received. Alternatively, if the method being requested was physically not present because no method was implemented, a 404 would be returned. Significantly for SOAPAction, a 414 may be returned if the requested URI is too large.

If the remote server fails, then one of the codes in Table 4-3 is returned.

Table 4-3. *HTTP Server Failure Codes*

Code	Definition
500	Internal server error
501	Not implemented
502	Bad gateway
503	Service unavailable
504	Gateway timeout
505	HTTP version not supported

These errors are generated from the client end, except for 500 and 501, which are typically generated from a service misconfiguration. In any case, if an HTTP error occurs, at least one error will be returned, and if practical, these errors should be handled in a context-sensitive fashion.

Since HTTP was not really built to support SOAP, a number of extensions to HTTP have been developed to provide extra functionality. The most important component of the extensions is support for globally unique namespaces; using these prevents any ambiguity when clients attempt to invoke a service on a particular server.

The HTTP extensions define a new type of HTTP request, M-POST, which is similar to a normal POST, except that it indicates that a new mandatory extension will be declared. This extension is defined by the Man element, which generally contains the unique namespace definition. As multiple Web services are deployed on the same server, or as search engines become available that "find" Web services with a specific name (e.g., BuyWidget), expect to see more widespread use of HTTP extensions.

RPC Example

This example creates a client for a retail application that sends an order and receives a receipt number if the server successfully receives the order. Here is the source code:

```
import java.io.*;
import java.net.URL;
import org.dom4j.*;
import javax.xml.soap.*;
import javax.xml.messaging.*;
import javax.xml.transform.*;
import javax.xml.transform.stream.*;
import javax.mail.internet.*;

public class Retailer
{
    public static void main(String args[])
    {
        // Construct and send message
        try
        {
            URLep ep = new URLep("http://jinx:8080/jaxm-simple/receiver");
            SOAPConnectionFactory factory = SOAPConnectionFactory.newInstance();
            SOAPConnection con = factory.createConnection();
            MessageFactory msg = MessageFactory.newInstance();
            SOAPMessage msg = msg.createMessage();
```

```
            SOAPPart sp=msg.getSOAPPart();
            SOAPEnvelope e = sp.getEnvelope();
            SOAPBody sb = e.getBody();
            sb.addChildElement(e.createName("GetReply" , "jaxm",
                "http://sun.com/jaxm/someuri/")).addChildElement("name").
                addTextNode("placeOrder");
             msg.saveChanges();
            System.err.println("Sending order to remote URL: "+ ep.getURL()+
                "….");
            SOAPMessage r = con.call(msg, ep);
            msg.writeTo(System.out);
            System.out.println("Order received. Receipt number for order:");
            TransformerFactory tf=TransformerFactory.newInstance();
            Transformer tfr = tf.newTransformer();
            Source src=r.getSOAPPart().getContent();
            StreamResult sr=new StreamResult( System.out );
            tfr.transform(src, sr);
            con.close();
        }
        catch(Exception e)
        {
            e.printStackTrace();
        }
    }
}
```

Creating a SOAP message, sending a request, and receiving a response follows a simple object factory pattern for creating the appropriate connections and messages. The application starts by creating a new a SOAPConnectionFactory object, from which a SOAPConnection is instantiated. Next, a MessageFactory object is created, from which a SOAPMessage is instantiated. As explained previously, a SOAP message has three parts; these are now created from the SOAPMessage instantiation. The message body, SOAPBody, is then derived from the envelope. At this point, the message is ready to be sent, and the SOAPConnection method call is invoked with both the message and the URL as arguments. If this was a simple one-way message, at this point you wouldn't need to do anything further; the message would simply be delivered and the client application could continue processing. However, because this example uses a request-response pattern, it must now process the response message, contained in SOAPMessage r, which is simply written to standard output after it has been received. In both cases, the request and response messages are printed to the screen, although in a real application, some business logic implementation would directly process the output. A sample output is shown here:

```
$ java Order
Sending message to URL: http://jinx:8080/jaxm-simple/receiver
<soap-env:Envelope xmlns:soap-env="http://schemas.xmlsoap.org/soap/envelope/">
<soap-env:Header/>
<soap-env:Body>
  <jaxm:GetReply xmlns:jaxm="http://sun.com/jaxm/someuri/">
    <name>placeOrder</name>
  </jaxm:GetReply>
</soap-env:Body></soap-env:Envelope>
Order received. Receipt number for order:
<?xml version="1.0" encoding="UTF-8"?>
<soap-env:Envelope xmlns:soap-env="http://schemas.xmlsoap.org/soap/envelope/">
<soap-env:Header/>
<soap-env:Body>
<Response>354543545</Response>
</soap-env:Body>
</soap-env:Envelope
```

Software

Since SOAP is the native remoting protocol for .NET, there is no special software required to use SOAP within the Visual Studio .NET environment. This is a great benefit, because you can seamlessly develop and deploy services as you would normal component interfaces.

One of the best J2EE toolkits with which to explore SOAP in its different contexts is Sun's Java Web Services Developer Pack (Java WSDP). This package contains software that supports the following technologies:

- JAXM (Java API for XML Messaging)

- JAXP (Java API for XML Processing)

- JAXR (Java API for XML Registries)

- JAX-RPC (Java API for XML-based RPC)

Because the implementation of Web services is hidden from potential clients, the actual implementation of services behind the scenes varies considerably from system to system. So, the sorts of classes that javax.xml.soap defines will be quite different to those specified for use with Apache SOAP, even though both are SOAP-based. The following interfaces for javax.xml.soap at least give you some idea of the sorts of elements required to build a basic SOAP server:

- SOAPBody: The body element in a SOAP message that allows methods to be added using addBodyElement, and faults to be thrown using addFault

- SOAPBodyElement: The actual content of a body element

- SOAPConstants: Contains constants for the SOAP protocol, including namespace identifiers for encoding and the envelope

- SOAPElement: Represents the different elements within a body, including the ability to create attributes and new child elements

- SOAPEnvelope: The envelope for a SOAP message

- SOAPFault: A body element that contains error messages

- SOAPFaultElement: Elements of individual faults

- SOAPHeader: The header element for the SOAP message

- SOAPHeaderElement: Individual elements of the SOAPHeader

The unwrapping of the SOAP header and body from message parts is shown in the following example:

```
SOAPPart a = msg.getSOAPPart();
SOAPEnvelope b = a.getEnvelope();
SOAPHeader c = b.getHeader();
SOAPBody d = b.getBody();
```

It is also possible to use the IBM Web Services Development Kit (WSDK) to develop and deploy similar projects.

Project

This project requires you to create a sample SOAP application based on a simple XML schema for processing ATM transactions from a remote terminal to a central server. Your application should pass the following data elements:

- Timestamp

- Customer ID

- Amount deposited/withdrawn

- Transaction ID

- ATM ID

You should be able to use either Sun's Java WSDP or Apache SOAP to implement a generic transaction method.

Summary

In this chapter, I have described the basic messaging requirements for building XML Web Services. The binding of XML-formatted messages to a simple protocol for exchanging these messages, across a standard web transport protocol, makes it easy to develop and deploy these services.

CHAPTER 5

∎∎∎

Description and Data Format

The Web services Description Language (WSDL) uses XML to define endpoints for messages that are either documents or RPCs. WSDL works with SOAP, along with a transport protocol like HTTP, to provide the infrastructure for supporting RPC with distributed object members (using remote methods and data). WSDL provides a platform-independent wrapper that allows existing methods to be exposed as services across any platform, given the endpoint specifications defined in the WSDL file. Developers rarely need to edit WSDL files directly, because development tools provide extensive support. In this chapter, I examine how to use WSDL to define endpoints for new and existing methods to provide remotely available services between loosely coupled clients and servers.

WSDL Overview

A WSDL file specifies a language- and platform-independent interface, generally for remote method invocation using SOAP, that is client/server in nature. Public methods (or functions) from virtually any programming language can be described using WSDL, including details of parameters and their data types that must be passed to invoke the method. Return types can also be specified. Details of the binding to a specific transport type must be specified, as must location details for the service to be invoked. Although current usage is for SOAP to be used in conjunction with WSDL, in fact the specification is quite general, allowing for future remote object access protocols to be utilized.

One of the nice features of WSDL is that many integrated development environments that support enterprise systems allow client application code to be automatically generated based on a URL that points to a WSDL file for a particular Web service. This saves valuable coding time and allows all developers to have access to a consistent set of methods generated from the same interface specification. Many tools will generate WSDL files from existing method code in projects created before Web services. In a matter of minutes, public methods for existing applications can be turned into Web services. Of course, with stateful interactions, this simplistic approach may not be adequate. However, for a heavily normalized SOA, services can be specified that are independent and do not require state to be recorded in middleware. For example, atomic method invocations like payment systems can be easily converted using these tools. .NET has one advantage over J2EE when integrating Web services with existing legacy applications: the native remoting protocol for .NET is already SOAP, so no further bridges between RMI or IIOP need to be considered.

The current WSDL version is 2.0 (originally 1.2), but WSDL 1.1 has been widely deployed in existing Web services. Some of the most prominent changes include

- Introducing interfaces as replacements for `PortTypes`

- Replacing ports with endpoints

- Making `targetNamespace` a mandatory attribute of the definitions element

An excellent overview of the changes can be found at `http://webservices.xml.com/pub/a/ws/2004/05/19/wsdl2.html`.

WSDL Format

A WSDL file defines eight key elements:

- `<binding>`: specifies the data format for a service and its protocol

- `<definitions>`: the base element that specifies basic identifying characteristics of the Web service, including its name

- `<message>`: data specification for a one-way message

- `<operation>`: specifies permissible procedures

- `<port>` or `<endPoint>`: specifies service details

- `<portType>` or `<interface>`: specifies type of operations permitted with one-way or roundtrip messages

- `<service>`: specifies URL location for invoking the service

- `<type>`: specifies types of data to be used, based on standard XML Schema data types (see Chapter 3 for a review)

The abstract specification of a service comprises the various <message>, <operation>, and <interface> elements; while the specific implementation of a service is described by <binding>, <service>, and <endPoint> elements.

In addition to the elements, a WSDL file can define up to four different operational procedures:

- Notification operation: a single message is sent from a server; no request is necessary.

- One-way operation: a single message is sent from a client; no response is necessary.

- Request-response operation: a client sends a message and receives a response from the server.

- Solicit-response operation: a server sends a message and receives a response from the client.

The most common of these is the request-response operation, since it mimics the most common client/server architectures (see Figure 5-1). However, the other operations are also worth considering in some architectures, since not all activities can be reduced to request/response interactions. I'll look at the elements in more detail before considering the specific operations that might be performed for different architectures.

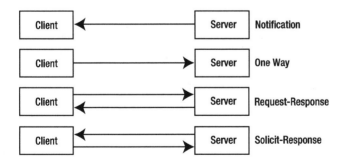

Figure 5-1. *WSDL-specific operations*

The `<definitions>` element defines many of the basic properties of a Web service. It contains namespace attributes, a set of types, message definitions (either one-way or request-response), and `portTypes`, which can encapsulate an operation.

Imagine I have developed a simple request-response application that returns the current spot price of gold. An example set of namespace definitions for this service would be as follows:

```
<definitions
  xmlns:s="http://www.w3.org/2001/XMLSchema"
  xmlns:tns="uri:com.somebroker.gold" targetNamespace="uri: com.somebroker.gold"
  xmlns="http://schemas.xmlsoap.org/wsdl/">
```

Here, I simply indicate that I will be using XML Schema and the WSDL specification to define a service that belongs to the target namespace `com.somebroker.gold`, which must be unique. Next, I specify the request message and the response message separately:

```
<message name="goldPriceRequest">
  <part name="exchangeName" type="s:xsd:string"/>
</message>
<message name="goldPriceResponse">
  <part name="goldPrice" type="s:xsd:float"/>
</message>
```

The `goldPriceRequest` message contains a single string parameter, the `exchangeName`, that represents the name of the exchange from which the quote should be obtained. The `goldPriceResponse` message contains a single float value, the `goldPrice`, which is returned from the exchange nominated. In both cases, the part element specifies individual parameters; more than one could be defined for the request message in normal practice, but only one for the response message.

The `portType` is related to the port, which is a messaging equivalent to a class or library. The `portType` encapsulates the operations defined by the passing of request and response messages between client and server. Since I've already defined the request and response messages, it's simply a matter of inserting their references into the operation definition:

```
<portType name="goldPort">
  <operation name="goldPrice">
    <input message="tns: goldPriceRequest"/>
    <output message="tns: goldPriceResponse"/>
  </operation>
</portType>
```

To operate, a `portType` must be bound to a specific protocol; otherwise, it does not have a transport! In this example, I am using SOAP over HTTP, but I just as easily could use SOAP over TCP, HTTPS, HTTPR, SMTP, or any other transport protocol, depending on requirements for guaranteed delivery, security, or message priority. The following entry specifies SOAP for our request and response methods:

```
<binding name="goldSoap" type="tns:goldPort">
  <soap:binding style="rpc"
    transport="http://schemas.xmlsoap.org/soap/http"/>
  <operation name="goldPrice">
    <soap:operation soapAction="/goldPrice" style="rpc"/>
    <input>
      <soap:body use="encoded" namespace="uri:com.somebroker.gold "
        encodingStyle="http://schemas.xmlsoap.org/soap/encoding/"/>
    </input>
    <output>
      <soap:body use="encoded" namespace="uri: com.somebroker.gold"
        encodingStyle="http://schemas.xmlsoap.org/soap/encoding/"/>
    </output>
  </operation>
</binding>
```

Having defined the portType and service bindings, I can define the port within a service description. This corresponds to the actual location of the service, and allows a client to invoke a service from a specific server location:

```
<service name="goldPrice">
  <port name="goldPort" binding="tns:com.somebroker.gold">
    <soap:address location=
      "http://webservices.somebroker.com/soap/servlet/rpcrouter"/>
  </port>
</service>
```

Building Web Services

So far, I've examined how to write WSDL files according to the elements and XML document structure specified in the WSDL specification. In reality, developers and/or system administrators rarely modify WSDL files directly on development or production servers, respectively. This is because most development and deployment environment that support Web services provide automated tools for generating WSDL from existing interfaces and/or method definitions. For example, the IBM's WSAD environment allows developers to nominate public methods for exposure as Web services, and to automatically generate the appropriate WSDL. The tool then initializes a test server and allows a test client and sample application to be generated. In the following section, I extend the gold price application by

building a Java application with methods that check the spot price of gold and place orders
"at market" price or for a specific price. I then walk through the steps of generating WSDL
and deploying the Web service to a test server.

The first step in developing the server code is to create a set of abstract interfaces
that define the operations that can be invoked from a client and that belong to a WSAD
"web project." The following code would therefore be contained within the source file
GoldBrokerIx.java:

```
public interface GoldBrokerIx
{
        // Returns current gold price from a specific exchange
        public float getGoldPrice(String exchangeName);
        // Places an order for a number of ounces of gold at market price
        public String buyGoldAtMarket(int ounces);
        // Places an order for a number of ounces of gold at a specific price
        public String buyGoldAtPrice(float price, int ounces);
}
```

While the getGoldPrice method returns the current spot gold price for a specific
exchange, the two buy methods (buyGoldAtMarket and buyGoldAtPrice) both return a
receipt number when the server acknowledges the order. Once the interfaces have
been specified, corresponding methods can then be instantiated in the source file
GoldBroker.java:

```
public class GoldBroker implements GoldBrokerIx
{
    public GoldBroker()
    {
        super();
    }

    public float getGoldPrice(String exchangeName)
    {
        float price=0;
        // execute method to return current gold price
        // and assign its value to price
        return price;
    }

    public String buyGoldAtMarket(int ounces)
    {
        String receiptNumber="";
        // execute method to buy ounces of gold at market price
        // with the receiptNumber being the returned value after
        // trade has been registered
```

```
        return receiptNumber;
    }

    public String buyGoldAtPrice(float price, int ounces)
    {
        String receiptNumber="";
        // execute method to buy ounces of gold at specific price
        // with the receiptNumber being the returned value after
        // trade has been registered
        return receiptNumber;
    }
}
```

Here, each method defined by the interface is implemented, with appropriate return value being assigned from some internal operation. To operate as a Web service, a new Web service is generated from the WSAD File menu. Firstly, the Web project from which the Web service will be generated must be selected, as shown in Figure 5-2. Developers can specify whether existing files in the test server deployment can be overwritten without warning, and whether folders can be created as necessary without user intervention.

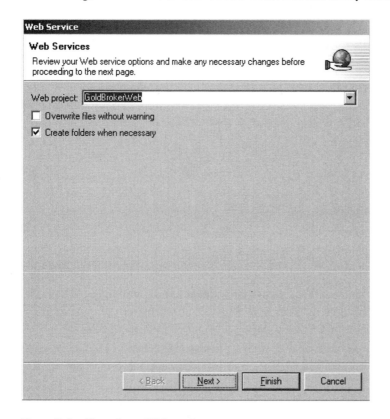

Figure 5-2. *Choosing a Web project*

Next, the name of the Java bean to utilize must be selected. In this example, the bean GoldBroker will be deployed as a Web service. The next screen, shown in Figure 5-3, allows the developer to configure the GoldBroker bean; the unique URI for the Web service must be entered (e.g., http://tempuri.org/GoldBroker), and the application's scope is also identified. The bean can be configured to use only static methods, and/or to utilize a secure transport layer rather than simple HTTP. Furthermore, the WSDL service, binding, and schema document names can all be modified for local conditions, but the defaults are usually sensible.

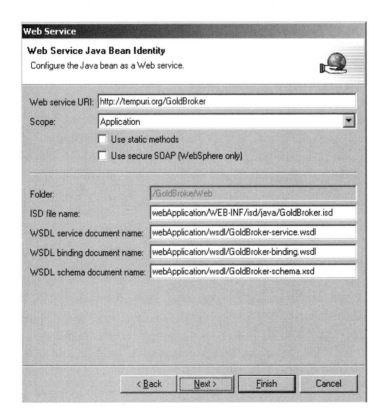

Figure 5-3. *Configuring a bean as a Web service*

The next screen, shown in Figure 5-4, allows individual methods within the GoldBroker bean to be selected for deployment as Web services (not all public methods need be selected). In this example, getGoldPrice, buyGoldAtPrice, and buyGoldAtMarket are all selected. Some further options are available, such as the use of Document/Literal, RPC/Literal, or RPC/Encoded encoding, and whether Java-to-XML mappings on the server should be displayed.

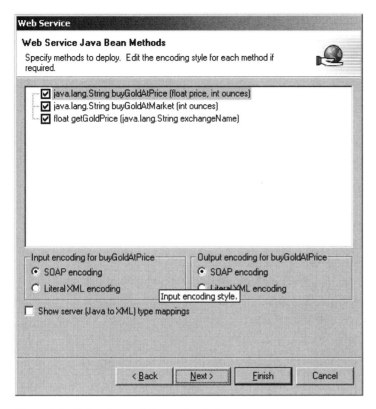

Figure 5-4. *Selecting public methods for exposure*

The final major screen in the deployment process, shown in Figure 5-5, involves the selection of WSDL bindings to protocols. Only SOAP is supported at this time. The proxy class name is also specified. The proxy class contains proxy methods for each method specified within the Web service. For example, here is the proxy method for the getGoldPrice method:

```
public synchronized float getGoldPrice(java.lang.String exchangeName)
    throws Exception
{
    String targetObjectURI = "http://tempuri.org/GoldBroker";
    String SOAPActionURI = "";

    if(getURL() == null)
    {
        throw new SOAPException(Constants.FAULT_CODE_CLIENT,
        "A URL must be specified via GoldBrokerProxy.setEndPoint(URL).");
    }
```

```
call.setMethodName("getGoldPrice");
call.setEncodingStyleURI(Constants.NS_URI_SOAP_ENC);
call.setTargetObjectURI(targetObjectURI);
Vector params = new Vector();
Parameter exchangeNameParam = new Parameter("exchangeName",
    java.lang.String.class, exchangeName, Constants.NS_URI_SOAP_ENC);
params.addElement(exchangeNameParam);
call.setParams(params);
Response resp = call.invoke(getURL(), SOAPActionURI);

//Check the response.
if (resp.generatedFault())
{
    Fault fault = resp.getFault();
    call.setFullTargetObjectURI(targetObjectURI);
    throw new SOAPException(fault.getFaultCode(), fault.getFaultString());
}
else
{
    Parameter refValue = resp.getReturnValue();
    return ((java.lang.Float)refValue.getValue()).floatValue();
}
}
```

Once the bean has been deployed to the server, a service binding must be specified in the appropriate WSDL file. The binding for GoldBroker is contained within the file GoldBroker-service.wsdl, as shown here:

```
<?xml version="1.0" encoding="UTF-8"?>
<definitions name="GoldBrokerService"
   targetNamespace=
   http://localhost:8081/GoldBrokerWeb/wsdl/GoldBroker-service.wsdl
   xmlns=http://schemas.xmlsoap.org/wsdl/
   xmlns:tns=http://localhost:8081/GoldBrokerWeb/wsdl/GoldBroker-service.wsdl
   xmlns:binding=
   http://www.goldbroker.com/definitions/GoldBrokerRemoteInterface
   xmlns:soap="http://schemas.xmlsoap.org/wsdl/soap/">
   <import namespace=
   http://www.goldbroker.com/definitions/GoldBrokerRemoteInterface
   location=
   "http://localhost:8081/GoldBrokerWeb/wsdl/GoldBroker-binding.wsdl"/>
   <service name="GoldBrokerService">
       <port name="GoldBrokerPort" binding="binding:GoldBrokerBinding">
```

```
        <soap:address location=
            "http://localhost:8081/GoldBrokerWeb/servlet/rpcrouter"/>
      </port>
    </service>
</definitions>
```

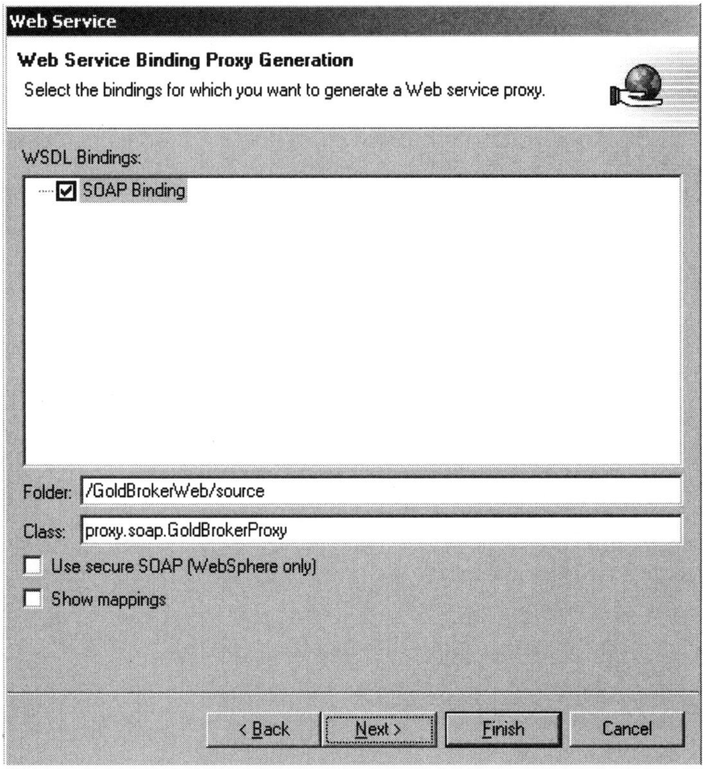

Figure 5-5. *Selecting a protocol binding*

The operations that form part of the portType, their bindings, and the request/
response messages are all contained within the GoldBroker-binding.wsdl file, as shown
here:

```
<?xml version="1.0" encoding="UTF-8"?>
    <definitions name="GoldBrokerRemoteInterface"
    targetNamespace=
    http://www.goldbroker.com/definitions/GoldBrokerRemoteInterface
    xmlns=http://schemas.xmlsoap.org/wsdl/
    xmlns:tns=http://www.goldbroker.com/definitions/GoldBrokerRemoteInterface
    xmlns:xsd=http://www.w3.org/2001/XMLSchema
```

```
      xmlns:soap="http://schemas.xmlsoap.org/wsdl/soap/">
  <message name="buyGoldAtPriceRequest">
    <part name="price" type="xsd:float"/>
    <part name="ounces" type="xsd:int"/>
  </message>
  <message name="buyGoldAtPriceResponse">
    <part name="result" type="xsd:string"/>
  </message>
  <message name="buyGoldAtMarketRequest">
    <part name="ounces" type="xsd:int"/>
  </message>
  <message name="buyGoldAtMarketResponse">
    <part name="result" type="xsd:string"/>
  </message>
  <message name="getGoldPriceRequest">
    <part name="exchangeName" type="xsd:string"/>
  </message>
  <message name="getGoldPriceResponse">
    <part name="result" type="xsd:float"/>
  </message>
  <portType name="GoldBrokerJavaPortType">
    <operation name="buyGoldAtPrice">
      <input name="buyGoldAtPriceRequest" message="tns:buyGoldAtPriceRequest"/>
      <output name="buyGoldAtPriceResponse"
message="tns:buyGoldAtPriceResponse"/>
    </operation>
    <operation name="buyGoldAtMarket">
      <input name="buyGoldAtMarketRequest"
message="tns:buyGoldAtMarketRequest"/>
      <output name="buyGoldAtMarketResponse"
            message="tns:buyGoldAtMarketResponse"/>
    </operation>
    <operation name="getGoldPrice">
      <input name="getGoldPriceRequest" message="tns:getGoldPriceRequest"/>
      <output name="getGoldPriceResponse" message="tns:getGoldPriceResponse"/>
    </operation>
  </portType>
  <binding name="GoldBrokerBinding" type="tns:GoldBrokerJavaPortType">
    <soap:binding style="rpc" transport="http://schemas.xmlsoap.org/soap/http"/>
    <operation name="buyGoldAtPrice">
      <soap:operation soapAction="" style="rpc"/>
      <input name="buyGoldAtPriceRequest">
```

```
        <soap:body use="encoded"
            encodingStyle=http://schemas.xmlsoap.org/soap/encoding/
            namespace="http://tempuri.org/GoldBroker"/>
      </input>
      <output name="buyGoldAtPriceResponse">
        <soap:body use="encoded"
            encodingStyle=http://schemas.xmlsoap.org/soap/encoding/
            namespace="http://tempuri.org/GoldBroker"/>
      </output>
    </operation>
    <operation name="buyGoldAtMarket">
      <soap:operation soapAction="" style="rpc"/>
      <input name="buyGoldAtMarketRequest">
        <soap:body use="encoded"
            encodingStyle="http://schemas.xmlsoap.org/soap/encoding/"
            namespace="http://tempuri.org/GoldBroker"/>
      </input>
      <output name="buyGoldAtMarketResponse">
        <soap:body use="encoded"
            encodingStyle=http://schemas.xmlsoap.org/soap/encoding/
            namespace="http://tempuri.org/GoldBroker"/>
      </output>
    </operation>
    <operation name="getGoldPrice">
      <soap:operation soapAction="" style="rpc"/>
      <input name="getGoldPriceRequest">
        <soap:body use="encoded"
            encodingStyle=http://schemas.xmlsoap.org/soap/encoding/
            namespace="http://tempuri.org/GoldBroker"/>
      </input>
      <output name="getGoldPriceResponse">
        <soap:body use="encoded"
            encodingStyle=http://schemas.xmlsoap.org/soap/encoding/
            namespace="http://tempuri.org/GoldBroker"/>
      </output>
    </operation>
  </binding>
</definitions>
```

Some versions of WSAD combine these files into a single WSDL file, but they are shown as separate here for clarity.

Systems Integration

In this section, I review some real Web services offered by third-party providers that you can integrate with your own applications. Some of these providers (such as FedEx) you will already be working with, so it will be possible for you to try a Web-services integration with some of your existing test systems.

FedEx Tracking

FedEx is one of the largest delivery companies in the world. The business process is quite simple in terms of inputs and outputs; a sender consigns a package to FedEx, who then delivers to a specific recipient. However, given the wide variety of destinations that FedEx ships to, it's not surprising that the internal mechanisms of delivery can be very complicated. Since FedEx provides time-based guarantees of delivery, senders typically want to know if a consignment has been delivered, whereas a recipient generally wants to know when it arrives. If a package has not been delivered on time, then a sender may contact FedEx and ask for a refund if the delivery time was guaranteed. Similarly, a recipient may contact FedEx and ask when the package will be delivered if it has not arrived on time. In both cases, the sender and recipient need a simple method for accessing FedEx's internal delivery systems to determine the consignment status. Rather than staffing a call center to provide this information, FedEx provides a Web site where senders and recipients can enter the tracking number and view the status.

This approach works for one or two packages, but if your company sends out hundreds and thousands of consignments every day, the browser interface is not scalable. Furthermore, if delivery is not made on time, typically you must follow a process, such as sending an e-mail to FedEx customer service. This means that the process should be automated, which can be easily achieved using a Web service. FedEx has created a Web service for just this purpose, and you can use it to track your packages.

A single method, getStatus, is defined in the WSDL interface for the Web service. It has a single input, the trackingNumber of type xsd:string, and it returns a status message also of type xsd:string. The SOAPAction is urn:xmethodsFedEx#getStatus, and the method namespace URI is urn:xmethodsFedEx. The complete WSDL file is shown here:

```
<?xml version="1.0" ?>
  <definitions name="FedExTrackerService"
  targetNamespace=http://www.xmethods.net/sd/FedExTrackerService.wsdl
  xmlns:tns=http://www.xmethods.net/sd/FedExTrackerService.wsdl
  xmlns:xsd=http://www.w3.org/2001/XMLSchema
  xmlns:soap=http://schemas.xmlsoap.org/wsdl/soap/
  xmlns="http://schemas.xmlsoap.org/wsdl/">
  <message name="statusRequest">
  <part name="trackingNumber" type="xsd:string" />
```

```
</message>
<message name="statusResponse">
<part name="return" type="xsd:string" />
</message>
<portType name="FedExTrackerPortType">
<operation name="getStatus">
<input message="tns:statusRequest" />
<output message="tns:statusResponse" />
</operation>
</portType>
<binding name="FedExTrackerBinding" type="tns:FedExTrackerPortType">
<soap:binding style="rpc" transport="http://schemas.xmlsoap.org/soap/http" />
<operation name="getStatus">
<soap:operation soapAction="urn:xmethodsFedEx#getStatus" />
<input>
<soap:body use="encoded" namespace="urn:xmethodsFedEx"
  encodingStyle="http://schemas.xmlsoap.org/soap/encoding/" />
</input>
<output>
<soap:body use="encoded" namespace="urn:xmethodsFedEx"
  encodingStyle="http://schemas.xmlsoap.org/soap/encoding/" />
</output>
</operation>
</binding>
<service name="FedExTrackerService">
<documentation>Provides access to a variety of FedEx delivery status
    information</documentation>
<port name="FedExTrackerPort" binding="tns:FedExTrackerBinding">
<soap:address location="http://services.xmethods.net:80/perl/soaplite.cgi" />
</port>
</service>
</definitions>
```

Exchange Rate Conversion

All companies in finance need to perform currency conversions on a regular basis. How many of our coworkers still use newspapers or Web page converters to do this manually? While proprietary systems exist for providing the conversion, a new interface needs to be created for each new program that uses these systems. Thus, by using a Web service, only a single interface needs to be specified for all clients wishing to access the system.

A major advantage in using a Web service is that the current, up-to-the-minute buy or sell exchange rate can be used in a transaction.

Two parameters are passed in with the request, country1 and country2, representing the currency to exchange from and exchange to, with the country names being used rather than the currency name. The return parameter is simply a floating-point number representing the conversion rate. Recall that the conversion rate for country1:country2 will be the inverse of country2:country1.

The WSDL file is shown here:

```xml
<?xml version="1.0" ?>
<definitions name="CurrencyExchangeService"
  targetNamespace=http://www.xmethods.net/sd/CurrencyExchangeService.wsdl
  xmlns:tns=http://www.xmethods.net/sd/CurrencyExchangeService.wsdl
  xmlns:xsd=http://www.w3.org/2001/XMLSchema
  xmlns:soap=http://schemas.xmlsoap.org/wsdl/soap/
  xmlns="http://schemas.xmlsoap.org/wsdl/">
<message name="getRateRequest">
<part name="country1" type="xsd:string" />
<part name="country2" type="xsd:string" />
</message>
<message name="getRateResponse">
<part name="Result" type="xsd:float" />
</message>
<portType name="CurrencyExchangePortType">
<operation name="getRate">
<input message="tns:getRateRequest" />
<output message="tns:getRateResponse" />
</operation>
</portType>
<binding name="CurrencyExchangeBinding" type="tns:CurrencyExchangePortType">
<soap:binding style="rpc" transport="http://schemas.xmlsoap.org/soap/http" />
<operation name="getRate">
<soap:operation soapAction="" />
<input>
<soap:body use="encoded" namespace="urn:xmethods-CurrencyExchange"
  encodingStyle="http://schemas.xmlsoap.org/soap/encoding/" />
</input>
<output>
<soap:body use="encoded" namespace="urn:xmethods-CurrencyExchange"
  encodingStyle="http://schemas.xmlsoap.org/soap/encoding/" />
</output>
</operation>
```

```
  </binding>
  <service name="CurrencyExchangeService">
  <documentation>Returns the exchange rate between the two currencies
    </documentation>
  <port name="CurrencyExchangePort" binding="tns:CurrencyExchangeBinding">
  <soap:address location="http://services.xmethods.net:80/soap" />
  </port>
  </service>
  </definitions>
```

A sample request for an exchange rate conversion between USD and AUD format is shown here:

```
<SOAP-ENV:Envelope xmlns:SOAP-ENV="http://schemas.xmlsoap.org/soap/envelope/"
  xmlns:xsi=http://www.w3.org/1999/XMLSchema-instance
   xmlns:xsd="http://www.w3.org/1999/XMLSchema">
<SOAP-ENV:Body>
<ns1:getRate xmlns:ns1="urn:xmethods-CurrencyExchange" SOAP
  -ENV:encodingStyle="http://schemas.xmlsoap.org/soap/encoding/">
<country1 xsi:type="xsd:string">united states</country1>
<country2 xsi:type="xsd:string">australia</country2>
</ns1:getRate>
</SOAP-ENV:Body>
</SOAP-ENV:Envelope>
```

The corresponding response is shown here:

```
<SOAP-ENV:Envelope xmlns:SOAP-ENV="http://schemas.xmlsoap.org/soap/envelope/"
  xmlns:xsi=http://www.w3.org/1999/XMLSchema-instance
   xmlns:xsd="http://www.w3.org/1999/XMLSchema">
<SOAP-ENV:Body>
<ns1:getRateResponse xmlns:ns1="urn:xmethods-CurrencyExchange" SOAP-ENV:
  encodingStyle="http://schemas.xmlsoap.org/soap/encoding/">
<return xsi:type="xsd:float">178.59</return>
</ns1:getRateResponse>
</SOAP-ENV:Body>
</SOAP-ENV:Envelope>
```

Let's examine how to implement a client interface to this interface by using Java:

```
import java.io.*;
import java.util.*;
import java.net.*;
```

```java
import org.apache.soap.*;
import org.apache.soap.rpc.*;
import org.apache.soap.util.xml.*;

public class CurrencyConversion
{
public static void main(String[] args)
{
    try
    {
        Call c = new Call ();
        c.setEncodingStyleURI(Constants.NS_URI_SOAP_ENC);
        c.setTargetObjectURI ("urn:xmethods-CurrencyExchange");
        c.setMethodName ("getRate");
        Vector p = new Vector ();
        p.addElement (new Parameter("country1", String.class, country1, null));
        p.addElement (new Parameter("country2", String.class, country2, null));
        c.setParams (p);
        Response r = c.invoke (http://services.xmethods.com:80/soap,"");
        if (r.generatedFault ())
        {
            System.out.println("System error");
        }
        else
        {
            Parameter result = r.getReturnValue ();
            Float rate=(Float) result.getValue();
            String country1= "united states";
            String country2= "australia";
            System.out.println(country1 + " -> "+ country2+
                " = "+getRate(u,country1,country2));
        }
    }
    catch (Exception e)
    {
        System.out.println("System error");
    }
}
```

Software Packages

If you don't use an integrated WSDL generator within your existing IDE, a number of software packages are available to work with WSDL files directly. The best-known tool is Altova's XMLSpy application, which acts as a SOAP client and debugging tool. It can interpret WSDL documents and validate them according to the 1.2 specification syntax. In addition, it can act as a SOAP client for any existing WSDL interface, and create a SOAP re-quest whose response can be validated on the client side. Support is provided for both simpleType and complexType elements. Figure 5-6 shows the binding WSDL for the GoldBroker example, with XMLSpy showing the detail of the request and response methods specified by the interface.

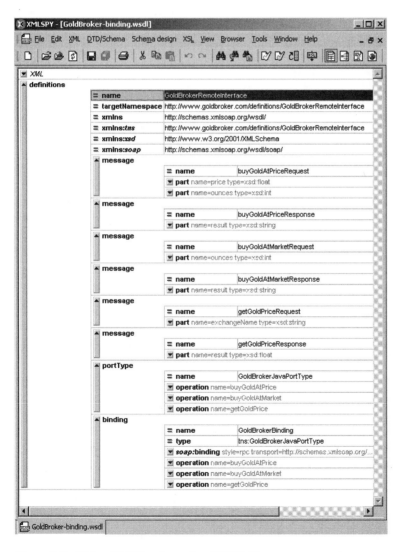

Figure 5-6. *Using XMLSpy to review WSDL files*

The IBM WSDL Explorer (http://www.alphaworks.ibm.com/tech/wsdlexplorer) is another useful demonstration package. It allows you to enter the URL for a WSDL file, and then it displays all available methods. Enter the parameters for the method you wish to invoke, and it displays the SOAP request and response for you, as shown in Figure 5-7.

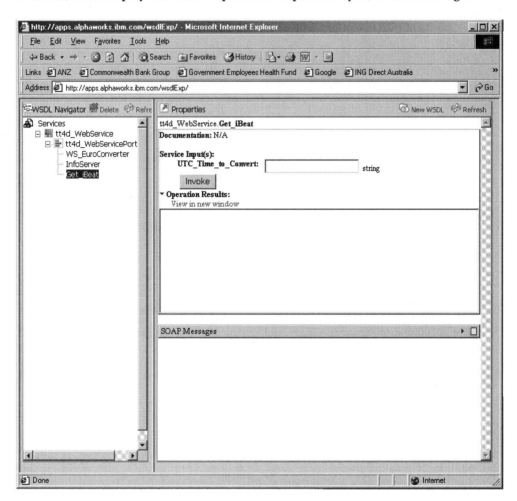

Figure 5-7. *Using WSDL Explorer to review request/response sequences*

For a more sophisticated solution to WSDL development, design, and maintenance, Cape Clear's Studio contains a WSDL editor that allows Web service interfaces to be specified using various wizards. It also allows the generation of Web services from existing EJB or CORBA objects, while providing rapid application development through the generation of sample applications and frameworks. JUnit test cases can also be generated allowing for test-driven and agile development of new Web services. A technical overview of the editor's capabilities are available at http://www.capeclear.com/products/whitepapers/ CapeClear4TechnicalOverview.pdf.

From the Web application perspective, the easiest way to interface dynamic Web applications with Web services is through Microsoft Front Page. Here, ASP.NET Web forms can be programmed to invoke Web services and display the results. More details are available at `http://msdn.microsoft.com/library/default.asp?url=/library/ en-us/dnfp2k2/html/odc_fpWSvc.asp`.

Existing Interfaces

After reading this chapter, you'll probably want to experiment with writing a client to an existing Web service rather than writing both a client and server at the same time. An excellent way to locate existing Web services is to use the service at `http://www. xmethods.com/`, which lists many different Web services and details of their interfaces.

Project

This project requires you to design and implement a Java server that performs a validity check on credit card numbers (the algorithm to do this is widely available on the Internet). After implementing the Java server, use WSAD to generate a Java bean to be deployed as a Web service, and deploy it to a test server. Then use XMLSpy to generate a SOAP client to interact with the server. Both Altova and IBM offer evaluation licenses to examine their Web services software; developers should make use of these offers to become familiar with the technology.

Summary

In this chapter, I've described how to specify interfaces for XML Web services. These interfaces provide the basis for interaction and data exchange between heterogeneous systems. In the next few chapters, I combine WSDL, SOAP, and XML to examine more sophisticated application requirements and protocols.

## CHAPTER 6

Discovery and Advertising

UDDI is the core Web services Universal Description, Discovery, and Integration proto-col that underlies service directories and discovery of those services through the effective management of service data and meta-data. Through White, Yellow, and Green Pages, public UDDI directories can be used to locate business partners dynamically, and private UDDI directories can be used internally for standard directory service functions. UDDI XML Schemas can define business entities, services, templates, and tModels (technical models), all of which I review in this chapter. The original UDDI concept now appears somewhat fanciful, in terms of searching and binding to these new (and untrusted) serv-ices based purely on UDDI listings. It appears that the UDDI concept has now evolved to cover both private and public repositories for WSDL files based on universal resource names (URNs). UDDI assures high availability because of full registry replication through geographically distributed nodes. Note that the phone book metaphor featured strongly in early descriptions of UDDI has been discarded in version 3 of the specification. To maintain backward compatibility with existing installations, and because the metaphor was quite powerful, I continue to use it in this chapter. I won't cover purely administra-tive functions such as internode operations and publishing to more than one registry.

Theory and Practice

Most enterprise operating environments have some kind of directory service that allows the characteristics of users, systems, and networks to be looked up dynamically on client request. This is because in large organizations, users come and go, systems are switched from subnet to subnet, and new networks are created when required. So, not all configu-ration data, such as security credentials, can be stored statically on each client system on the network. Trying to maintain consistency between hundreds or thousands of statically stored copies of the same directory is a nightmare, especially in fast-changing environ-ments. Thus, protocols like LDAP can be used to allow dynamic access to a logically centralized service that provides up-to-date, often-replicated data about entities that clients and applications typically work with.

Originally, the X.500 standard was introduced to provide a directory service for entire organizations. LDAP is the "lightweight" version of the Directory Access Protocol (DAP), and it provides various interfaces for managing directory data (updates, insertions, and deletions) and queries on the directory for security purposes. LDAP is quite a flexible protocol; it allows both text and multimedia data to be stored about principals on the network. Note that UDDI is a standard feature of the Windows 2003 operating environment, providing an extra layer of integration with existing Active Directory services.

To some extent, UDDI can be seen as an extension of LDAP that goes beyond organizational boundaries to facilitate the location and invocation of Web services. Strictly speaking, you don't need UDDI to invoke a method exposed through WSDL and SOAP; if you know the appropriate interface URL and parameters, then these can be used statically by a client application for invocation. However—just like the consistency problem for organizations in locating local entities—in a fast-changing external environment, URLs will also change. So, clients should be able to locate a desired service dynamically rather than having to rely on static data.

Organizations typically utilize two types of UDDI registries: public registries set up by the major vendors, each hosting an individual "node" to promote the global exchange of business and service details; and private registries, which are accessible only to clients behind the corporate firewall. Public registries provide the kind of service-finding techniques necessary for integration with business partners and external organizations, and private registries provide the integration within existing application architectures. When moving away from centralized stovepipes to more distributed application architectures internally, using the dynamic service lookups provided by UDDI can provide a platform for integration. Note that a node can be a member of only one registry, since it provides a complete replica of the logical registry data. Maintaining consistency between replicated copies of registry data is an ongoing research problem.

At this stage, UDDI has not reached the level of sophistication that may be required to ensure the integrity and confidence of dynamic lookups for services, or the promise of the dynamic selection of business partners identified from a public directory. There certainly is a large-scale effort underway through the UDDI Business Registry (UBR) to act as a single logical registry for the world's Web services. Currently, more than 10,000 businesses are registered in the UBR, publishing more than 7,000 services, with the core nodes hosted by IBM, Microsoft, SAP, and NTT Communications. Service entries created at one node are automatically propagated to the other core nodes.

Versions 2 and 3 of UDDI certainly allow organizations to publicize their business details in public directories, and run private directories that act in the same way as a cross-platform version of LDAP. UDDI is quite flexible in that a single UDDI registry can support both private and public access to certain types of data and entities. All data is exposed as an XML Web service in its own right.

UDDI makes a distinction between business data and service data, which are spread across three different directory types: White Pages, Yellow Pages, and Green Pages. The two former directory types are concerned with business data, and the latter is primarily concerned with service data. Five original different data types are supported in the directory: businessEntity, businessService, bindingTemplate, tModel, and publisherAssertion. I'll examine each in the context of the directory type to which they belong. In UDDI version 3, there is also a subscription API to describe standing requests to keep track of changes (http://uddi.org/pubs/uddi_v3_features.htm).

White Pages are responsible for storing business contact information in the businessEntity format. This contains the main contact information for an organization, very much like an alphabetically ordered standard phone directory. Listings can be made in multiple languages through the use of Unicode, as can the accompanying descriptions. A publisherAssertion describes the association between different entities in the White Pages.

The Yellow Pages uses a businessService data type. The latter provides a corollary to a standard Yellow Pages directory; organizations and their services can be located using category-based classifications, permitting discovery of the providers of specific goods and services. Logically, each grouping of services described by a businessService is associated with one and only one businessEntity.

The Green Pages store specific service invocation information (details clearly not found in a traditional phone book). Both a bindingTemplate data type and a tModel data type are used. A bindingTemplate is used to store details of individual Web services, and a tModel provides a catalog-like specification. The bindingTemplate contains all the details required to invoke a Web service, including access points. Logically, each bindingTemplate is associated with a single businessService.

A tModel is an independent model specification that can be reused by multiple bindingTemplates, enabling the easy sharing of data between instances and even different systems. It contains URLs pointing to specification documents and their associated meta-data and model identification.

The interaction between the different types of pages is shown in Figure 6-1.

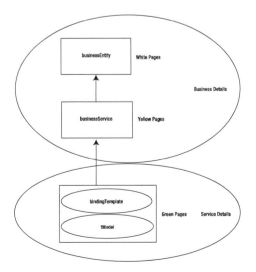

Figure 6-1. *UDDI data types*

Three types of users are permitted to access a UDDI registry: publishers, inquirers, and subscribers. Just like in a normal telephone book, a publisher is the company that places an advertisement for a specific good or service, while an inquirer wants to locate a company that provides a specific good or service. The types of access controls implemented for publishers and subscribers ensure that subscribers cannot overwrite the records of publishers; otherwise, all users of the registry could change each other's details at will, either maliciously or accidentally. In addition to preventing write access for subscribers on publishers' data, one publisher should also not be able to overwrite data belonging to another publisher.

Passing a user name and password within the context of the publishing API typically authenticates publishers. These data are usually encrypted between the publisher application and the registry by using Secure HTTP (HTTPS). Inquirers make queries about available services and can access the inquiry API over a normal HTTP connection. IBM has a test registry for publishing methods and an inquiry API available at `http://www-306.ibm.com/software/solutions/webservices/uddi/`.

The fact that inquirers are not authenticated is problematic for public registries, since you may want to restrict access to certain organizational groups or subgroups. Presently, if you have sensitive data stored in a registry, the best solution is to make the entire registry private. Hopefully, this restriction will change in future versions. One possible compromise is to utilize a subscriber role rather than an inquirer; the subscription API does support client authentication (using the `authInfo` token), but provision for this API is not currently mandatory. The UDDI subscription API sets up the registry framework as a traditional "pub/sub" system; subscribers listen for broadcasts of new types of entries being inserted (e.g., `businessEntity`, `businessService`, `bindingTemplate`, `tModel`), and update their activities accordingly. For example, a quality-of-service monitoring application for the banking industry may monitor all current and new services operating and "ping" them regularly to test availability. If the monitoring application is a registry subscriber, then it will be automatically notified of new banking entities and services when their corresponding entries are inserted. The entries listened for can be set in the monitoring application by means of a list of preferences.

One reason why subscription is useful is that client applications can dynamically maintain references to service location data, thereby minimizing downtime resulting from configuration file changes. Thus, dynamic applications can be bound together at run time by the invocation of services located through subscription. This may include discovery of new information and service providers throughout the life of the application. While the mechanisms to appropriately select new services are largely undefined, this is the type of reflection that is desirable in an application context. As mentioned previously, being able to monitor quality of service is also a key property of subscription-based services, since endpoints can be looked up during execution. Thus, if one server is failed-over, another can be dynamically located.

A unique property of UDDI is that it supports many different categorization schemes, so different "views" on a single element can be utilized. Thus, while the description of industries and products is taxonomic, multiple systems can be implemented to describe data in the registry.

API Review

Searching a UDDI registry can be based on a number of different criteria from the client's perspective. Services can be identified through interfaces matching a specification, through standard industry or product codes, or based on simple keywords. There are two separate API sets: one intended for developers who work with nodes, the other for client inquiries.

White Pages

A businessEntity is the key data structure for the White Pages, comprising elements and attributes. The businessEntity attributes include a businessKey that exclusively names each organization's entry by way of Universally Unique Identifier (UUID). The UUID acts as a unique primary key in the database of businessEntity entries, ensuring that they cannot be confused. In addition, an authorizedName attribute identifies the contact person for the organization, and the operator attribute identifies the organization managing the records for the organization.

Several key elements also contain details for the White Pages. These include the name of the businessEntity, its description, a list of contacts, a description of businessServices provided, a discoveryURL that specifies a discovery mechanism, an identifierBag that is related to the organization's main industry (such as a Dun & Bradstreet D-U-N-S number), and a categoryBag that may contain product information from the Universal Standard Products and Services Classification System (UNSPSC—[http://www.unspsc.org/] or industry information from the North American Industry Classification System (NAICS) http://www.census.gov/epcd/www/naics.html). To ensure authenticity, each businessEntity can be digitally signed using an XML digital signature.

The discoveryURL simply points to a URL specifying a discovery document. For example, the businessKey uddi:cassowary.net:registry:engineer:21 can be associated with a discovery document using the following syntax:

```
<discoveryURL >
    http://www.cassowary.net?businessKey= uddi:cassowary.net:registry:engineer:21
</discoveryURL>
```

While the default assumption is that a useType attribute of businessEntity will be used, it is possible to specify an alternative data structure if required.

Multiple name elements can be associated with each businessEntity, which can be useful when a company has multiple trading names or abbreviations, or where it trades under different names in different countries. The following example shows that the company Bank One, which trades under the acronym B1, would have name definitions as follows:

```
<name>Bank One</name>
<name>B1</name>
```

Like names, an organization can have multiple descriptions in any language. For example, Bank One may trade in both the United States and France, with the following descriptions entered into the registry:

```
<description xml:lang="en">A large bank </description>
<description xml:lang="fr">Une banque grand</description>
```

The contacts list contains a set of contact items, which themselves describe individuals who have specific responsibilities within an organization. For example, a stockbroking firm may have a contact for Equities Support, Derivatives Support, and so on. These could be defined in the following way:

```
<contact useType="Equities Support">
    <personName>Jane Doe</personName>
    <description>Chief Equities Officer</description>
</contact>
<contact useType="Derivatives Support">
    <personName>John Lee</personName>
    <description>Chief Derivatives Officer</description>
</contact>
```

Details including phone, e-mail, and address may also be included. One nice feature of UDDI is that addressing formats are standardized, removing some of the ambiguity in resolving different address components by using tModels. Again, this is very useful when dealing with international addresses that do not conform to a standard U.S. model. The following example shows the address for the Derivatives Support office:

```
<address useType="Derivatives Support" xml:lang="en">
   <addressLine>678 Richmond Rd</addressLine>
   <addressLine>Richmond</addressLine>
   <addressLine>VA</addressLine>
   <addressLine>23227</addressLine>
</address>
```

The identifierBag contains identification information for the organization that typically comes from an external source. The identifier is encapsulated within a keyedReference, where the unique keyValue associated with a keyName could be used as a primary key for local searching. The following identifierBag shows the D-U-N-S details for Bank One:

```
<identifierBag>
    <keyedReference
        tModelKey="uddi:ubr.uddi.org:identifier:dnb.com:D-U-N-S"
        keyName="BANK ONE"
        keyValue="93-342-3333" />
</identifierBag>
```

A categoryBag contains similar details, except that a higher level of categorization can be achieved on the basis of tModels. The keyedReference structure is once again used, and related multiple keyedReferences can be combined into a single keyedReferenceGroup. For example, to specify the geographic location of Bank One, the following code could be used:

```
<keyedReferenceGroup tModelKey="uddi:ubr.uddi.org:categorizationGroup:wgs84" >
    <keyedReference
        tModelKey="uddi:ubr.uddi.org:categorization:wgs84:latitude"
        keyName="Latitude"
        keyValue="+40.0000" />
    <keyedReference
        tModelKey="uddi:ubr.uddi.org:categorization:wgs84:longitude"
        keyName="Longitude"
        keyValue="+10.0000" />
</keyedReferenceGroup>
```

Yellow Pages

The businessService data structure encapsulates all the details for an organization's entry, including four elements and two attributes. The name element is the business name, and the description indicates the nature of its operations. A technical definition of the available services is provided by a number of bindingTemplates in the Green Pages (one for each service), and a categoryBag is also provided, as per the White Pages businessEntity.

As with the White Pages, a businessKey element is provided, but so is a UUID, called a serviceKey, which identifies each service provided; this can be issued on request by the registry, or it can be supplied. For example, many organizations would use unique codes to identify the services they offer. Some similarities exist between businessService and businessEntity: both have a name and description, a categoryBag for categorization, and can be digitally signed for authenticity.

Green Pages

One of the main features is the inclusion of bindingTemplates, which contain all the technical details required to define an individual Web service. The bindingTemplate has a serviceKey and a bindingKey, which like the serviceKey can be supplied by the user or generated by the registry. In addition to a description, an accessPoint URL is supplied to indicate the service's address. A group of tModelInstanceInfo elements that define the technical blueprint for the service is encapsulated within a tModelInstanceInfo element.

The accessPoint defines a network endPoint, which is the address where the service is located. A bindingTemplate can be used to indicate a shared service description, and a hostingRedirector is used to indicate when requests are to be forwarded to another registry. WSDL description is supported by the wsdlDeployment attribute.

A sample bindingTemplate for a stock trading service called is shown here.

```
<bindingTemplate bindingKey="uddi:bank.one.net:stock">
    <description xml:lang="en">
        Stock Trading Service - Bank One
    </description>
    <accessPoint useType="endPoint">
        http://bank.one.net/StockWebService
    </accessPoint>
    <tModelInstanceDetails>
        <tModelInstanceInfo tModelKey="uddi:bank.one.net:stock_interface"/>
        <tModelInstanceInfo tModelKey="uddi:uddi.org:transport:http"/>
    </tModelInstanceDetails>
</bindingTemplate>
```

Here, you can see a bindingKey and its associated accessPoint, which then has two constituent tModelInstanceInfo tModelKeys: one for the trading interface, and one for the HTTP transport protocol. Alternative transports are also supported—even the humble phone, as shown in the following example:

```
<bindingTemplate bindingKey="uddi:bank.one.net:stock">
    <description xml:lang="en">
        Stock Trading Service - Bank One
    </description>
    <accessPoint useType="endPoint">
        tel:+1-804-358-1877
    </accessPoint>
    <tModelInstanceDetails>
        <tModelInstanceInfo tModelKey="uddi:uddi.org:transport:telephone"/>
    </tModelInstanceDetails>
</bindingTemplate>
```

Preferably, WSDL description would be used instead of a static accessPoint such as a phone number or URL. This approach provides more flexibility, as shown in the following example:

```
<bindingTemplate bindingKey="uddi:bank.one.net:stock">
    <description xml:lang="en">
        Stock Trading Service - Bank One
    </description>
    <accessPoint useType="wsdlDeployment">
        http://bank.one.net/StockWebService.wsdl
    </accessPoint>
    <categoryBag>
        <keyedReference keyName="uddi-org:types:wsdl" keyValue="wsdlDeployment"
        tModelKey="uddi:uddi.org:categorization:types"/>
    </categoryBag>
</bindingTemplate>
```

In addition to bindingTemplates, tModels are the key data structures utilized in the Green Pages. The tModel is a general description or technical specification that can describe specifications and expectations that ensure compatible services can be invoked dynamically. For example, if two banks offer compatible payment services, then an end-user application should be able to select either one based on cost or availability considerations. The tModel allows clients to verify that a particular Web service supports a specification.

Sometimes, humans need to interact with Web services to understand what services are actually available. One way to do this is through an overview document specified by a tModel. The following example shows instance details about the StockWebService:

```
<tModelInstanceInfo tModelKey="uddi:bank.one.net:stock_interface">
    <instanceDetails>
        <overviewDoc>
            <description xml:lang="en">
                The StockWebService returns current stock prices.
            </description>
            <overviewURL useType="text">
                http://bank.one.net/StockWebService.pdf
            </overviewURL>
        </overviewDoc>
    </instanceDetails>
</tModelInstanceInfo>
```

Inquiry API

From the client side, the most commonly used API is the Inquiry API. This provides a number of methods through HTTP POST that allow different types of searching to be performed. The following are the most commonly used methods:

- `find_binding`: returns bindings contained in a `businessService` data structure in the form of a `bindingDetail` data structure

- `find_business`: returns details of businesses in a `businessList` data structure

- `find_relatedBusinesses`: returns details of businesses related to the one specified in the search term (usually a key)

- `find_service`: returns one or more services in a `serviceList` data structure resulting from a search of recorded organizations

- `find_tModel`: returns one or more tModels in a `tModelList` structure based on a query

- `get_bindingDetail`: returns the details of one or more `bindingTemplates` in a `bindingDetail` structure

- `get_businessDetail`: returns the details of one or more sets of `businessEntity` details in a `businessDetail` structure

- `get_operationalInfo`: returns operational information for organizations using an `operationalInfo` structure

- `get_serviceDetail`: returns service details for one or more instances of `businessService` data encapsulated in a `serviceDetail` structure

- `get_tModelDetail`: returns tModel details for one or more instances of tModel data encapsulated in a `tModelDetail` structure

Publisher API

Obviously, queries can be performed only on a populated registry, and this data must be entered and continually managed by using the Publisher API. The major methods that can be invoked are listed here.

- add_publisherAssertions: adds a publisher assertion to the set of currently defined assertions

- delete_binding: removes a specific bindingTemplate

- delete_business: removes a specific businessEntity

- delete_publisherAssertion: removes a specific publisherAssertion

- delete_service: removes a specific businessService

- delete_tModel: logically removes but does not delete a tModel

- get_assertionStatusReport: provides feedback using an assertionStatusReport data structure on a businessEntity

- get_publisherAssertions: retrieves a set of assertions using a publisherAssertions structure relating to a publisher

- get_registeredInfo: returns a list of organizations and tModels hosted by a specific publisher

- save_binding: saves a new bindingTemplate or updates an existing entry

- save_business: saves a new businessEntity or updates an existing entry

- save_service: saves new service details or updates an existing entry

- save_tModel: saves a new tModel or updates an existing entry

- set_publisherAssertions: sets the assertions for a specific publisher

Schemas and APIs

The schemas for UDDI implementations are divided into two broad categories: Node API sets and Client API sets. The schema details for Node API sets are listed here.

- UDDI Schema (http://uddi.org/schema/uddi_v3.xsd)

- UDDI Policy (http://uddi.org/schema/uddi_v3policy.xsd)

- UDDI Policy Instance
  (`http://uddi.org/schema/uddi_v3policy_instanceParms.xsd`)

- UDDI Custody (`http://uddi.org/schema/uddi_v3custody.xsd`)

- UDDI Subscription (`http://uddi.org/schema/uddi_v3subscription.xsd`)

- UDDI Replication (`http://uddi.org/schema/uddi_v3replication.xsd`)

The schema details for the Client API sets are

- UDDI Subscription Listener (`http://uddi.org/schema/
  uddi_v3subscriptionListener.xsd`)

- UDDI Value Set Validation (`http://uddi.org/schema/uddi_v3valueset.xsd`)

- UDDI Value Set Caching (`http://uddi.org/schema/uddi_v3valuesetcaching.xsd`)

Commands

The following examples show how to use sample clients to interrogate a UDDI directory, and how to search entries in the White, Yellow, and Green Pages.

Sample Clients

Most public UDDI directories provide user-friendly Web interfaces to enter and modify entries in the White, Yellow, and Green pages. For example, IBM has a public test registry located at `http://uddi.ibm.com/`. To act as a publisher, you can enter the details or a real (or fictitious) business, and later perform a query. The first stage in the publishing process is to define a business name, and then, as shown in Figure 6-2, enter the description of a business and language details on the Add a new Description screen.

Next, the business's main contact details, which can include a name and role, are entered on the Add a Contact screen, as shown in Figure 6-3.

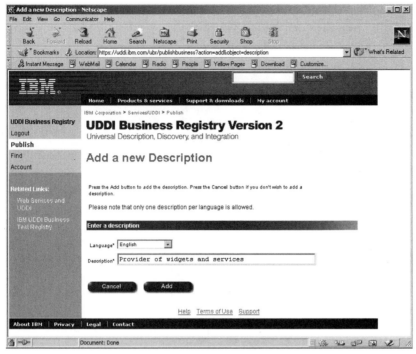

Figure 6-2. *Entering business description details*

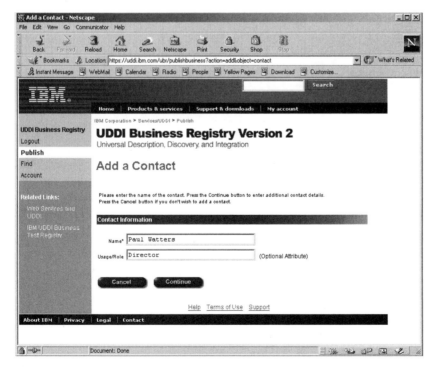

Figure 6-3. *Adding contact details*

In terms of Yellow Pages data, the Add a Locator screen is for selecting an appropriate industry-specific category for the organization. NAICS codes ranging from Agriculture to Public Administration appear in Figure 6-4.

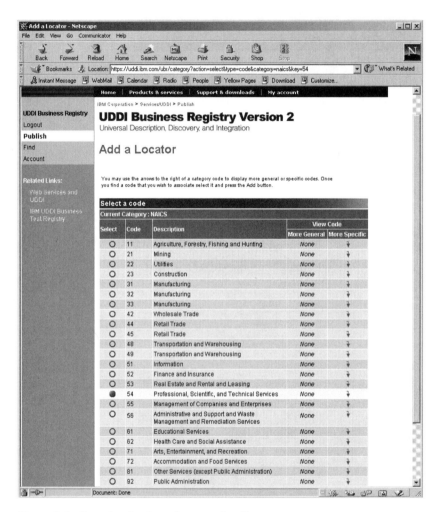

Figure 6-4. *Entering business locator details*

Once the data is saved, you can confirm the entry in the Add a Business screen, as shown in Figure 6-5. You can make changes before the entry is committed to the registry. tModels can also be entered on the appropriate screen by clicking on the Edit link.

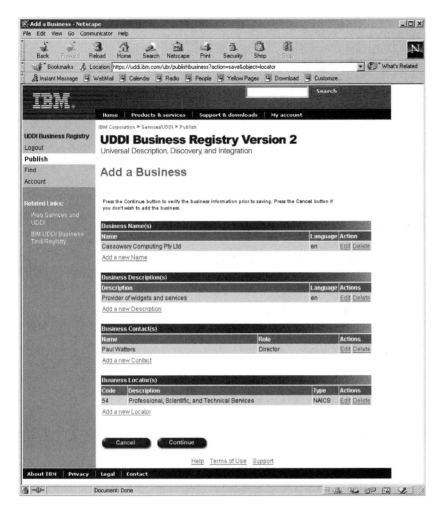

Figure 6-5. *Validating business details*

Once a description is published, an inquirer can use the Find a Business screen to perform a query on that entry in the registry, as shown in Figure 6-6. Here, a case-sensitive or case-insensitive search can be performed on a full or partial business name. Alternatively, identifiers or locator strings can be used to perform lookups.

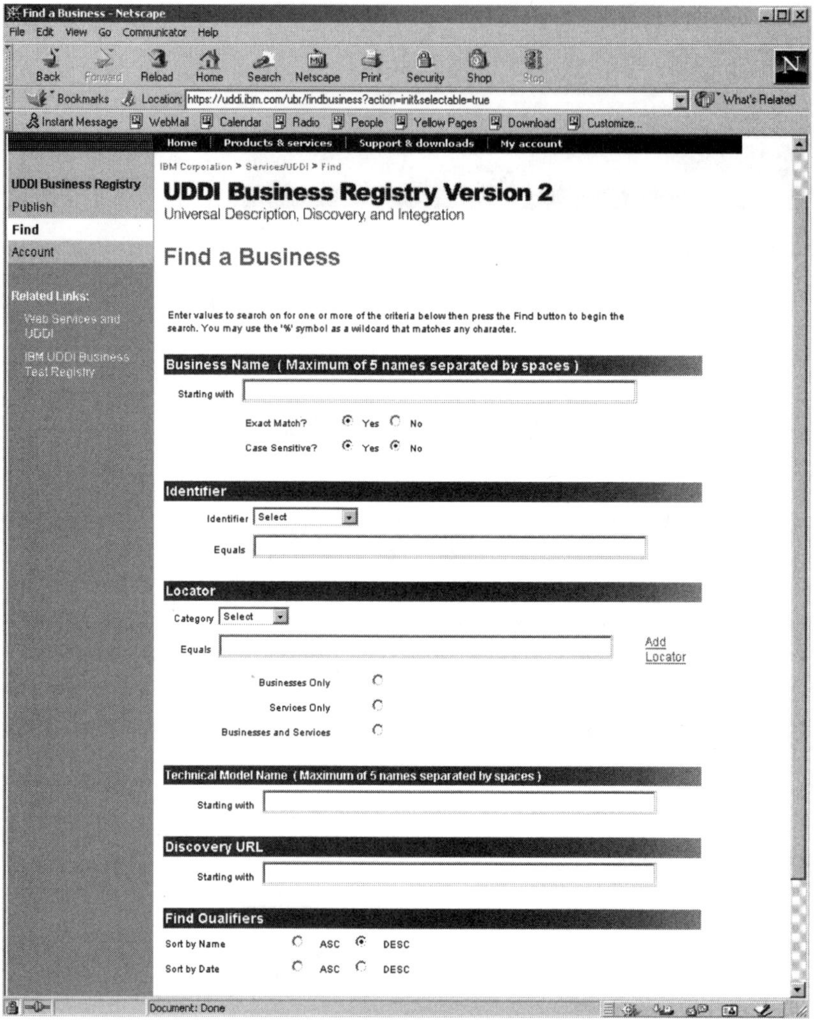

Figure 6-6. *Searching for business details*

Searching

UDDI registries allow several types of searching, and most clients, depending on the purpose of the application, will support these. Browsing involves starting with a wide-ranging query, reviewing some search results, and then perhaps drilling down to find specific details. A good example is when a client might search for a specific supplier to see what services it provides. The supplier's name is passed to the find_business method, which then returns a businessList set comprising a list of businessEntity records. The supplier's name could be specified fully or partially, so "Bank One" and "Bank O*" (using a findQualifier) should return a businessList with the correct bank's details. All of the records retrieved in the businessList can then be used to further query the registry for the relevant businessService by using the find_service method and tModel entries associated with that business. For example, if Bank One provided a credit card validation method as a Web service, then the tModel describing the data format and the service endpoint should be retrievable once the businessEntity for Bank One has been located.

The alternative approach to searching is to drill down first. This requires knowledge of the key for one of the uniquely identifying elements of a businessEntity, business-Service, or tModel. If you have identifying information for one of these data structures, you can use this key and the get_businessDetail method to retrieve any of the related data structures. Drilling down is appropriate when a local record of keys is cached to speed up processing. For example, a mortgage broker might cache the businessService keys for all of the home loan approval services provided by the major financial institutions. Each of these can be queried in turn to determine whether an application for credit is likely to be approved.

Dynamic location of business data is provided through invocation. This provides real-time binding of search queries to live registry nodes and the associated bindingTemplates for available services. Thus, if a bank has two separate data centers to provide failover, and the primary site does fail, then the bank's business partners, on detecting a failure, will refresh their bindingTemplates using the cached bindingKey for each service. This will return, from the registry, the current bindingTemplate for the secondary site. This kind of high-availability strategy is one of the key benefits of using UDDI to maintain directory services for services that must be up 24-7.

Many findQualifiers are available for enhanced searching in UDDI. Table 6-1 provides the findQualifier names available for each API .

Table 6-1. *UDDI Enhanced Search Qualifiers*

find_business	find _service	find_binding	find_tModel
andAllKeys	andAllKeys	andAllKeys	approximateMatch
approximateMatch	approximateMatch	approximateMatch	caseInsensitiveSort
binarySort	binarySort	binarySort	caseInsensitiveMatch
bindingSubset	bindingSubset	bindingSubset	caseSensitiveSort
caseInsensitiveSort	caseInsensitiveSort	caseInsensitiveSort	caseInsensitiveMatch
caseInsensitiveMatch	caseInsensitiveMatch	caseInsensitiveMatch	diacriticInsensitiveMatch
caseSensitiveSort	caseSensitiveSort	caseSensitiveSort	diacriticSensitiveMatch
caseInsensitiveMatch	caseInsensitiveMatch	caseInsensitiveMatch	exactMatch
combineCategoryBags	combineCategoryBags	diacriticInsensitiveMatch	signaturePresent
diacriticInsensitiveMatch	diacriticInsensitiveMatch	diacriticSensitiveMatch	orAllKeys
diacriticSensitiveMatch	diacriticSensitiveMatch	exactMatch	orLikeKeys
exactMatch	exactMatch	signaturePresent	sortByNameAsc

Continued

Table 6-1. *UDDI Enhanced Search Qualifiers (Continued)*

find_business	find_service	find_binding	find_tModel
signaturePresent	signaturePresent	orAllKeys	sortByNameDesc
orAllKeys	orAllKeys	orLikeKeys	sortByDateAsc
orLikeKeys	orLikeKeys	sortByDateAsc	sortByDateDesc
serviceSubset	sortByNameAsc	sortByDateDesc	UTS-10
sortByNameAsc	sortByNameDesc		
sortByNameDesc	sortByDateAsc		
sortByDateAsc	sortByDateDesc		
sortByDateDesc	suppressProjectedServices		
suppressProjectedServices	UTS-10		
UTS-10			

Clearly, many of these qualifiers cannot be used in conjunction with each other; for instance, you can't search on andAllKeys, orAllKeys, and orLikeKeys, or an error will be returned. This could have been better implemented by using attribute-value pairs, such as "sort=caseSensitive" or "sort=caseInsensitive". The function of each qualifier is summarized here.

- andAllKeys: substitutes logical AND for OR in identifierBag searches

- approximateMatch: supports wildcard searches; uses % and _ for multiple-letter or single-letter wildcards, respectively

- binarySort: arranges search by name

- bindingSubset: makes use of just the categoryBag elements from nominated bindingTemplate elements

- caseInsensitiveSort: ignores case in sorting

- caseInsensitiveMatch: ignores case in searching

- caseSensitiveSort: uses case in sorting

- caseSensitiveMatch: uses case in searching

- combineCategoryBags: groups together categoryBag elements and returns a match if any of the categoryBag elements has a match

- diacriticInsensitiveMatch: ignores diacritic marks in search

- diacriticSensitiveMatch: uses diacritic marks in search

- exactMatch: search string must exactly match a target

- signaturePresent: will return only registry entries that have been digitally signed

- orAllKeys: substitutes logical AND for OR in tModelBag and categoryBag searches

- orLikeKeys: substitutes logical AND for OR in tModelBag and categoryBag searches containing more than one keyedReference element

- serviceSubset: makes use of just the categoryBag elements from nominated businessService elements

- sortByNameAsc: sorts alphabetically ascending by name

- sortByNameDesc: sorts alphabetically descending by name

- sortByDateAsc: sorts alphabetically ascending by date

- sortByDateDesc: sorts alphabetically descending by date

- suppressProjectedServices: ensures that service projections are never returned from a query

- UTS-10: makes use of the Unicode Collation Algorithm and Collation Element Table to organize search results

Let's look at some example queries to see how these qualifiers can be used in practice. To locate business entries that start with the letters "Bank" followed by any number of subsequent characters, the following find_business method invocation would be used:

```
<?xml version = "1.0" encoding = "UTF-8"?>
<find_business xmlns = "urn:uddi-org:api_v3"
xmlns:xsi = "http://www.w3.org/2001/XMLSchema-instance">
  <findQualifiers>
    <findQualifier>
      uddi:uddi.org:findQualifier:approximateMatch
    </findQualifier>
  </findQualifiers>
  <name>Bank%</name>
</find_business>
```

Similarly, if entries containing all business names that started with "Bank On" with only one possible trailing character (e.g., Bank On**e**), then the following query would be used:

```
<?xml version = "1.0" encoding = "UTF-8"?>
<find_business xmlns = "urn:uddi-org:api_v3"
xmlns:xsi = "http://www.w3.org/2001/XMLSchema-instance">
  <findQualifiers>
    <findQualifier>
      uddi:uddi.org:findQualifier:approximateMatch
    </findQualifier>
  </findQualifiers>
  <name>Bank On_</name>
</find_business>
```

To locate all of the businesses whose name starts with "Bank" and ends with "Limited", the following query would be used:

```
<?xml version = "1.0" encoding = "UTF-8"?>
<find_business xmlns = "urn:uddi-org:api_v3"
xmlns:xsi = "http://www.w3.org/2001/XMLSchema-instance">
  <findQualifiers>
    <findQualifier>
      uddi:uddi.org:findQualifier:approximateMatch
    </findQualifier>
  </findQualifiers>
  <name>Bank%Limited</name>
</find_business>
```

To do a search using a NAICS code for all businesses in a specific industry, a similar approach is taken. The following example returns listings for all businesses in the Finance and Insurance industries:

```
<?xml version = "1.0" encoding = "UTF-8"?>
<find_business xmlns = "urn:uddi-org:api_v3"
xmlns:xsi = "http://www.w3.org/2001/XMLSchema-instance">
  <findQualifiers>
    <findQualifier>
      uddi:uddi.org:findQualifier:approximateMatch
    </findQualifier>
  </findQualifiers>
  <categoryBag>
    <keyedReference
```

```
        keyValue = "54%"
        tModelKey = "uddi:ubr.uddi.org:categorization:naics:1997"/>
    </categoryBag>
</find_business>
```

Case Study

This case study demonstrates how to integrate UDDI with other server-side technologies in the data access layer. In the following example called BusinessSearch.java, a manufacturer wants to reward the retailer who sells $1,000,000 of goods each month. These data are stored in a local database called sales, and the name of the business is stored in the field bus_name. Thus, by using the JDBC API within our application, we can create a connection to the database, select the retailer with the appropriate level of sales, and return the business name to the calling application. The application then creates a SOAP connection to a UDDI registry to retrieve the business details of the retailer, and prints it to the screen. This job could be automated on UNIX by creating a cron job that ran once each month and e-mailed the output to the manufacturer's CEO. Obviously, the report might also include other relevant details, like how many retailers achieved the milestone, and perhaps return all their details in rank order. However, as the example shows, it's quite easy to combine UDDI and SOAP with JDBC to create powerful searching tools. Note that a retailer seeking credit card clearance payment facilities could also search a UDDI directory to find a local bank with the lowest commission. Interestingly, the retailer's application could also use Web services to process the transactions.

```java
import javax.xml.soap.*;
import javax.xml.messaging.*;
import java.util.*;
import java.io.*;
import java.sql.*;

public class BusinessSearch
{
    public static void main(String[] args)
    {
        String businessName=selectTopSeller();
        if (businessName!=null)
        {
            printBusinessDetails(businessName);
        }
        else
```

```java
    {
        System.out.println("No million dollar sales");
    }
}

private String selectTopSeller()
{
    String businessName;
    Connection con;
     String url = "jdbc:mysql://dbserver:3306/business";
    try
    {
        Class.forName("org.gjt.mm.mysql.Driver");
    }
        catch(java.lang.ClassNotFoundException e)
    {
        System.err.print("ClassNotFoundException()");
        }
    try
    {
        con = DriverManager.getConnection(url, username, password);
    }
        catch (SQLException e)
        {
            throw(new UnavailableException(this, e.getMessage())));
        }
    try
    {
        Statement stmt = con.createStatement();
        String query="select bus_name from sales where total=1000000";
        ResultSet rs = stmt.executeQuery(query);
         rs.next();
         businessName=rs.getString(1);
    }
    catch (SQLException ex )
    {
        out.println("Message:    " + ex.getMessage ());
}

    return businessName;
}

private void printBusinessDetails(String businessName)
```

```
{
    try
    {
        String URL="http://www-3.ibm.com/services/uddi/testregistry/inquiryapi";
            URLEndpoint ep = new URLEndpoint(URL);
            MessageFactory mf = MessageFactory.newInstance();
        SOAPMessage msg = mf.createMessage();
        SOAPEnvelope e = msg.getSOAPPart().getEnvelope();
        SOAPBody b = e.getBody();
        b.addChildElement(e.createName("find_business", "",
            "urn:uddi-org:api"))
            .addAttribute(e.createName("generic"), "1.0")
            .addAttribute(e.createName("maxRows"), "10")
            .addChildElement("name").addTextNode(businessName);
        msg.saveChanges();
        SOAPConnectionFactory fac = SOAPConnectionFactory.newInstance();
        SOAPConnection con = fac.createConnection();
        SOAPMessage r = con.call(msg, ep);
        System.out.print("Business details for "+businessName+": ");
        r.writeTo(System.out);
        con.close();
    }
    catch (Exception ex)
    {
        ex.printStackTrace();
    }
}
}
```

Note that you will need to use UDDI4J to access a UDDI registry with Java, or use the Microsoft UDDI SDK in a .NET context.

Project

In this project, you should connect to a test registry and create the appropriate entries in the White, Yellow, and Green Pages. Using UDDI, can you then retrieve the location of the WSDL file for your services by creating a UDDI client?

Summary

In this chapter, I've examined UDDI and the role of directory services in automating application integration. UDDI has so far failed to make a significant impact on the development and deployment of Web services, but future revisions may come closer to meeting market demands for highly available and secure service directories. However, private UDDI registries behind the firewall appear to be a growth area; here, internal applications can dynamically bind the latest WSDL files in an application integration scenario. Clearly, this can be extended to trusted trading partners by granting access to the private UDDI registry, subject to the security requirements and frameworks described in Chapter 8.

CHAPTER 7

■■■

Alternative Transports

In all previous chapters, I have assumed that SOAP is bound to the HTTP protocol to provide a transport layer. While this protocol supports the request-response nature of the SOAP-RPC type operations, SOAP does not actually specify a protocol for transport. Thus, since SOAP is based on message passing, it can be used asynchronously across a wide variety of transports that may support security, asynchronous messaging, and reliable delivery. However, as I will show in the code examples presented, this conversion is not exactly "plug and play," because code modifications are necessary to support the alternative bindings. In this chapter, I examine how to bind different transports to SOAP, and how such bindings can be used to implement enterprise applications that rely on loose coupling.

SMTP

E-mail is a ubiquitous, asynchronous message exchange system based around two core protocols for server-server exchange between Mail Transport Agents (MTAs): the Simple Mail Transfer Protocol (SMTP), proposed by RFC 821, and the Extended Simple Mail Transfer Protocol (ESMTP). MTAs operate on many different platforms and operating systems and, since they run on TCP, can be interrogated manually for mail sending and reading.

SMTP and ESMTP have a long and stable history, and are supported by all servers that send and receive e-mail. In addition to MTAs, Mail User Agents (MUAs) are required to transfer mail from the central SMTP server to clients. This can be achieved by using the Post Office Protocol (POP) 3 or the newer Internet Message Access Protocol (IMAP). POP is a "disconnected" service, in that requests and responses require a new connection to be created each time. IMAP attempts to preserve a connection to the server. POP clients typically retrieve messages and retain them on the client system, while IMAP stores them on the server. The benefit of POP is that users can retain control over their own mail storage, while IMAP users can access all of the folders and files from any location. Applications using SOAP over SMTP could bypass the existing client protocols by pretending to be a SMTP server, but given the large number of APIs available for talking POP or SMTP, it seems more reasonable to reuse.

While HTTP is often touted as the transport protocol of choice for Web services, this choice may not suit all applications, particularly those with some deferred processing requirement or which take a long time to run. This is particularly the case for back-end systems that do not run on "Internet time." For example, during the day at a mail order company, multiple clients may send requests to batch print envelopes after midnight to minimize computational and network resources. Clearly, clients can't wait around for a success message, so an asynchronous message protocol is more sensible. Once all the envelopes have finished printing, each client can be sent another message indicating 1) how many envelope printing requests were received, 2) how many were printed successfully, and 3) how many others have been reserved for reprinting during the next evening. If the total number of jobs received by the server for any particular client is less than what was sent, then the missing jobs can be re-sent.

HTTP can traverse firewalls, since most leave port 80 unblocked, but SMTP has the same capability. The main advantages of HTTP over SMTP for transporting SOAP messages are reduced latency, and, where HTTPS is used, data confidentiality. But the processing and bandwidth costs are higher with HTTPS, so it may not be suitable for congested networks or back-end systems with limited capacity. SMTP supports public key encryption systems of various kinds, so confidential material could be encrypted prior to transmission using SMTP, rather than implementing the full heavyweight HTTPS protocol.

One major advantage of SMTP over HTTP is that if an HTTP delivery request cannot be delivered because of a temporary network or system outage, then the request will fail immediately. In contrast, SMTP requests will be relayed from an intermediate SMTP server until the remote server can be contacted. If the remote server does not respond for several days, then a specific error code will be returned to the client so that further action can be taken. In this way, SMTP is far more tolerant of errors than HTTP and is highly scalable. Authentication is provided between client and POP server by way of a user name and password. J2EE support for working with SMTP is automatically provided through the JavaMail API, so very little extra coding is required to run SOAP over SMTP.

One disadvantage of using e-mail for SOAP message exchange is that while HTTP is a simple client-server protocol, SMTP must generally be combined with POP or IMAP to provide true end-to-end messaging. A mail handler like `procmail` may also be required. This provides advantages over HTTP—messages can be queued, stored on the server archivally, etc.—but it also created new client-server, server-server, and server-client interactions that must be managed. While SOAP and most e-mail use this approach, other protocols may not be so complex; the Unix-to-Unix Copy Program (UUCP) and X.400 messaging are older systems that potentially could be used if bindings were developed. Other proprietary and nonstandard protocols might also provide greater efficiencies in terms of binary transfer reducing network traffic, but given the ubiquity of SMTP, it seems unlikely that any of these will be adopted as a standard binding for SOAP.

Both HTTP and SMTP operate over TCP and are text-based, meaning that commands can be directly issued from the command-line by using telnet, and the output recorded. This is very useful for troubleshooting. Ultimately, the choice of HTTP, SMTP, or another transport mechanism depends on an application's requirements for asynchronous and/or guaranteed delivery.

Figure 7-1 shows the basic message flow between clients and servers that use SOAP over SMTP. The client application creates messages that are sent to the client MTA by the MUA using POP, and these are then sent to the server MTA over SMTP. These messages are then picked up by the server MUA using IMAP, and ultimately delivered to the server application. It's possible that client and server applications may bypass the MUA intermediary and directly implement utilize SMTP command-set, since this is supported by the JavaMail API.

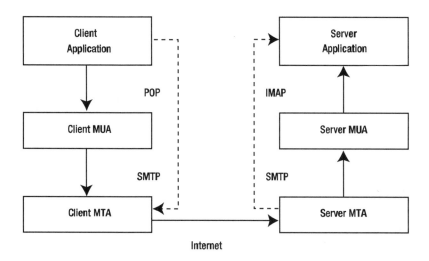

Figure 7-1. *Basic message flow for sample client/server applications using SOAP over SMTP*

SMTP Commands

Before I examine how to transmit SOAP messages in SMTP messages, I will first investigate the SMTP protocol and how it is used in practice. The exchange between sending and receiving MTAs consists of a number of commands and associated parameters sent to the receiver. The receiver then acknowledges each request with a specific code, much like HTTP.

The SMTP commands most commonly used are the following:

- DATA: specifies that the transmitted data is a message

- EHLO: specifies that ESMTP will be used

- EXPN: returns the members of local mailing lists

- HELO: specifies that SMTP will be used

- MAIL: specifies the sender's e-mail address

- QUIT: terminates an SMTP session

- RCPT: specifies the recipient's address

- VRFY: checks that a recipient's e-mail address is valid on the remote system

In addition to these SMTP commands, the ESMTP command set provides the following operations:

- VERB: uses verbose style

- 8BITMIME: uses MIME data

- DSN: supports delivery status notification to the sender

- SIZE: specifies the message size

- ONEX: specifies a transmission of a single message

- ETRN: starts the queue for remote messages

- XUSR: specifies user data

This command set can be used on the server side for many purposes. For example, message sizes larger than a maximum limit can be detected and rejected before being delivered. This prevents e-mail "bombs" from clogging systems. In a messaging environment, it may also prevent denial-of-service attacks from preventing the delivery of messages.

Sample SMTP Session

Now that I've reviewed basic SMTP commands, let's see how the exchange of messages actually operates. Imagine a messaging application where salespeople make a sale and record it on their local point-of-sale device, which in turn sends a message to a print manager to print an invoice during a batch process after hours. The user julian@sales.cassowary.net, for example, might want to send a message to the user lp@print.cassowary.net. An SMTP session would be created for each sale that julian made, which would subsequently see a message delivered to lp's mailbox.

While it's possible to use the sendmail MTA to issue SMTP commands, it's also possible to use telnet for the same purpose. The first step is to create a connection from sales.cassowary.net to print.cassowary.net on TCP port 25.

```
% telnet print.cassowary.net 25
```

The remote host print.cassowary.net will then acknowledge the request, as long as a compatible MTA is running.

```
220 print.cassowary.net sendmail 8.1.1 #1 ESMTP ready at Mon, 21 Jul 2003
    10:30:00 -1100
```

Once the acknowledgement is received and an ESMTP server is identified, I begin issuing commands.

```
>>> HELO sales.cassowary.net
```

This identifies the sender. Next, the sender is acknowledged.

```
250 print.cassowary.net Hello sales.cassowary.net
```

Now, the sender is identified.

```
>>> MAIL From:<julian@sales.cassowary.net>
```

Once again, an acknowledgement is sent.

```
250 (verified non-local) Ok
```

The recipient is next identified.

```
>>> RCPT To:<lp@print.cassowary.net>
```

As long as the user identified has a local account, the following response will be issued:

```
250 (verified local) Ok
```

Next, the sender indicates that the message now be sent.

```
>>> DATA
```

The receiver then indicates the format in which message data should be sent.

```
354 Start mail input; end with <CRLF>.<CRLF>
```

The message data can now be transmitted. The following example shows invoice data that could be further populated on the server side by retrieving the appropriate records from a database:

```
Invoice 8475866
Item: 5869704
Cost: $34.30
Deliver to: 7485695
>>> .
```

After the message data, has been transmitted, the successful receipt is acknowledged by the receiver.

```
250 2.6.0 Roger
```

The session can now be terminated.

```
>>> QUIT
```

The receiver once again acknowledges.

```
221 2.0.0 print.cassowary.net Out
```

SMTP Headers

SMTP-delivered messages have a number of standard headers that can be used to identify senders, recipients, and other message properties. Server-side applications may make use of these characteristics to organize incoming messages. For example, all messages from the user "sales" might be directed to one mailbox that is used to print spool invoices, while all messages from "payments" may be redirected to a bookkeeping application for processing.

When the message is being delivered (and afterward), the following headers are available for processing:

- Content-Length: specifies the length of the message in lines, e.g.,

  ```
  Content-Length: 1024
  ```

- Content-Type: specifies the type of multimedia data (supported by MIME) encoded in the message, e.g.,

  Content-Type: text/plain; charset="iso-8859-1"

- Date: contains a timestamp from the message receipt, e.g.,

  Date: Thu, 24 Jul 2003 09:00:00 +1000

- From: the user who sent the message, e.g.,

  From jones@sales.cassowary.net Thu Jul 24 09:00 2003

- Message-Id: a unique identifier generated by the sending MTA, e.g.,

  Message-Id: <200307241000.a487YTG87575@sales.cassowary.net>

- Received: records details of the message's delivery including MTA identifiers and client host, e.g.,

  Received: from jones.cassowary.net (root@ jones.cassowary.net
      [10.64.16.12])
      by lp.cassowary.net (8.9.1a/8.9.1) with ESMTP id MAA09867
      for <lp@lp.cassowary.net>; Thu, 24 Jul 2003 09:00:00 +1000 (AEST)

- Subject: contains a description of the message, e.g.,

  Subject: Print Job 287564

- To: the user to whom the message is addressed, e.g.,

  To: Invoice Printing Web Service < lp@lp.cassowary.net>

POP

As mentioned previously, the MUA provides connectivity between the client application and the MTA, just as if the client application were a normal mail client like pine, elm, or the many other clients currently in use. One protocol to allow the client retrieval of e-mail from a server is the Post Office Protocol (POP), which was originally defined in RFC 1725 and runs on TCP port 110. POP is particularly useful in situations where the mail client runs on a separate system from the mail server, since it provides a mechanism for off-line message distribution. While POP allows messages to be retained on the server, it supports a handshaking mechanism to ensure that once messages have been copied successfully to the client, they can be safely deleted from the user's server-side mailbox. In these days of fast PCs, it is possible for individual users to run their own MTAs on the client-side, but this prevents the site-wide enforcement of rules and aliases, and also links mail delivery to individual machines whose configuration can change rapidly. Using a central server with RAID technology, automated failover, etc. ensures that messaging facilities can be highly available.

POP uses a simple sequence of commands including the following:

- DELE *i*: removes message *i* from the mail queue on the server

- LIST: returns a list of messages available on the server for download the client

- PASS *p*: specifies a password *p* to match the username *u* for remote authentication

- QUIT: terminates a POP connection

- RETR *i*: requests the contents of message *i* to be downloaded from the server

- USER *u*: specifies a username *u* to be used with a password *p* for server auth entication

Typically, a client connects with USER and PASS, requests a LIST, and then a RETR for every message, a DELE once the message has been successfully downloaded, and a QUIT to end the session. Each request made to the POP server is acknowledged by a status code like +OK for affirmative requests, and negative requests receive an –ERR code.

Obviously, passing user names and passwords in the clear seems pretty naive given today's transport layer security measures, because a rogue user could intercept these authentication tokens.

IMAP

The alternative to POP is the Internet Message Access Protocol (IMAP), which was originally put forward in RFC 2060. IMAP clients on remote systems are able to simulate the kind of on-line connectivity utilized by local mail clients. While IMAP clients can operate in a disconnected mode, they make much use of folder synchronization to ensure data integrity, and other more advanced management features. For example, the typical POP request sequences discussed earlier are based on whole message retrieval, but IMAP provides facilities to selectively retrieve message headers and other message parts. This makes scanning e-mail very quick, which may be important in the sorts of process auto-mation that Web services are useful for.

As an example, a print server could use IMAP to scan for the size headers on all invoice messages received during the past business day and queued for overnight printing; then alert the printer operator to provide the actual number of blank pages to complete all jobs. With POP, all messages would need to be retrieved to obtain this data, but with IMAP, a quick scan of the headers could be performed. Alternatively, the scanning could identify only messages received by a specific user, estimate their printing costs, and then automati-cally send them an invoice. Given that the contents of an e-mail message could potentially contain the payload of any Web service, the possibilities are endless. Also, since the pro-cessing occurs on the MTA server side, systems on the sending side and receiving side are not tied up with back-end processing.

MIME

SOAP message data must be text-based, although conceivably, binary data may need to be transferred. For example, if our invoice was created in Microsoft Word format and attached to the message, this would be made possible by MTA support for the Multipur-pose Internet Mail Extensions (MIME), specified in RFC 2045. Using MIME means that binary data can be recoded as base64 text data and transferred as a normal text part in a multipart message. Most modern SMTP servers support MIME, so it is now very easy to send messages that contain images, movies, and other document formats. MIME types are specified in the message header, so it would be possible to scan server-side messages using IMAP to determine whether any images had been received by a print manager, for example, and redirect these to a color printer rather than a black-and-white system.

As discussed in Chapter 2, Microsoft has also developed the DIME standard, which allows binary data to be encapsulated and transported with SOAP messages. DIME has bet-ter performance than MIME and has a simpler header structure. For more details on DIME, see http://msdn.microsoft.com/library/default.asp?url=/library/en-us/dnservice/html/service01152002.asp.

Subscription Example

Before I move on to examine how to develop Java applications that can use SMTP bind-ings for SOAP messages by using the JavaMail API, it might be worth exploring a sample SOAP header that uses SMTP to see how it differs from those based on HTTP. The follow-ing example describes a simple subscription interface for a news scanning system for the financial press. When new messages are received, they are processed with a text analysis application to determine whether they contain anything of interest for particular compa-nies, and the items are then redirected to the appropriate analyst. The interface between the client and server for a specific new service, in this case, is very simple.

```
<?xml version="1.0"?>
<definitions name="NewsWire"
          targetNamespace="http://news.cassowary.net/newswire.wsdl"
          xmlns:tns="http://news.cassowary.net/newswire.wsdl"
          xmlns:xsd1="http://news.cassowary.net/newswire.xsd"
          xmlns:soap="http://schemas.xmlsoap.org/wsdl/soap/"
          xmlns="http://schemas.xmlsoap.org/wsdl/">

    <message name="MessageSubscribe">
        <part name="body" element="xsd1:MessageSubscribe"/>
        <part name="msgSubHeader" element="xsd1:SubHeader"/>
    </message>

    <portType name="NewsWirePortType">
        <operation name="MessageSubscribe">
           <input message="tns:MessageSubscribe"/>
        </operation>
    </portType>

    <binding name="NewsWireSoap" type="tns:NewsWirePortType">
        <soap:binding style="document"
transport="http://news.cassowary.net/smtp"/>
        <operation name="MessageSubscribe">
           <input message="tns:MessageSubscribe">
              <soap:body parts="body" use="literal"/>
              <soap:header message="tns:MessageSubscribe" part="msgSubHeader"
                  use="literal"/>
           </input>
        </operation>
    </binding>

    <service name="NewsWireService">
        <port name="NewsWirePort" binding="tns:NewsWireSoap">
           <soap:address location="mailto:stories@news.cassowary.net"/>
        </port>
    </service>

    <types>
        <schema targetNamespace="http://news.cassowary.net/newswire.xsd"
               xmlns="http://www.w3.org/2000/10/XMLSchema">
           <element name="MessageSubscribe">
               <complexType>
```

```
        <all>
            <element name="serviceName" type="string"/>
        </all>
        </complexType>
        </element>
    </schema>
    </types>
</definitions>
```

The real differences here are in the service definition, where the SOAP address location is given as the URL mailto:stories@news.cassowary.net, rather than an HTTP URL. In the XML schema defined by http://news.cassowary.net/newswire.xsd, one or more news wire services can be defined by the element serviceName, since stories on multiple news services could be listened for.

JavaMail

JavaMail is the standard Java API for developing applications that make use of SMTP, IMAP, and POP mail protocols. Its base classes are used by application developers who need to include some mail functionality in their system, such as e-mailing status and error messages around a distributed system. It can also be used to build new types of e-mail clients, such as those that operate through Web browsers, or through paging systems and other mobile devices.

You could always implement your own classes and methods to transfer mail using the MTA and MUA mail exchange protocols discussed previously. However, the main advantage of using JavaMail is that components already developed to undertake standard e-mail functions can be reused. This reduces development time for operations common to all e-mail platforms, especially when catering for exceptions. JavaMail builds on other widely used APIs, such as the Java Activation Framework (JAF), which provides basic data types and supports complex and simple mail types, formats, transports, and operations through subclassing.

JavaMail architecture has two main components: the abstract layer, which specifies all the abstract classes that support all the different types of messages and messaging; and the implementation layer, which instantiates the abstract classes to support existing e-mail messaging services. This architecture allows new types of messaging to be supported in the future, but still using the same basic toolkit and API.

Applications that utilize JavaMail operate by creating a bean that invokes methods in the e-mail implementation layer, which in turn creates subclasses of the abstract methods defined in the abstract layer. The implementation layer then provides the interface to communicate with MTAs or MUAs as required. Executing a "send" mail command consists of the following steps:

1. A mail message is constructed with the header and body containing the required data, as just described.

2. An authentication and global user properties object, known as a Session object, is created to access the corresponding mailbox.

3. The message is then sent by invoking the Transport.send() method.

Retrieving a message follows a similar path, since a Session object is also required before a message can be retrieved from the correct mailbox. Listening for messages employs standard Java event-based programming using the MailEvent class. JavaMail can be used at both ends of an application: sending and submitting messages on one client, and receiving and distributing messages to another client.

The main base interface in JavaMail is the Part, which is implemented by the Message class, Mimepart interface, and Bodypart class. In the case of multipart messages, Bodypart will be contained within a Multipart container class. The MimeMessage and MimeBodyPart classes implement the Mimepart interface. The MimeMessage class also extends the basic Message class, and the MimeBodyPart class also extends the Bodypart and MimeMultipart container classes. Sets of messages are represented by Store objects, just like a normal hierarchical mailbox. MUAs can then perform operations on a Store class implementation.

The Message class contains all of the abstract properties associated with an e-mail message, including addresses and content types. Many of the methods implemented in the Message class are defined in Part, including all of the details required for message routing. The user preferences for sending messages are contained within the Session object created for each user.

Single Part Messages

Before I examine how you can use SMTP directly as a transport for SOAP, let's see how a simple JavaMail application could be used to send an ordinary message. The Send-Invoice.java class, shown in the following code sample, contains a message subject and body sent from a salesperson to the line printer's inbox. A cron job could then be scheduled to print and the file all received invoices once each day using a batch process. The sample code looks like this.

```java
import javax.mail.*;

public class SendInvoice
{
    public static void main(String[] args)
    {
```

```java
    String invoice = "Invoice: 576665\nQuantity: 10\nPrice: 45.66";
    Properties p = new Properties();
    p.put("mail.smtp.host", "sales.cassowary.net");
    Session s = Session.getDefaultInstance(p, null);
    try
    {
        Message m = new MimeMessage(s);
        m.setSubject("Invoice: 576665");
        m.setContent(invoice, "text/plain");
        InternetAddress from = new
            InternetAddress("jenny@sales.cassowary.net");
        InternetAddress[] to =
        {
            new InternetAddress(args["lp@print.cassowary.net"])
};
        m.setFrom(from);
        m.setRecipients(Message.RecipientType.TO, to);
        Transport.send(m);
    }
    catch (Exception e)
    {
        e.printStackTrace();
    }
  }
}
```

Let's examine each step in turn. First, I create the message contents by inserting them into a string (called invoice), where individual lines are separated by newline delimiters \n. Here, I've used colon-delimited fields on each line to specify the values for each variable; the invoice number is 576665, the quantity of items is 10, the price is $45.66, and so on. There is no restriction about the content used here, so it could easily translate into XML.

```java
String invoice = "<?xml version=\"1.0\" encoding=\"UTF-8\"?>\n"+
    "<invoice>576665</invoice>\n"+
    "<quantity>10</quantity>\n"+
    "<price>45.66</price>";
```

Next, a Properties object is created, into which the SMTP delivery host's name is entered. A Session object is also created, along with a Message of type MimeMessage. The members of MimeMessage contain most of the message meta-data, including InternetAddress objects for the sender and receiver, the subject line, and the text encoding type. Once all of the meta-data has been set, then the message can be sent by invoking the `Transport.send()` method. Any exceptions can be caught and handled within this code block.

Multipart Messages

In the previous example, I have shown how a message can be sent in real time using JavaMail. In a distributed system where connectivity is transient, messages may well be queued for delivery in batch mode. So, a sender may send a single message with a large number of individual messages attached at the end of each day. The following example shows how to construct a MIME multipart message, where each message contains a separate XML invoice:

```java
import javax.mail.*;

public class SendMultipleInvoices
{
    public static void main(String[] args)
    {
        String invoice1 = "<?xml version=\"1.0\" encoding=\"UTF-8\"?>\n"+
            "<invoice>576665</invoice>\n"+
            "<quantity>10</quantity>\n"+
            "<price>45.66</price>";
        String invoice2= "<?xml version=\"1.0\" encoding=\"UTF-8\"?>\n"+
            "<invoice>576666</invoice>\n"+
            "<quantity>45</quantity>\n"+
            "<price>28.99</price>";
        Properties p = new Properties();
        p.put("mail.smtp.host", "sales.cassowary.net");
        Session s = Session.getDefaultInstance(p, null);
        try
        {
            Message m = new MimeMessage(s);
            m.setSubject("Invoices: 27_07_2003");
            MimeBodyPart m1 = new MimeBodyPart();
            m1.setContent(invoice1, "text/plain");
            MimeBodyPart m2 = new MimeBodyPart();
            m2.setContent(invoice2, "text/plain");
            Multipart multi = new MimeMultipart();
            multi.addBodyPart(m1);
            multi.addBodyPart(m2);
            msg.setContent(multi);
            InternetAddress from = new
```

```
                InternetAddress("jenny@sales.cassowary.net");
            InternetAddress[] to =
            {
                new InternetAddress(args["lp@print.cassowary.net"])
        };
            m.setFrom(from);
            m.setRecipients(Message.RecipientType.TO, to);
            Transport.send(m);
        }
        catch (Exception e)
        {
            e.printStackTrace();
        }
    }
}
```

In this example, two `MimeBodyPart` objects are created and attached to a single
`Multipart` object, which is then used as the message contents, rather than a single part,
as in the first example. Again, XML-formatted data, or any type of text data, can be used.

SOAP Messages

So far, I've examined how to create and send single messages containing plain text and
XML, and how to create and send multipart XML messages. Putting all of these elements
together, I can now move forward to create a sample SOAP application that performs the
same function as I've just shown: an invoice created by the sales department to be printed
by a central printing facility. In this case, however, the message just contains a reference
number that the print facility selects from a customer database, which instructs it to print
all pending invoices. This saves message traffic, since the printer application can generate
this data on the fly. It also prevents the proliferation of message data in multiple places.

```
import java.util.Date;
import javax.mail.*;

public class SOAPInvoices
{
    public static void main(String[] args)
    {
        String sender="julian@sales.cassowary.net";
        String recipient="lp@print.cassowary.net";
        String subject="Print Outstanding Invoices";
        try
        {
```

```
        MimeMessage m = new MimeMessage();
        m.setFrom(new InternetAddress(sender));
        m.setRecipients(Message.RecipientType.TO,new
            InternetAddress(recipient));
        m.setSubject(subject);
        m.setSentDate(new Date());
        m.addHeaderLine("SOAPAction: \"http://lp.cassowary.net/\"");
        m.addHeaderLine("Content-Type: text/xml; charset=utf-8");
        m.setText(
        "<?xml version=\"1.0\" encoding=\"UTF-8\"?>\n" +
        "<SOAP-ENV:Envelope SOAP-ENV:encodingStyle"+
         "=\"http://schemas.xmlsoap.org/soap/encoding\" " +
        "xmlns:SOAP-ENV=\"http://schemas.xmlsoap.org/soap/envelope/\" " +
        "xmlns:xsd=\"http://www.w3.org/2001/XMLSchema\" " +
        "xmlns:xsi=\"http://www.w3.org/2001/XMLSchema-instance\" " +
        "xmlns:SOAP-ENC=\"http://schemas.xmlsoap.org/soap/encoding/\">\n" +
        "  <SOAP-ENV:Body>\n" +
        "    <ns1:lp xmlns:ns1=\"http://lp.cassowary.net/\">\n" +
        "      <CustomerNumber xsi:type=\"xsd:string\">80956654"+
        "</CustomerNumber>\n    </ns1:lp>\n" +
        "  </SOAP-ENV:Body>\n" +
        "</SOAP-ENV:Envelope>\n";
        );
        Transport.send(m);
    }
    catch (Exception e)
    {
        System.out.println("Send Failed: ");
        e.printStackTrace(System.out);
    }
  }
}
```

The major difference between this application and the previous examples is the message content; instead of being plain text or plain XML, the message is actually a SOAP message, complete with headers, body, and envelope. The message is transmitted the same way as normal text. So, using SOAP over SMTP with JavaMail is just a simple extension of normal SMTP messaging.

Receiving SOAP Messages

I've shown how JavaMail can be used to send SOAP messages, but how would an application actually receive these messages and implement them? In the following example, I use IMAP to connect to the lp user's mailbox and check for any new invoice messages. Going one step further, I could then extract the messages, print them, and file them for future reference.

```java
import java.io.*;
import javax.mail.*;
import javax.mail.event.*;

public class CheckNewInvoices
{
    public static void main(String argv[])
    {
        String pr = imap";
        String ho = "mail.cassowary.net";
        String u = "lp";
        String p = "8gj5jjhg";
        String mb = "inbox";
        try
        {
            Session s = Session.getDefaultInstance(System.getProperties(), null);
            Store st = s.getStore(pr);
            st.connect(ho, u, p);
            Folder f = st.getFolder(mb);
            f.open(Folder.READ_WRITE);
            f.addMessageCountListener(new MessageCountAdapter()
            {
                public void messageCount(MessageCountEvent mce)
                {
                    Message[] ms = mce.getMessages();
                    System.out.println("New Invoices: " + ms.length);
                }
            }
        });
        catch (Exception e)
        {
            e.printStackTrace();
        }
    }
}
```

This example only prints the SOAP Message, which is of little practical use. More advanced code using DOM/SAX parsers to extract the individual elements for processing would be required to implement business logic.

Project

In this project, you will take the GoldBroker application described in previous chapters and convert the transport from HTTP to SMTP. What issues arise in doing this conversion? Is it "plug and play" (i.e., no code modification required)? Does the move from a synchronous protocol to an asynchronous protocol require different exception handling?

Summary

In this chapter, I have described how to make Web services more flexible by using alternative transports. The e-mail protocol SMTP is very suitable to building a more reliable asynchronous messaging for Web services transport because it has built-in failure modes. However, many other alternatives deserve consideration. For example, ebXML. org proposed a reliable messaging protocol that could work with SOAP. Given the (purported) strength of ebXML in Europe and the current talk about somehow merging the ebXML standards with Web services, it is ebXML's reliable messaging over HTTP that could add the most value to the WS protocols. It may also be possible to use other application layer protocols like FTP.

CHAPTER 8

■■■

Security

Security is a major nonfunctional requirement for enterprise systems, alongside availability, maintainability, manageability, and scalability. Given that Web services are seen as the great enablers of B2B e-commerce and external application integration for the enterprise, security takes on an even greater significance. Most existing enterprise applications operate within very tightly controlled security domains. Centralized application and system architectures deployed within dedicated data centers, operated at great expense, emphasize the strong business requirement for effective security. Running applications within a single security domain endows a high level of trust in the integrity and authenticity of operations undertaken by such applications. However, because Web services allow the remote execution of RPC-style services across firewalls and across domains, a high level of security (and implicitly, a high level of trust) is clearly required. This chapter outlines the security requirements of Web services applications and covers the major specifications under development in this area.[1]

Security Requirements

Enterprise application security involves controlling risk arising from inadvertent or deliberate actions that result in a compromised system. Possible outcomes of this state include data interception by unauthorized third parties, repudiation of permanently recorded data, partial data corruption, complete data loss, and fraudulent use of data. Techniques utilized to achieve these ends include impersonation, spoofing, cryptanalysis, sniffing, and various denial-of-service attacks. If the loss of data integrity is accidental, the potential causes are numerous; accidents, naivete, downright stupidity, and insufficiently rigorous security standards and policies can severely affect the reliability of any enterprise system. Physical attacks on systems may result in financial loss, but for most firms, loss of data can lead to lawsuits, loss of business, and bankruptcy. For systems that operate in batch mode at the back end, the impact may be less time-sensitive than with real-time front-end systems.

---

1. For more details on individual specifications, see *Web Services Security* by Mark O'Neill et al. (New York: McGraw-Hill/Osborne, 2003).

Take batch processing of financial statements as an example. If the database is wiped because of a virus and must be reloaded from backups, this may delay printing by a couple of hours. The end result for customers is unchanged; they still receive their statements in the mail. However, if an electronic payments system is unavailable because an intruder has managed to delete configuration files or prevent the system from returning to operation momentarily, then financial losses will begin to mount very rapidly until service is restored. These differences are reflected in the synchronous-vs.-asynchronous messaging types used by SOAP, and are one reason for the interest in developing reliable, resilient protocols for invoking services and exchanging data.

Providing security for Web services reflects many of the same issues experienced in real-time enterprise systems, so it follows that many of the solutions can be translated and implemented in the Web services world. Many applicable techniques are available for performing authentication, authorization, and related operations to protect data and systems from attacks. In this section, I examine some of the key requirements of mission-critical systems and explore how they are relevant to Web services. In the subsequent section, I look at the current set of standards and how they can be utilized in the enterprise.

Integrity

At one level, data integrity is concerned with issues like ensuring that corruption of physical memory can be easily detected and rectified, or that transmitted data matches an accompanying checksum. So Error Correcting Coding (ECC) and Cyclic Redundancy Checking (CRC) are fundamental coding and integrity checking mechanisms of most computer systems. But the checksum computed from one bit of (say) an octet is not unique, in the sense that it exclusively verifies the integrity of that byte. If a message whose integrity must be verified consists of many or a variable number of bytes, and where its integrity must be determined on an unconditional basis, then one-way hash functions, like message digests (described later), can be used. Other integrity issues arise from multiple copies of the same logical data item being stored physically in multiple places. In this case, message digests and similar techniques can be used to ensure that replicas agree with the original/authentic data in question. Message digests can also detect and reconcile discrepancies between data entered multiple times by different users.

In Web services, data integrity of SOAP messages is critical, as the default HTTP transport layer does not provide any data secrecy. So, messages could potentially be intercepted by a third party and modified en route between a client and server. For example, a stockbroking system may collect data on entry and exit fees for 500 mutual funds to generate dynamic recommendations for purchase or sale by its clients. By using SOAP to retrieve these prices in real time, clients can receive an aggregated overview of market performance. However, if a "man in the middle" attack occurs, and the prices of the funds were modified maliciously (e.g., prices multiplied by a factor of 10), then the results would be unfortunate!

While SSL would certainly prevent this tampering at the transport layer, methods to ensure message integrity are still required. Message digests are the most common technique for achieving this. Thus, when an input string of any length is passed to the hash function, the result is a nearly unique digest; at the very least, the probability of a collision is very low. As the number of digest bits increases, this probability is even further reduced. Thus, while MD5 produces a 128-bit digest, like 5ef09da5727837f13a2975cfb6795776, Hans Dobbertin has recently shown that collisions can actually be generated in practice (i.e., different source files could have the same message digest computed from them). In contrast, the more recent SHA-1 algorithm produces a 160-bit digest, where collisions have yet to be experienced in practice.

Authenticity

When a SOAP message has been received, how can the recipient establish its authenticity? In other words, if a bank receives a message from a customer requesting a withdrawal, how can the bank be sure that the message has been sent from the actual customer and not an imposter? In synchronous systems, a number of authentication techniques (reviewed in the next section) may be used. But embedding these in a message that may be archived and passed to multiple users isn't very secure. What we really need is a method to ensure that a message is authentic, in much the same way as physically signing a contract or payment authorization.

This is the approach taken by digital signature technology, which is based on public key cryptography and message digests, and associated software and systems usually labeled as Public Key Infrastructure (PKI). Digital signing can be implemented by encrypting the message digest of a file. PKI is based on the idea that a central certification authority (CA) has the means to establish the identity of organizations and individuals, and that CAs issue certificates verifying that an organization is who it says it is. For example, the managing director of a retailing company would submit credentials to a CA (like VeriSign) for authentication. Once the details have been scrutinized, the CA issues an electronic certificate to the retailer. Client browsers can use certificates issued by a certifying authority to tell consumers that a site is what it claims to be. Without this independent scrutiny of certification, it would be difficult if not impossible to establish trust on the Internet, since spoofing attacks are now commonplace.

The two concepts of certification and encryption can be combined to ensure that data integrity is preserved, and that trust can be established, by the use of public key cryptography. Traditional symmetric key encryption operates by using a single key's algorithm to encrypt data, and then using the same key to decrypt the data. Although symmetric key algorithms are conceptually simple to use and develop, they suffer from a fatal flaw: You must surrender a copy of the key to any external to whom you send encrypted material. This means that the same key can be used to decrypt other documents sent by you, even to other parties, unless a one-time cipher pad is used. This is impractical for individuals, since a database of all keys used must be maintained and secured against interception.

Asymmetric encryption operates on the principle that two keys are required to secure data: a public key, which can be sent to all individuals and organizations who want to send encrypted material to you, and a private key, which is never publicly released, but which can be used to unlock data that has been signed with your public key. So, to encrypt data to send to a specific recipient, you must have a copy of the recipient's public key. If you are not sure whether the public key is genuine, you can compute a small footprint (like a checksum) that can be compared to a footprint computed from the recipient's private key, often over a telephone. Using public keys to sign data ensures that documents intended to be decrypted by you alone can be safely unencrypted without comprising your entire data protection scheme.

Although it is possible that someone could guess or deduce your private key through brute force, in practical terms this is likely to take thousands of computer years of CPU power. The current key length standard is 128 bits, although military-grade technology typically uses 168 bits. Until recently, such high-level encryption technology was only available within North America. However, the efforts of Phil Zimmerman's Pretty Good Privacy (PGP) product have ensured that international users can make use of this technology. PGP avoids the very CPU-intensive encryption of a long message with PKI by 1) encrypting the message with a simpler key and 2) encrypting this simple key with the original PKI key.

CAs use PKI technology to ensure that an organization's public key is valid and matches the organization to which it was originally assigned. Since an organization's private key will decrypt only data encrypted with its public key, a bona fide organization would have its private key available; a spoofer would not have the private key, and would be unable to access encrypted data intended for the genuine organization. This is the cornerstone of SSL authenticity: only a bona fide organization, whose private key could decrypt the certified public key, would be able to read a consumer's credit card transmitted across the Internet. The client browser also gives a symmetric key to the server, which is used once for a single session, which if delayed will time out.

Digital signatures utilize PKI by allowing messages to be digitally signed in such a way that it is difficult for others to forge that signature. Users can sign messages in a unique way by using their private keys. Signing also prevents repudiation of data, since the message contents cannot be modified once the signature has been applied. To achieve this, a message digest is computed from the source message, then the digest is encrypted using the signer's private key; the encrypted message digest is the digital signature, which is then attached to the message. This is the technique used by PGP to avoid another lengthy encryption of the entire message with the digital signature (sender's private key) by using the sender's private key to encrypt only the message digest.

The receiver can verify a message's authenticity by decrypting the digital signature into its original message digest by using the sender's public key. The message digest is then computed from the received message. If it matches the digest decrypted from the signature, it can be considered authentic.

Obviously, risks are involved in determining authenticity if the CA colludes with other third parties to undermine the process. This requires companies using digital signing technology to trust CAs. Trust is discussed further on.

Authentication

Authentication provides that an asserted identity is genuine. Tokens for identification include arbitrary identifiers like user names, and those based on unique or pseudo-unique biometric characteristics, such as fingerprints, iris patterns, and DNA. Since biometric characteristics cannot be easily forged, they are often considered strong identification. Because a user could be coerced into supplying DNA, viewing an iris scanner, or pressing a thumbprint scanner, identity must be proven, most often by revealing a secret. In most authentication systems, this is a password known only to the user. The password is not stored directly by the authenticating service; instead, a message digest is computed from the password and stored in the authentication database. Thus, when a user presents a password, its message digest is computed and compared to the digest in the database. A match indicates authentication. Of course, a malicious login program could just store the password plaintext received at the socket level—which is a good reason to store the message digest of the original login program somewhere safe and compare it to the message digest of the executing program!

Passwords are problematic because, although known only to the user, many users create passwords that can be found in a dictionary, and are therefore susceptible to a brute force password-guessing programs that simply compute the message digests from all dictionary entries and attempt to use these to compare with the entries stored in the authentication database (if it is compromised). Otherwise, dictionary words—or other words strongly associated with a specific user, such as their name, car type, birth month, pet's name, etc.—can be passed directly to a login program. Even a randomly chosen password is not safe; the length of a password is the most significant determinant of its "guessability," assuming a random distribution of password probabilities. An ATM PIN with four numeric digits has 10,000 possible combinations, while the Windows registry setting `MinPwdLen` can be used to ensure a minimum of eight-character alphanumeric passwords, giving around 6,095,689,385,410,816 possible combinations.

User name and password authentication is usually referred to as simple authentication. More-sophisticated techniques are available, and may be more relevant to SOAP messaging (although some simple user name and password SOAP extensions have been proposed).[2] These include the digital signature technique discussed previously, and certificate-based methods for distributing public keys and their meta-data in a standard, centralized fashion. For example, certifications typically contain an individual's name, public key, serial numbers, etc. all signed by a CA for verification.

Simple authentication can also be enhanced significantly by the use of more than two factors; for example, a one-time pad can be used to supplement fixed user name and password access. Once a user has been primarily authenticated by two factors, then an additional challenge is presented by the server, which is only ever used once. The client must carry a hardware device that prints out the appropriate response in a predefined sequence. The device cannot be used if the primary password is unknown, nor does the password alone suffice without the one-time pad.

A number of systems are available to manage certificates and assist in the production of technology that utilizes certificates based on technologies like SSL, X.509 certificates, X.509 PKI, the Public Key Cryptography Standard (PKCS) #11, and the Federal Information Processing Standards Publications (FIPS PUBS) standard 140-1. These systems should be able to support core methods in symmetric and asymmetric key encryption, and implementation of certificate-based authentication. In addition, messages and other kinds of data should be digitally signable by using these toolkits, making them especially suited for deployment within e-commerce systems using SSL technology, whether between clients and browsers, or for protecting all sensitive data transmitted within a network. Management of certificates is particularly important for deleting certificates that have expired or are no longer required. This is an important activity, since many certificates will have been received or generated by an organization during its lifetime. However, only a small subset will be active at any one time. In addition, data previously encrypted and stored (in a database table, for example) will require a private key to unlock its contents.

Authorization

Authorization is concerned with both defining and enforcing access controls to resources based on authenticated identity or group membership. A simple example of authorization are the access permissions that can be set on files. File owners can be authorized to read, write, and execute files, and these permissions can be extended to group members or other users as a whole. This very gross-scale scheme has been refined in recent years to include more fine-grained access controls on a per-user basis, where the user is not the file owner. These Access Control Lists (ACLs) must be maintained for deciding about access and for enforcing those decisions. These complementary roles in enforcing security policies are known as Policy Decision Points (PDPs) and Policy Enforcement Points (PEPs), respectively. As I'll show soon, some approaches to Web services security provide explicit mechanisms for defining and enforcing access controls to individual services

---

2. See http://www.whitemesa.com/soapauth.html for one proposal by Robert Cunnings and Richard Salz.

based on a PDP and PEP architecture. In production environments, the PDP and PEP are typically located on physically different systems to ensure that decisions and enforcement procedures are kept quite separate, just as the courts (legal decision) and police (law enforcement) have very different roles that do not overlap.

Role-Based Access Control (RBAC) is a complementary authorization approach based on the idea that individual roles (rather than users or groups) should have authority to execute a group of operations defined in a profile. This makes it easier to disassociate specific users from roles when they leave an organization or are promoted. In terms of services, specific roles are required to undertake various tasks in an organization, and access rights can be easily associated with these. For example, a service that accepts electronic payments should not have the right to cancel a payment. Payment cancellations must be handled by a different supervisory service that does not accept payments in its own right. By correctly mapping distinct functions onto organizational structures, very fine-grained RBAC schemes can be devised.

While authorizations should be enforced as a matter of course, there may well be occasions when this enforcement must be overridden, usually in emergencies. For example, if a customer traveling in a foreign country loses a credit card, the issuing bank will generally extend them a small line of credit, even without confirming their identity by means of a card (since it has been lost). This debit is then eventually applied to the customer's account when the card has been reissued and the customer's identity confirmed. If the bank strictly followed security procedures, then the PDP should not have extended the credit, but this is a good example of where flexibility is required.

Secrecy

In my discussion of authenticity, I covered the concept of PKI and how it is useful in identification and certification. PKI is one application of asymmetric cryptography concerned with sharing secrets; simpler and perhaps more common schemes, based on symmetric cryptography, are widely used to ensure data confidentiality. Cryptographers generally are concerned either with developing new techniques to ensure the secrecy of data (cryptology) or with trying to "crack" those techniques (cryptanalysis).

When "plaintext" data is encoded using an algorithm to ensure that its real contents remain confidential, a "ciphertext" is generated. Central to most algorithms is a very large number, known as the key, which must be known to retrieve the plaintext from the ciphertext. In symmetric schemes, the key is used to encrypt and decrypt the data. In asymmetric schemes, multiple keys are involved in the process; each user has a private key, known to only that user, and a public key, which is widely published. Thus, when User A wants to encipher a plaintext for User B, User A obtains User B's public key and uses this to encrypt the plaintext. Now, only User B can decrypt the ciphertext using User B's private key.

The various algorithms used in cryptography are covered in great detail elsewhere[3]—and although secrecy is an important aspect of security, issues of identification and access control are of equal importance for Web services.

Trust

In e-commerce systems, trust is king: if customers cannot trust their retailers, and if retailers cannot trust their wholesalers, and if wholesalers cannot trust their manufacturers, and if manufacturers can't trust the government, then the whole cycle of economic activity over the Internet would be flawed. The concept of trust here does not cover attitudes of consumers toward the quality of their retailer's products or staff; rather, trust simply means being able to determine whether a participant in commercial transactions is who it says. Consumers need to ensure that the site they are transmitting their details to is a genuine retailer and not an imposter. Retailers need to ensure that their purchasing data is being transmitted to the appropriate wholesaler and is not being intercepted by a competitor. Wholesalers need to know that their manufacturing partners are genuine and not part of an elaborate scheme cooked up by a cracking group. Manufacturers need to be assured that, when dealing electronically with the government, their data is secure and is being received by the appropriate department. When customers walk into a physical department store, they know who they are dealing with; consumers should experience the same sense of trust when dealing electronically with organizations over the Internet.

Given that Web services involve a greater level of automation than other Internet applications, establishing trust is crucial. While technology solutions such as UDDI may well enable the automated screening and potential selection of business partners based on financial considerations, establishing trust could be quite challenging in this scenario. A CA may be able vouch for the identity of a specific firm, but perhaps in another country, many risk-management issues arise from allowing computer applications to run a business!

Also, Web services over the Internet are a far cry from the typical ISDN or dedicated lines used today by companies to transact with banks and other financial institutions. For example, I don't think there has been any serious suggestion of replacing dedicated Electronic Funds Transfer at Point Of Sale (EFTPOS) lines with a Web service for authenticating cardholders and authorizing transactions, yet this would be technically easy to achieve using the security standards for Web services described in this chapter.

A key concept for trust is the notion of a "trust domain" or a "security domain." These can be defined as the set of systems and services encapsulated within an entity that can authenticate principals and authorize their activities. These may be systems within an

---

3. An excellent reference is *Fundamentals of Computer Security* by Josef Pieprzyk, Thomas Hardjono, and Jennifer Seberry (Berlin: New York: Springer-Verlag, 2003).

intranet and all of their users. Alternatively, users on an extranet may be authenticated within the local domain, in which case they can also belong to a trust domain. The real problem is that all possible businesses in the world cannot hold authentication tokens for all their possible partners; this would result in a combinatorial explosion of authentication tokens. In addition, all principals acting on behalf of a firm would have to have their own authentication tokens stored remotely in order for this scheme to operate.

It seems more sensible and efficient for trust domains to be responsible for their own authentication, and to then when dealing with business partners, make assertions about principals who are thus authenticated. This reduces much of the administrative burden on trusted partner domains to perform authentication and maintain sets of credentials.

The concept of a trust domain is important, since it has the following two properties:

- Principals make no omissions.

- Principals do not participate in collusions.

In terms of Web services, an authenticated, trusted service can guarantee that it will perform a specific function as requested—no more and no less. Thus, when an assertion of trust is made between domains, we are really saying that we expect the service to perform just as if it were part of the trusted domain, and that it won't fail or launch a Trojan horse *just because* it's trusted by our domain.

Standards

Web services security has two major standards: WS-Security and SAML. The WS-Security standard (developed by Microsoft, VeriSign, and IBM) is a SOAP extension that describes how Web services can or should make use of authentication, encryption for data secrecy, and data integrity in a standard way. WS-Security is concerned with the mechanics of how to format security within SOAP headers and/or messages. WS-Security provides methods to support data confidentiality and digital signing of data. At a much higher level, the tokens used to actually make assertions about security are covered by SAML, while WS-Security provides a mechanism for actually transmitting SAML tokens.

Secure Web services may make use of a number of ancillary standards. XML Encryption, for example, provides a set of techniques to encrypt parts of XML documents, and also to express encrypted data as an XML document. While transport-layer security (such as HTTPS) provides encryption and data confidentiality between client and server, XML Encryption provides confidentiality even when messages and data are not in transit. This makes XML Encryption appropriate for archiving sensitive data, such as client records, particularly where privacy is an issue. For instance, credit reference agencies maintain databases of consumer credit activity. These records should not be held in plaintext form and should only be decipherable by a user with the appropriate authorization. HTTPS will not provide this type of security.

Previously, I've discussed the importance of digital signatures to nonrepudiation. XML Signature is a standard for applying signatures to XML and also for expressing signatures in XML. It allows messages and individual headers to be signed, making it useful for the electronic exchange of contract data. This level of granularity ensures that headers containing static data are not changed during the routing process, even if some other headers are modified.

Once PKI becomes distributed around the Internet, key management becomes more difficult. Indeed, PKI has a reputation of being difficult to install, maintain, and manage, even though it has many potential uses. The XML Key Management Specification (XKMS) enables services to be registered, validated, and located using XML messaging. XKMS operations can even be implemented as Web services!

The following sections focus on WS-Security and SAML as the most widely endorsed standards for enhancing and implementing Web services security.

WS-Security

The main purpose of WS-Security is to ensure the security of SOAP messages. While XML digital signatures and XML Encryption are certainly an important part of overall SOAP security, WS-Security is SOAP-specific. In fact, WS-Security is the first of many standards in the WS-Security framework that have been proposed as an overall framework for ensuring security for Web services. WS-Security was also accepted as OASIS standard in April 2004. Following is a summary of the WS-Security protocols' main features:

- *WS-Policy*: Policy-based framework for specifying security requirements of Web services, including privacy, data confidentiality, dynamic bindings and signatures

- *WS-Trust*: Specifies the mechanisms for establishing trust relationships

- *WS-Privacy*: Specifies mechanisms for ensuring that the privacy policies, particularly regarding user data, are respected by invoked Web services

- *WS-SecureConversation*: Builds a secure transport layer that does not rely on HTTPS, since the Web services transport layer is entirely pluggable

- *WS-Federation*: Permits the exchange of security tokens in a federated manner, allowing different security services (such as authentication) to interoperate seamlessly

- *WS-Authorization*: Specifies how access controls can be utilized to build on role-based and access control list authorization models

Specifications for WS-Policy, WS-Trust, WS-SecureConversation, and WS-Federation are now available. Only WS-Authorization and WS-Privacy are yet to be released. Figure 8-1 shows the logical layering of these protocols.

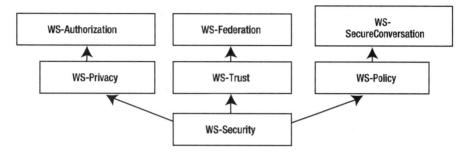

Figure 8-1. *Basic security layers provided by complementary standards*

Throughout the rest of this section on standards, I'll provide an overview of WS-Security and its application to ensuring the security of Web services, alongside complementary technologies.

The Specification

WS-Security specifies a number of security tokens that are simply XML elements that can be attached to a normal SOAP message. A number of tokens are available to support the basic required elements of security discussed earlier in this chapter, including user name and password authentication, certificates, digital signatures, and encryption. The security tokens for these elements are UsernameToken and X509v3Certificate, and <ds:Signature> and <n4:encryptedData>, respectively. Before I examine these tokens in detail, I'll first cover the architectural issues involved in designing applications using WS-Security.

WS-Security covers authentication, data authenticity, and encryption in a wide-ranging framework that is expandable, in the sense that WS-Security does not specify the sorts of tokens that must be exchanged. This provides the flexibility required for authentication performed in different contexts; proof of identity may be either individual or group-based (i.e., assertion of individual identity or, potentially, group membership). It builds on top of existing SOAP and security infrastructure, so we're talking about additional elements primarily within the header for SOAP, and about integrating with existing security systems. For example, Kerberos is a commonly used network authentication system that provides authentication and single sign-on for "Kerberized" applications. It consists of a certificate-based system for granting access to specific systems for predefined periods of a set amount of time, during certain hours, or both. A ticket is issued by a dedicated server that must then be renewed if a session is to be maintained. A random session key ensures backward and forward confidentiality. The main problem with Kerberos is that not many applications are Kerberized, even though its authentication model is quite strong; it is supported for authentication within security domains, and by external networks known as realms. Because it is widely used, WS-Security provides the ability to encode binary Kerberos tickets and use them in conjunction with text X.509 certificates, whether generated locally or issued by a CA.

To demonstrate how this works, I'll examine this sample "secured" SOAP message.

```
<?xml version="1.0" encoding="utf-8"?>
  <S:Envelope xmlns:S="http://www.w3.org/2001/12/soap-envelope"
    xmlns:ds="http://www.w3.org/2000/09/xmldsig#">
  <S:Header>

...

  </wsse:Security>
          xmlns:wsse="http://schemas.xmlsoap.org/ws/2002/04/secext">
       wsse:UsernameToken Id="http://namespaces.xmethods.com/xspace/">
          <wsse:Username>JaneDoe</wsse:Username>
    <wsse:Password>859gbgdf</wsse:Password>
        </wsse:UsernameToken>
       <ds:Signature>
          <ds:SignedInfo>
            <ds:CanonicalizationMethod
                Algorithm=
                     "http://www.w3.org/2001/10/xml-exc-c14n#"/>
            <ds:SignatureMethod
                   Algorithm=
                   "http://www.w3.org/2000/09/xmldsig#hmac-sha1"/>
            <ds:Reference URI="#cassowary-id-8FE432-7DAB-8EDA-8765-
                8AB5434321AC">
              <ds:DigestMethod
                     Algorithm=
                     "http://www.w3.org/2000/09/xmldsig#sha1"/>
              <ds:DigestValue>c8f+dcjgfj49945grggrdI=</ds:DigestValue>
            </ds:Reference>
          </ds:SignedInfo>
          <ds:SignatureValue>JSB8fndjJHlkdkjH8d8743ddf3</ds:SignatureValue>
          <ds:KeyInfo>
              <wsse:SecurityTokenReference>
                <wsse:Reference URI="#cassowary-id-8FE432-7DAB-8EDA-8765-
                   8AB5434321AC"/>
              </wsse:SecurityTokenReference>
          </ds:KeyInfo>
```

```
        </ds:Signature>
      </wsse:Security>
    </S:Header>
    <S:Body Id="#cassowary-id-8FE432-7DAB-8EDA-8765-8AB5434321AC">
...
    </S:Body>
</S:Envelope>
```

The most interesting part of the preceding message, in terms of security, is that the WS-Security lines for authentication take up only a few lines in the header; the other security-related material provides a digital signature for nonrepudiation! The security-specific elements include `<wsse:Password>` for the password and `<wsse:Username>` for the user name. In the sections that follow, I examine each of these elements and the ancillary digital signature and encryption issues in more detail.

Two-Factor Authentication

A sample UsernameToken is shown next, with the `<wsse:Username>` of "root" and the corresponding `<wsse:Password>` of "23hfd6re". As previously mentioned, possession of both the user name and password usually indicates that the user has been authenticated.

```
<soap:Header>
  <wsse:Security xmlns:wsse="http://schemas.xmlsoap.org/ws/2002/07/secext">
    <wsse:UsernameToken xmlns:wsu="http://schemas.xmlsoap.org/ws/2002/07/utility"
        Id="http://namespaces.xmethods.com/xspace/">
      <wsse:Username>root</wsse:Username>
      <wsse:Password>23hfd6re</wsse:Password>
    </wsse:UsernameToken>
  </wsse:Security>
</soap:Header>
```

WS-Security is not restricted to simple user name and password authentication; other security tokens, such as X.509 certificates, are also acceptable. Here is a sample X.509 v3 certificate:

```
<soap:Header>
  <wsse:Security xmlns:wsse="http://schemas.xmlsoap.org/ws/2002/07/secext">
    <wsse:BinarySecurityToken ValueType="wsse:X509v3"
        EncodingType="wsse:Base64Binary"
      xmlns:wsu="http://schemas.xmlsoap.org/ws/2002/07/utility"
      Id="cassowary-id-8FE432-7DAB-8EDA-8765-8AB5434321AC">
```

```
            JSU8f8fd09gj78sdnHGbdf….
        </wsse:BinarySecurityToken>
      </wsse:Security>
</soap:Header>
```

Here, you can see the certificate encoded using `Base64Binary`, having a unique identifier and a truncated version of the certificate data.

Digital Signatures

Digital signatures (`http://www.xml.com/pub/a/2001/08/08/xmldsig.html`) can be added
to a SOAP security header as shown in the following example:

```
<soap:Header>
  <wsse:Security xmlns:wsse="http://schemas.xmlsoap.org/ws/2002/07/secext">
    <ds:Signature xmlns:ds="http://www.w3.org/2000/09/xmldsig#">
      <ds:SignedInfo>
        <ds:CanonicalizationMethod Algorithm=
            "http://www.w3.org/2001/10/xml-exc-c14n#" />
        <ds:SignatureMethod Algorithm=
            "http://www.w3.org/2000/09/xmldsig#rsa-sha1"/>
        <ds:Reference URI="#cassowary-id-8FE432-7DAB-8EDA-8765-8AB5434321AC">
          <ds:Transforms>
            <ds:Transform Algorithm="http://www.w3.org/2001/10/xml-exc-c14n#" />
          </ds:Transforms>
          <ds:DigestMethod Algorithm="http://www.w3.org/2000/09/xmldsig#sha1"/>
<ds:DigestValue>c8f+dcjgfj49945grggrdI=</ds:DigestValue>
        </ds:Reference>
      </ds:SignedInfo>
<ds:SignatureValue>JSB8fndjJHlkdkjH8d8743ddf3</ds:SignatureValue>
      <ds:KeyInfo>
        <wsse:SecurityTokenReference>
          <wsse:Reference URI="#cassowary-id-8FE432-7DAB-8EDA-8765-8AB5434321AC"/>
        </wsse:SecurityTokenReference>
      </ds:KeyInfo>
    </ds:Signature>
  </wsse:Security>
</soap:Header>
```

In this example, the signature algorithm being used is RSA on SHA-1
(`http://www.w3.org/2000/09/xmldsig#rsa-sha1`), and the exclusive canonicalization

technique (http://www.w3.org/2001/10/xml-exc-c14n#) is employed. The message digest algorithm is also SHA-1 (http://www.w3.org/2000/09/xmldsig#sha1), and the computed digest is also displayed. The Reference URI for the signature is always linked back to the message.

Data Confidentiality

If data confidentiality for the message is required, then such encrypted data can be stored as part of an XML file by using the following method:

```
<?xml version='1.0' encoding='UTF-8'?>
<soap:Envelope
  <soap:Header>
    <wsse:Security>
      <n4:ReferenceList>
        <n4:DataReference URI='#cassowary-id'/>
      </n4:ReferenceList>
    </wsse:Security>
  </soap:Header>
  <soap:Body
    <n4:encryptedData' Id=cassowary-id'>
      <n4:encryptionMethod Algorithm=
          'http://www.w3.org/2001/04/xmlenc#tripledes-cbc'/>
      <ds:keyInfo>
        <ds:keyName>crypto</ds:keyName>
      </ds:keyInfo>
      <n4:cipherData>
      <n4:cipherValue>AfU8JKjn89b980fLL/GSJdvbf98erOg</n4:cipherValue>
</n4:cipherData>
</n4:encryptedData>
</soap:Body>
</soap:Envelope>
```

Here, we can see that the 3DES encryption is used (http://www.w3.org/2001/04/xmlenc#tripledes-cbc), with both the key name (keyName) and cipher details (cipherValue) embedded within the body rather than the header. This is because it is the message that is encrypted rather than encryption details being specified for digital signatures in the header. This technique is quite general and could be used in any enterprise application using Web services where message confidentiality is required.

SAML

WS-Security is a SOAP extension that describes how Web services should make use of authentication, encryption for data secrecy, and data integrity in a standard way. But WS-Security does not define which tokens are used to actually make assertions about security. These are provided by the Security Assertion Markup Language (SAML), although there is by no means universal acceptance of this scheme (SAML is very complete, however, and has been adopted by OASIS). The following section focuses on SAML and how it can be used to specify trust assertions about authentication and access control within, and most importantly between, trust domains.

SAML is based on the notion of assertions made about principals from a specific trust domain, which are claims that can then be taken as legitimate depending on the level of trust vested in the authority making the claim. If a CA is the eventual root in a chain of trust, and the end-user party trusts the CA, then the authority of the claim can be accepted.

The assertion of claims concerning authentication and authorization are significant for highly scalable Web services that have fine-grained access control. SAML promises to deliver single sign-on for accessing these resources, without having to be reauthenticated every time a service is invoked. This could significantly reduce technical overhead, but more importantly, it simplifies the business processes required to implement cross-domain applications. Also, potential business exists for the provision of authentication services across trust domains; Microsoft's Passport and the Liberty Alliance's offerings are the most prominent current implementations.

To assist in this goal, SAML also specifies a request/response protocol using XML for communicating assertions: `samlp:` indicates that this protocol is being used, while `saml:` indicates individual claims. SAML does not provide the underlying authentication service; Kerberos or some similar standard implementation will likely do this. While Kerberos can work across firewalls, an administrative headache is created if users from one trust domain must be authenticated individually within another domain. The problem is compounded if a number of business partners are involved in a virtual enterprise or similar joint undertaking. This proliferation of authentication can lead to the perverse situation in which foreign principals could be authenticated by a nonlocal domain and use that authentication to access services illegally—all without the local domain being involved! Evidently, it's better to allow trust domains to maintain their primary role in authentication, but to provide some mechanism for domains to exchange claims about authentication—particularly in the loosely coupled environment of Web services, where there are no guarantees about transport protocols or operating-system-specific security mechanisms.

Assertion Elements

The set of claims associated with a principal is called a *profile* in SAML terminology. The claims can be derived from different trust domains, with the underlying tokens being exchanged using SOAP and other Web services protocols. SAML supports three assertion types: Attribute, Authorization, and Authentication. These assertions encapsulate individual attributes, profiles, and policies. Assertions may have all of the following elements:

- `<Advice>` holds extra data relevant to the assertion.

- `<Assertion>` contains the data for specific claims.

- `<AssertionIDReference>` is associated with each claim.

- `<Audience>` specifies the intended end-users or viewers of the claims.

- `<AudienceRestrictionCondition>` restricts audience use.

Additional general conditions can also be applied to the claims.

Assertions must be created using a particular syntax derived from a base `AssertionType`, which has the following elements:

- `<AttributeStatement>` is simply a declaration associated with an attribute.

- `<AuthenticationStatement>` is a similar declaration associated with authentication.

- `<AuthorizationDecisionStatement>` is associated with access control issues.

- `<ds:signature>` serves the same role in SAML as for WS-Security.

- `<Statement>` relates to schemas for programs.

- `<SubjectStatement>` relates to schemas for principals.

The remaining elements—`<AssertionID>`, `<IssueInstant>`, `<Issuer>`, `<MajorVersion>`, and `<MinorVersion>`—are version-control elements relating to the time claims were made and versions of the assertion.

The final level of element specification is a set of complements to `<Assertion>` claims, which are collectively grouped as `<Statement>` elements. These include the `<NameIdentifier>` and `<SubjectConfirmation>`, which specify principal names and protocols for authentication, respectively.

Using Assertions

I'll now examine how each assertion type (Authorization, Authentication, and Attribute) is used in practice. Authorization assertions are used to determine whether access should be granted to a specific principal for a nominated resource. The authorization decision is handled by two different entities within the SAML architecture: the PDP for making decisions, and the PEP for enacting them. The PEP is capable of making three decisions: allowing access (Permit), denying access (Deny), or failing to determine whether access should be granted (Indeterminate). A decision is formed as an `<AuthorizationDecisionStatement>` comprising a URI of the resource about which the decision is concerned, the decision text, and any auxiliary details, such as the evidence used to reach the decision.

The PDP may be external, while the PEP must always be internal. If the PDP is not local, then a Policy Retrieval Point (PRP) must be accessed to retrieve policies as required. The sorts of decisions a PDP routinely makes include whether a principal is a member of a group or a firm, and whether the principal has a valid authentication assertion. Other tests are based on run-time factors, such as whether a client supports encrypted communication channels, or whether a granted right that is valid for a specific time or day. These factors are not independent, so compound conditions can be specified (e.g., principal must belong to a specific group and only access a resource between 10 and 12 p.m.).

The topic of security policy management is beyond the scope of this book, but the Internet Engineering Task Force/Distributed Management Task Force (IETF/DMTF) has a policy framework available at `http://www.ietf.org/html.charters/policy-charter.html` that discusses the role of a Policy Repository, and the separate role of enforcement versus decision. A number of available tools provide integrated management of policies for whole systems or networks to ensure consistent decisions and enforcement across the board. The framework describes the operational issues surrounding the PDP and PEP model. As discussed previously, this framework is important to the overall implementation of SAML.

Before an authorization decision can be made about a principal, the principal's credentials must be evaluated through the authentication process. The Credentials Collector passes the credentials to the Authentication Authority, which then evaluates them according to a policy. If the authentication is validated, an `<AuthenticationStatement>` is issued, and then Attribute and Authorization assertion evaluations can proceed. The authentication process is more sophisticated than many two-factor systems, since the validity of the decision can be specified for a certain time period before reauthentication is required. Authentication details are stored in the `<SubjectLocality>` element of the `<AuthenticationStatement>`.

SAML does not specify that only one type of authentication is possible; many standard techniques are supported, including user name/password, Kerberos, Secure Remote Password (SRP), hardware tokens, certificate-based client authentication (SSL),

XML digital signature, and a number of PKI systems, such as X.509, PGP, Simple PKI (SPKI), and XKMS.

A principal's privileges are specified using a set of attributes in an Attribute assertion, which is then evaluated by a PDP with respect to specific requests for authorization. Attributes are specified in an `<AttributeStatement>` that contains elements specifying confirmation methods, attributes, subjects, and various identifiers.

Authorizations in SAML can be specified in such a way that they are compatible with most operating systems or platforms. For example, five basic permissions can be set on resources—read, write, execute, delete, and control—and these can be set generically using the URI `urn:oasis:names:tc:SAML:1.0: action:rwedc`. Alternatively, UNIX-style permissions can be set by using the URI `urn:oasis:names:tc:SAML:1.0:action:unix`. This method provides the ability to specify symbolic and octal permissions codes.

Implementations

A number of commercial applications now use SAML in production, including Entegrity's AssureAccess, Entrust's GetAccess portal, Netegrity's AffiliateMinder, Securant's RSA Cleartrust, Sun's iPlanet Directory Server with Access Management, Sun's ONE Network Identity, and Systinet's WASP Secure Identity. Several vendors have also developed SDKs to support development in the SAML area, including the Netegrity JSAML toolkit, and VeriSign's Trust Services Integration Kit (TSIK), which can be downloaded from `http:// www.xmltrustcenter.org/developer/verisign/tsik/faq.htm`, and which has a bulletin board at `http://www.xmltrustcenter.org/developer/verisign/tsik/ forum.htm`. TSIK provides a number of factory classes to generate the objects for performing requests and responses, and for processing assertions. The main classes include `SOAPAssertionProviderFactory`, `XMLAssertionGeneratorFactory`, `XMLRequestGeneratorFactory`, `XMLResponseGeneratorFactory`, and `XMLSecurityParameters`.

There is also a proposal to standardize Java support for SAML through Java Community Process (JCP) JSR 155 (Web Services Security Assertions). Further debate continues on this fundamental technology both within the SAML community and beyond. For example, given Microsoft's investment in existing single sign-on technology through Passport, they may not use SAML with their Web services. However, given that SAML can be used with WS-Security, many vendors may support its use in the future.

Sample Application

The sample request/response cycle shown here demonstrates the key features of SAML when implemented. A `<samlp: Request>` is sent by the client, and the server responds with a `<samlp: Response>`. The scenario involves a user (`Janedoe`) who wants to access resources within the `somebank.com SecurityDomain`. The `username` for the principal is contained within the `AttributeName`, whose namespace is equivalent to the `SecurityDomain`. The specific request is shown in the `AttributeQuery`.

```
<samlp: Request>
        <samlp: AttributeQuery>
                <saml: Subject>
                        <saml: NameIdentifier
SecurityDomain="somebank.com" Name="janedoe"/>
                </ saml: Subject>
                <saml: AttributeDesignator AttributeName="username"
AttributeNamespace="somebank.com">
                </ saml: AttributeDesignator>
        </ samlp: AttributeQuery>
</ samlp: Request>
```

After the Request is processed, the Response is generated; either the principal will be authenticated, or the request will be rejected. The following response shows user name and password authentication being used, as well as time restrictions being placed on the resource access for the principal:

```
<samlp: Response
MajorVersion="2"
MinorVersion="1"
RequestID="192.169.204.23.83766354"
InResponseTo="192.170.205.33.87365532"
StatusCode="Success">
        <saml: Assertion
MajorVersion="1"
MinorVersion="0"
AssertionID="192.170.205.33.87365532"
Issuer="somebank.com"
IssueInstant="2003-09-16T10:00:23Z">
                <saml: Conditions
NotBefore="2003-09-16T10:01:00Z"
NotAfter="2003-09-23T10:01:00Z" />
                <saml: AuthenticationStatement
AuthenticationMethod="Password"
AuthenticationInstant="2003-09-16T10:00:00Z">
                        <saml: Subject>
                                <saml: NameIdentifier
SecurityDomain="somebank.com"
Name="janedoe" />
                        </ saml: Subject>
                </ saml: AuthenticationStatement>
        </ saml: Assertion>
</ samlp: Response>
```

This sample application is very simple compared to what would actually be required for deployment in a production financial system. You should explore the many excellent examples provided in the WS-Security implementation from IBM or Microsoft.

Project

Take the GoldBroker application and implement an authentication system based on WS-Security and SAML tokens. Test whether the integration is successful across platforms; i.e., does an authentication service provided by Windows successfully authenticate J2EE clients? What problems do you encounter?

Summary

In this chapter, I have examined the security issues addressed in current Web services standards and how to implement them. Although two major standards for Web services security, WS-Security and SAML, exist today, rationalization may well be in the future. Because WS-Security is the basis of a standard that requires at least other standards to operate successfully, WS-Security's use in production environments may have limited applicability. But since security is a major nonfunctional requirement of enterprise applications and their integration, this will continue to be the most interesting area of development in Web services.

Given the differences between WS-Security and SAML, and that a uniform approach between all point-to-point trading partners will be required for end-to-end security, the security standards for Web services may not be ready for large-scale implementations, especially those being devised by and for financial institutions. Nevertheless, institutions can easily deploy a reasonable level of security over the Internet by using some existing technologies; SSL provides confidentiality of data transmission, as well as client and server authentication using client and server certificates.

CHAPTER 9

■■■

Quality of Service

For any serious enterprise applications in finance, quality of service must often be assured, whether through strategies for high availability, redundancy, reliability, or failover. In this chapter, I discuss how to specify quality of service levels for Web services, and how to implement this throughout the protocol stack. I also explore a number of strategies for achieving different quality of service levels.

Theory and Practice

In the previous chapters, I have examined how to implement basic Web services—from the underlying data representation, through various transport protocols for messaging. Regardless of the actual combination of these bindings and services that compose a Web service application, we need to view the entire set of services and applications that underlie the delivery and deployment of the application as a "system." If the system as a whole is stable and operational, the application will be delivered successfully. If one or more components fail, however, the system may fail entirely or partially—in the latter case, possibly cascading errors leading to data loss or corruption without system administrators or service developers being aware.

The NASA controllers of the Apollo missions had a saying: Failure is not an option. This saying holds very true for supporting Web services in the finance industry, where enterprise systems are supporting billions of dollars of transactions. Since these transactions are not conducted on paper—even settlement is completely electronic—loss of data is catastrophic.

To prevent data loss and system failure, it is necessary to be constantly aware of the system's *status*: the set of states, operationalized as specific system variables, that collectively determine whether the system is "up" (system success) or "down" (system failure). Any system has many possible variables to measure, but you need to monitor only those with potential to cause system failure, either alone or in combination. For any specific system, determining the set of possible simple or interacting failure modes requires systematic testing, but I do discuss some generic scenarios in this chapter.

Some system variables are directly measurable, such as the hard disk capacity. If disk capacity is full, and you are running a relational database to store user state, perhaps through a J2EE stateful session bean, then running out of disk space is a critical fault. Monitoring the level of disk space in a system is one of the most basic but often overlooked system variables. However, from a status perspective, you don't need to just examine the raw figures; you want to know if disk status is OK, or whether it is at a warning, critical, or failed level—probably representing 95 percent, 99 percent, or 100 percent capacity, respectively. By determining a set of margins, alerts can be issued, and the problem can be rectified before the system fails.

In this chapter, I examine some strategies for supporting both stateless and stateful services, and develop a sample application for monitoring the status of one variable in a distributed system—the "heartbeat"—that determines whether a Web service client can connect to a server in an end-to-end sense. The heartbeat request should be sent on a regular basis, such as once every minute. If the heartbeat fails, a critical alert can be issued and the various status variables can be examined to determine the source of the fault.

System Status

The selection of system status variables for monitoring depends on the operating system and enterprise architecture used to deploy Web services. In a general sense, the following sections apply equally well to Microsoft Windows, UNIX, and Linux systems, but the specific commands and examples are targeted at Sun Microsystems' Solaris operating system.

CPU

CPU activity is often expressed as a percentage or fraction of total capacity. Since a multitasking operating system can process multiple jobs concurrently, it is possible for this percentage to exceed 100 percent of capacity, in which case processes are executed proportionally slower. If your server running a mission-critical authentication Web service for Internet banking was running with a load of 2.0 and it had only one CPU, then responses would be expected to be at least twice as slow compared to a load of 1.0. I say "at least" because of process and thread switching overhead incurred by executing multiple processes, depending on the current process priority. If one process must be executed, such as the authentication service, but another service like batch processing of contract notes for share trading could be performed at a lower priority, then the processes should be set with higher and lower priority correspondingly.

On Solaris, each individual user can reduce the process priority by using the `renice` command, but only the super-user can increase the priority of a process. Also, in a multiprocessor system, it is usually possible to use resource-management facilities to bind a process to execute on a specific CPU. For example, if a J2EE application server process was started with a process identifier of 168, and you wanted to bind it to CPU 0, then the following command could be used:

```
# pbind -b 0 168
```

Resource management also provides for policy-based allocation of CPU resources to specific applications and groups of users who execute them. On Solaris, these groups are known as sgroups. Imagine a scenario where you wanted to partition CPU resources between a J2EE application server (user java), an Oracle database (user oracle), and an MQSeries message queue (user jms). You can create an sgroup for each group of users that operate each application by using the limadm command.

```
# limadm set sgroup=java
# limadm set sgroup=oracle
# limadm set sgroup=jms
```

If you wanted to allocate 50 percent of the CPU capacity to the user java, 30 percent to the user oracle, and 20 percent to the user jms, the following limits would be set:

```
# limadm set cpu.shares=50 java
# limadm set cpu.shares=30 oracle
# limadm set cpu.shares=20 jms
```

Resource usage can be monitored according to the set limits by using the liminfo command.

```
# liminfo -c jms
Login name:     jms         Uid (Real,Eff):    1024 (-,-)
Sgroup (uid)    jms(1024)  Gid (Real,Eff):    10(-,-)

Shares:20        Myshares:       1
Share: 20 %      E-share:        0 %
Usage: 0         Accrued usage:  0

Mem usage:       0 B      Term usage:      0s
Mem limit:       0 B      Term accrue:     0s
Proc mem limit: 0 B       Term limit:      0s
Mem accrue:      0 B.s

Processes:       2        Current logins:  1
Process limit:   0
```

If not using explicit CPU sharing, it is still possible to obtain the whole of system resource usage by using the w command.

```
$ w
9:10pm     up 2:37,     3 users,   load average: 0.07, 0.09, 0.08
User       tty          login@     idle          JCPU PCPU what
root       console      6:34pm     2:36                     /usr/dt/bin/sdt_shell -c
root       pts/3        6:34pm     2:31            4    3   bash
pwatters   pts/4        6:41pm                         14   w
```

Here, the 1-minute, 5-minute, and 15-minute load averages are reported in the top right-hand corner of the display (0.07, 0.09, and 0.08, respectively). The load average output is combined with a list of users and processes, which is not relevant if you want a raw CPU load figure to trigger an alert. The easiest way to get the 1-minute system load is to write a small shell script to filter out irrelevant values. Here is an example script:

```
$ w | grep "load average" | awk 'BEGIN {FS = " "}{print $10}
' | awk 'BEGIN {FS = ","}{print $1}'
```

The output is then given as

```
0.07
```

This value could be passed to a heartbeat status monitor of the kind described in the case study I provide further on.

Memory

Running out of physical memory is a common enough occurrence, which is why virtual memory is often used. Although using virtual memory slows processing, it does save on physical memory costs, which, for enterprise systems, can be much more expensive than for a standard PC. One problem with virtual memory is that it is generally finite; memory blocks are read from RAM and written to a disk file of a certain predetermined size, such as 512MB. If your RAM requirements exceed this, then your applications will begin to fail. Thus, virtual memory monitoring is a commonly used system status metric.

Solaris provides the swap -l command to determine how much virtual memory is available and how much is being used.

```
$ swap -l
swapfile            dev     swaplo blocks   free
/dev/dsk/c0t0d0s1   136,9   16 1049312      1049168
```

Here, we can see that the virtual memory consisting of 1,049,312 512-byte blocks is hardly used, since there 1,049,168 blocks free. Just as with the w command, extraneous text surrounds the important figures of allocated and used virtual memory blocks, so you could use the following script statements to extract the appropriate values from swap -1 and assign them to the variables $allocated and $free:

```
set allocated=`swap -l | grep "/dev/dsk" | awk 'BEGIN {FS = " "}{print $4}'`
set free=`swap -l | grep "/dev/dsk" | awk 'BEGIN {FS = " "}{print $5}'`
```

You could then use $allocated and $free inside a script to calculate the percentage of free virtual memory, watching especially for 95, 99, or 100 percent usage (warning, critical, or failed levels). Again, an alert could be issued when usage exceeds these targets.

Storage

Imagine you are running a relational database server that stores client state. You know that if the database manager process fails, you can always rely on your log to regenerate the tables. But what if the file system on which the log was written were 100 percent full? You may well have to restore the database log from backups, potentially losing all data since the previous backup. This is just one example of what can happen when file systems are full. Many system services rely on temporary space in /tmp, for example, and will crash if they cannot write anything to /tmp. So, just like monitoring virtual memory and CPU activity, storage availability also needs to be monitored.

To monitor disk usage on Solaris, the df ("disk free") command is used.

```
# df -k
Filesystem          kbytes    used      avail     capacity  Mounted on
/dev/dsk/c0t0d0s0   2942926   1614084   1269984   56%       /
/devices            0         0         0         0%        /devices
/proc               0         0         0         0%        /proc
mnttab              0         0         0         0%        /etc/mnttab
fd                  0         0         0         0%        /dev/fd
swap                536104    56        536048    1%        /var/run
swap                536064    16        536048    1%        /tmp
/dev/dsk/c0t0d0s7   4809630   20095     4741439   1%        /export/home
```

Here, the amount of space available on each file system is shown in kilobytes. Normally, you would need to monitor the / and /tmp file systems in particular, and any database server partitions. To check the space specifically for the / file system, you would use the following command:

```
$ df -k | grep /dev/dsk/c0t0d0s0
/dev/dsk/c0t0d0s0    2942926 1614084 1269984    56%    /
```

Again, you can use UNIX pattern-matching tools to extract the relevant field showing the available capacity.

```
$ df -k | grep /dev/dsk/c0t0d0s0 | awk 'BEGIN {FS = " "}{print $4}'
1269984
```

The amount of free space could be used inside a script to calculate the percentage of free disk space, once again watching for 95, 99, or 100 percent usage to produce an alert when usage exceeds these targets.

Case Study

In this case study, we will develop a heartbeat system-monitoring application that determines the end-to-end connectivity status of a Web services client and server; that is, whether a client SOAP message sent via HTTP has reached a destination server, and whether an expected SOAP response from the server has been received. If the expected response is not received, then an alert can be issued on the client side, and the server administrators can be notified to examine their set of status variables for any problems. The heartbeat can also be used to return notifications to the client for specific error conditions on the server, even if network connectivity is guaranteed. For example, if a server needs to be rebooted, this can be reported back to the client, which can then cease sending real service requests until a heartbeat request receives a response from the server that the reboot is complete and the system is ready for servicing once again.

The system-monitoring application is developed in Visual Studio .NET, giving you the opportunity to observe an alternative to the primarily J2EE examples presented in previous chapters, and to observe the development and deployment process from start to finish.

First, you create a new ASP.NET Web Service from the File ➤ New Project menu of Visual Studio .NET, under the Visual C# tree of wizards (see Figure 9-1). We then specify the service's name and the host on which it will run: `http://localhost/HeartBeat`. The local system is used as both client and server in this example, but obviously in a real-world monitoring scenario, they would run on different machines.

Once the project has been created, a default service called Service1 is created, corresponding to the C# class `Service1.asmx.cs`. You can change this service name to something more descriptive if you like. Initially, you will be presented with the Design View in the IDE, but you need to switch to the code view to define your individual services and their corresponding `WebMethods`.

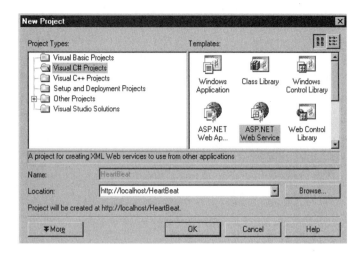

Figure 9-1. *Creating the HeartBeat project in Visual Studio .NET as an ASP.NET Web Service*

A skeleton class containing a `HelloWorld` WebMethod is created by default for you.

```csharp
using System;
using System.Collections;
using System.ComponentModel;
using System.Data;
using System.Diagnostics;
using System.Web;
using System.Web.Services;

namespace HeartBeat
{
    /// <summary>
    /// Summary description for Service1.
    /// </summary>
    public class Service1 : System.Web.Services.WebService
    {
        public Service1()
        {
            //CODEGEN: This call is required by the ASP.NET Web Services Designer
            InitializeComponent();
        }
```

```csharp
#region Component Designer generated code

//Required by the Web Services Designer
private IContainer components = null;

/// <summary>
/// Required method for Designer support - do not modify
/// the contents of this method with the code editor.
/// </summary>
private void InitializeComponent()
{
}

/// <summary>
/// Clean up any resources being used.
/// </summary>
protected override void Dispose( bool disposing )
{
    if(disposing && components != null)
    {
        components.Dispose();
    }
    base.Dispose(disposing);
}

#endregion

// WEB SERVICE EXAMPLE
// The HelloWorld() example service returns the string Hello World
// To build, uncomment the following lines then save and build the project
// To test this web service, press F5

//      [WebMethod]
//      public string HelloWorld()
//      {
//          return "Hello World";
//      }
    }
}
```

The service does not actually implement any methods at this point, because the HelloWorld method is commented out. So, to define the heartbeat method, insert a new WebMethod, declared as public, with an appropriate message that indicates if the SOAP message has been received by the server.

```
[WebMethod]
public string AreYouThere()
{
    return "I am here";
}
```

The IDE at this point is shown in Figure 9-2.

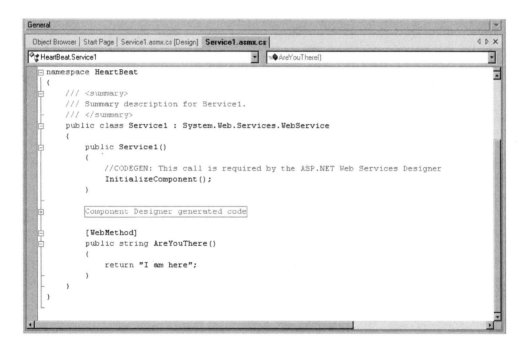

Figure 9-2. *Declaring the* AreYouThere *service in Visual Studio .NET as an ASP.NET Web Service*

When you press F5, the service code compiles, and you can execute and test the service by using a dynamically generated harness. When running the service as declared, you'll see the results shown in Figure 9-3. The Areyouthere operation is supported, but the harness notes that the default tempuri.org namespace is being used. Every Web service should have a unique namespace, as described in Chapter 3, so you should change the namespace to something unique before making it public.

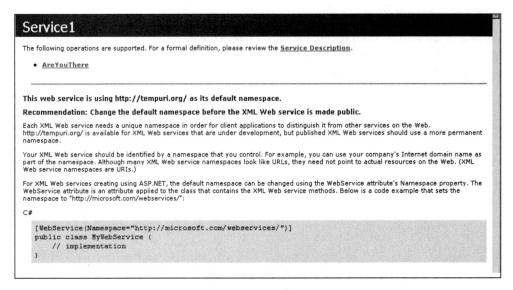

Figure 9-3. *Testing the* AreYouThere *service in Internet Explorer*

To make the namespace unique, simply modify the class declaration as follows, using the cassowary.net namespace:

```
[WebService(Namespace="http://cassowary.net/webservices/")]
    public class Service1 : System.Web.Services.WebService
    {
        public Service1()
        {
...
```

Now, the Service1 (http://localhost/HeartBeat/Service1.asmx) method AreYouThere is available for review through the browser (http://localhost/HeartBeat/Service1.asmx?op=AreYouThere). A sample SOAP request for the method would look like this.

```
POST /HeartBeat/Service1.asmx HTTP/1.1
Host: localhost
Content-Type: text/xml; charset=utf-8
Content-Length: length
SOAPAction: "http://cassowary.net/webservices/AreYouThere"

<?xml version="1.0" encoding="utf-8"?>
<soap:Envelope xmlns:xsi="http://www.w3.org/2001/XMLSchema-instance"
    xmlns:xsd=http://www.w3.org/2001/XMLSchema
    xmlns:soap="http://schemas.xmlsoap.org/soap/envelope/">
```

```
    <soap:Body>
        <AreYouThere xmlns="http://cassowary.net/webservices/" />
    </soap:Body>
</soap:Envelope>
```

The corresponding SOAP response would then look like this.

```
HTTP/1.1 200 OK
Content-Type: text/xml; charset=utf-8
Content-Length: length

<?xml version="1.0" encoding="utf-8"?>
<soap:Envelope xmlns:xsi="http://www.w3.org/2001/XMLSchema-instance"
    xmlns:xsd=http://www.w3.org/2001/XMLSchema
    xmlns:soap="http://schemas.xmlsoap.org/soap/envelope/">
    <soap:Body>
        <AreYouThereResponse xmlns="http://cassowary.net/webservices/">
          <AreYouThereResult>string</AreYouThereResult>
        </AreYouThereResponse>
    </soap:Body>
</soap:Envelope>
```

If invoked through HTTP GET, the request would look like this.

```
GET /HeartBeat/Service1.asmx/AreYouThere? HTTP/1.1
Host: localhost
```

The corresponding HTTP GET response would then look like this.

```
HTTP/1.1 200 OK
Content-Type: text/xml; charset=utf-8
Content-Length: length

<?xml version="1.0" encoding="utf-8"?>
<string xmlns="http://cassowary.net/webservices/">string</string>
```

ASP.NET supports HTTP GET, HTTP POST, and SOAP. However, Web services use SOAP, and SOAP uses HTTP POST for the body part to be encoded. Therefore, using HTTP GET is rare for a Web service, but just serves to demonstrate the request/response cycle in this example. The WSDL for the service is shown here.

```
  <?xml version="1.0" encoding="utf-8" ?>
  <definitions xmlns:http=http://schemas.xmlsoap.org/wsdl/http/
  xmlns:soap=http://schemas.xmlsoap.org/wsdl/soap/
```

```
xmlns:s=http://www.w3.org/2001/XMLSchema
xmlns:s0=http://cassowary.net/webservices/
xmlns:soapenc=http://schemas.xmlsoap.org/soap/encoding/
xmlns:tm=http://microsoft.com/wsdl/mime/textMatching/
xmlns:mime=http://schemas.xmlsoap.org/wsdl/mime/
targetNamespace=http://cassowary.net/webservices/
xmlns="http://schemas.xmlsoap.org/wsdl/">
<types>
<s:schema elementFormDefault="qualified"
  targetNamespace="http://cassowary.net/webservices/">
<s:element name="AreYouThere">
<s:complexType />
</s:element>
<s:element name="AreYouThereResponse">
<s:complexType>
<s:sequence>
<s:element minOccurs="0" maxOccurs="1" name="AreYouThereResult"
  type="s:string" />
</s:sequence>
</s:complexType>
</s:element>
<s:element name="string" nillable="true" type="s:string" />
</s:schema>
</types>
<message name="AreYouThereSoapIn">
<part name="parameters" element="s0:AreYouThere" />
</message>
<message name="AreYouThereSoapOut">
<part name="parameters" element="s0:AreYouThereResponse" />
</message>
<message name="AreYouThereHttpGetIn" />
<message name="AreYouThereHttpGetOut">
<part name="Body" element="s0:string" />
</message>
<message name="AreYouThereHttpPostIn" />
<message name="AreYouThereHttpPostOut">
<part name="Body" element="s0:string" />
</message>
<portType name="Service1Soap">
<operation name="AreYouThere">
<input message="s0:AreYouThereSoapIn" />
<output message="s0:AreYouThereSoapOut" />
```

```
</operation>
</portType>
<portType name="Service1HttpGet">
<operation name="AreYouThere">
<input message="s0:AreYouThereHttpGetIn" />
<output message="s0:AreYouThereHttpGetOut" />
</operation>
</portType>
<portType name="Service1HttpPost">
<operation name="AreYouThere">
<input message="s0:AreYouThereHttpPostIn" />
<output message="s0:AreYouThereHttpPostOut" />
</operation>
</portType>
<binding name="Service1Soap" type="s0:Service1Soap">
<soap:binding transport="http://schemas.xmlsoap.org/soap/http"
  style="document" />
<operation name="AreYouThere">
<soap:operation soapAction=
"http://cassowary.net/webservices/AreYouThere" style="document" />
<input>
<soap:body use="literal" />
</input>
<output>
<soap:body use="literal" />
</output>
</operation>
</binding>
<binding name="Service1HttpGet" type="s0:Service1HttpGet">
<http:binding verb="GET" />
<operation name="AreYouThere">
<http:operation location="/AreYouThere" />
<input>
<http:urlEncoded />
</input>
<output>
<mime:mimeXml part="Body" />
</output>
</operation>
</binding>
<binding name="Service1HttpPost" type="s0:Service1HttpPost">
<http:binding verb="POST" />
```

```
<operation name="AreYouThere">
<http:operation location="/AreYouThere" />
<input>
<mime:content type="application/x-www-form-urlencoded" />
</input>
<output>
<mime:mimeXml part="Body" />
</output>
</operation>
</binding>
<service name="Service1">
<port name="Service1Soap" binding="s0:Service1Soap">
<soap:address location="http://localhost/HeartBeat/Service1.asmx" />
</port>
<port name="Service1HttpGet" binding="s0:Service1HttpGet">
<http:address location="http://localhost/HeartBeat/Service1.asmx" />
</port>
<port name="Service1HttpPost" binding="s0:Service1HttpPost">
<http:address location="http://localhost/HeartBeat/Service1.asmx" />
</port>
</service>
</definitions>
```

To test the service in the browser, the URL http://localhost/HeartBeat/
Service1.asmx/AreYouThere? can be invoked, giving the following response:

```
<?xml version="1.0" encoding="utf-8" ?>
  <string xmlns="http://cassowary.net/webservices/">I am here</string>
```

The basic heartbeat is a very useful gross status monitoring tool, but it can be
extended in a number of useful ways. For example, the return message could indicate
whether a server system failure had occurred; a series of methods could be called in a
predetermined sequence, so that if one method reported a failure, then those called previously would already have been verified. The example code shows a nested if-then-else
decision structure checking the system states in order of priority and returning the
appropriate message.

```
[WebMethod]
public string AreYouThere()
{
    if (!checkFreeDiskSpace())
    {
```

```
        return "Not enough disk space";
    }else if (!checkSystemLoad())
    {
        return "System load too high";
    }
    else if (!checkSystemSecurity())
    {
        return "System is compromised";
    }
    else
        return "I am here";
}
```

Each status method would then be declared private in the HeartBeat class or prefer-ably, from a design perspective, in a separate class.

A more sophisticated approach involves creating a series of threads that could be spawned to check the status of each system variable then return a set of error messages once the threads are synchronized. A sample XML schema for this service is shown here.

```
<?xml version="1.0" encoding="UTF-8"?>
<xsd:schema xmlns:xsd=http://www.w3.org/2001/XMLSchema
  xmlns:binding=http://www.breezefactor.com/2002/xml-schema-binding
  <xsd:element name="SystemStatusResponse">
      <xsd:complexType>
          <xsd:sequence>
              <xsd:element name="System" type="xsd:string" />
              <xsd:element name="Membership">
                  <xsd:complexType>
                      <xsd:sequence>
                          <xsd:element name="ErrorMessages"
                                  type="xsd:string" minOccurs="0"
                                  maxOccurs="unbounded" />
                      </xsd:sequence>
                  </xsd:complexType>
              </xsd:element>
          </xsd:sequence>
      </xsd:complexType>
  </xsd:element>
</xsd:schema>
```

For each System, an unbounded list of ErrorMessages is defined, which could be an empty set if the system status is OK. It would also be possible to collect the raw status variable values and return them to the client, and let the client decide whether to proceed with invoking a service. In the following example, you create a new service called GetSystemStatus, which returns an array of strings comprising the CPU load average, percentage of free virtual memory, and the percentage of free hard disk space. Returning this information would allow the client to determine which server to invoke a service from.

```
[WebMethod]
public string[] GetSystemStatus()
{
    string[] status=new string[3];
    status.SetValue(getCPULoadAverage(),0);
    status.SetValue(getFreeVirtualMemory(),1);
    status.SetValue(getFreeDiskSpace(),2);
    return status;
}

private string getCPULoadAverage()
{
    // Implement method
    return "25%";
}

private string getFreeVirtualMemory()
{
    // Implement method
    return "68%";
}

private string getFreeDiskSpace()
{
    // Implement method
    return "28%";
}
```

Here, I have left the implementation of the system status methods as an exercise for you, with the actual code varying depending on the system being used. Now, the Service1 (http://localhost/HeartBeat/Service1.asmx) method GetSystemStatus is available for review through the browser (http://localhost/HeartBeat/Service1.asmx?op=GetSystemStatus). A sample SOAP request for the method would look like this.

```
POST /HeartBeat/Service1.asmx HTTP/1.1
Host: localhost
Content-Type: text/xml; charset=utf-8
```

```
Content-Length: length
SOAPAction: "http://cassowary.net/webservices/GetSystemStatus"

<?xml version="1.0" encoding="utf-8"?>
<soap:Envelope xmlns:xsi="http://www.w3.org/2001/XMLSchema-instance"
  xmlns:xsd=http://www.w3.org/2001/XMLSchema
  xmlns:soap="http://schemas.xmlsoap.org/soap/envelope/">
  <soap:Body>
    <GetSystemStatus xmlns="http://cassowary.net/webservices/" />
  </soap:Body>
</soap:Envelope>
```

The corresponding SOAP response would then look like this.

```
HTTP/1.1 200 OK
Content-Type: text/xml; charset=utf-8
Content-Length: length

<?xml version="1.0" encoding="utf-8"?>
<soap:Envelope xmlns:xsi=http://www.w3.org/2001/XMLSchema-instance
  xmlns:xsd=http://www.w3.org/2001/XMLSchema
    xmlns:soap="http://schemas.xmlsoap.org/soap/envelope/">
  <soap:Body>
    <GetSystemStatusResponse xmlns="http://cassowary.net/webservices/">
      <GetSystemStatusResult>
        <string>string</string>
        <string>string</string>
      </GetSystemStatusResult>
    </GetSystemStatusResponse>
  </soap:Body>
</soap:Envelope>
```

If invoked through HTTP GET, the request would look like this.

```
GET /HeartBeat/Service1.asmx/GetSystemStatus? HTTP/1.1
Host: localhost
HTTP/1.1 200 OK
Content-Type: text/xml; charset=utf-8
Content-Length: length
```

The corresponding HTTP GET response would then look like this.

```
<?xml version="1.0" encoding="utf-8"?>
```

```
<ArrayOfString xmlns="http://cassowary.net/webservices/">
  <string>string</string>
  <string>string</string>
</ArrayOfString>
```

The WSDL for the service is shown here.

```
<?xml version="1.0" encoding="utf-8" ?>
<definitions xmlns:http="http://schemas.xmlsoap.org/wsdl/http/"
 xmlns:soap=http://schemas.xmlsoap.org/wsdl/soap/
 xmlns:s=http://www.w3.org/2001/XMLSchema
 xmlns:s0=http://cassowary.net/webservices/
 xmlns:soapenc=http://schemas.xmlsoap.org/soap/encoding/
 xmlns:tm=http://microsoft.com/wsdl/mime/textMatching/
 xmlns:mime=http://schemas.xmlsoap.org/wsdl/mime/
 targetNamespace=http://cassowary.net/webservices/
 xmlns="http://schemas.xmlsoap.org/wsdl/">
<types>
<s:schema elementFormDefault="qualified"
 targetNamespace="http://cassowary.net/webservices/">
<s:element name="GetSystemStatus">
 <s:complexType />
 </s:element>
<s:element name="GetSystemStatusResponse">
<s:complexType>
<s:sequence>
 <s:element minOccurs="0" maxOccurs="1" name="GetSystemStatusResult"
   type="s0:ArrayOfString" />
 </s:sequence>
 </s:complexType>
 </s:element>
<s:complexType name="ArrayOfString">
<s:sequence>
 <s:element minOccurs="0" maxOccurs="unbounded" name="string"
   nillable="true" type="s:string" />
 </s:sequence>
 </s:complexType>
 <s:element name="ArrayOfString" nillable="true" type="s0:ArrayOfString" />
 </s:schema>
 </types>
<message name="GetSystemStatusSoapIn">
 <part name="parameters" element="s0:GetSystemStatus" />
```

```
  </message>
<message name="GetSystemStatusSoapOut">
 <part name="parameters" element="s0:GetSystemStatusResponse" />
 </message>
 <message name="GetSystemStatusHttpGetIn" />
<message name="GetSystemStatusHttpGetOut">
 <part name="Body" element="s0:ArrayOfString" />
 </message>
 <message name="GetSystemStatusHttpPostIn" />
<message name="GetSystemStatusHttpPostOut">
 <part name="Body" element="s0:ArrayOfString" />
 </message>
<portType name="Service1Soap">
<operation name="GetSystemStatus">
 <input message="s0:GetSystemStatusSoapIn" />
 <output message="s0:GetSystemStatusSoapOut" />
 </operation>
 </portType>
<portType name="Service1HttpGet">
<operation name="GetSystemStatus">
 <input message="s0:GetSystemStatusHttpGetIn" />
 <output message="s0:GetSystemStatusHttpGetOut" />
 </operation>
 </portType>
<portType name="Service1HttpPost">
<operation name="GetSystemStatus">
 <input message="s0:GetSystemStatusHttpPostIn" />
 <output message="s0:GetSystemStatusHttpPostOut" />
 </operation>
 </portType>
<binding name="Service1Soap" type="s0:Service1Soap">
 <soap:binding transport="http://schemas.xmlsoap.org/soap/http"
   style="document" />
<operation name="GetSystemStatus">
 <soap:operation soapAction=
   "http://cassowary.net/webservices/GetSystemStatus" style="document" />
<input>
 <soap:body use="literal" />
 </input>
<output>
 <soap:body use="literal" />
 </output>
```

```
  </operation>
  </binding>
<binding name="Service1HttpGet" type="s0:Service1HttpGet">
  <http:binding verb="GET" />
<operation name="GetSystemStatus">
  <http:operation location="/GetSystemStatus" />
<input>
  <http:urlEncoded />
  </input>
<output>
  <mime:mimeXml part="Body" />
  </output>
  </operation>
  </binding>
<binding name="Service1HttpPost" type="s0:Service1HttpPost">
  <http:binding verb="POST" />
<operation name="GetSystemStatus">
  <http:operation location="/GetSystemStatus" />
<input>
  <mime:content type="application/x-www-form-urlencoded" />
  </input>
<output>
  <mime:mimeXml part="Body" />
  </output>
  </operation>
  </binding>
<service name="Service1">
<port name="Service1Soap" binding="s0:Service1Soap">
  <soap:address location="http://localhost/HeartBeat/Service1.asmx" />
  </port>
<port name="Service1HttpGet" binding="s0:Service1HttpGet">
  <http:address location="http://localhost/HeartBeat/Service1.asmx" />
  </port>
<port name="Service1HttpPost" binding="s0:Service1HttpPost">
  <http:address location="http://localhost/HeartBeat/Service1.asmx" />
  </port>
  </service>
  </definitions>
```

To test the service in the browser, the URL http://localhost/HeartBeat/
Service1.asmx/GetSystemStatus? can be invoked, giving the following response:

```
<?xml version="1.0" encoding="utf-8" ?>
<ArrayOfString xmlns:xsd="http://www.w3.org/2001/XMLSchema"
  xmlns:xsi=http://www.w3.org/2001/XMLSchema-instance
  xmlns="http://cassowary.net/webservices/">
  <string>25%</string>
  <string>68%</string>
  <string>28%</string>
</ArrayOfString>
```

Project

Define a new class called SystemStatus that has private methods checkVirtualMemory, checkDiskUsage, and any other status variables you want to monitor on the server side. Implement these methods and rewrite the AreYouThere method by using a set of threads to concurrently invoke each variable. You should then return a set of status strings to the client using AreYouThere if an error condition has been detected.

Summary

In this chapter, I have discussed the nonfunctional requirements of Web services that are mission-critical, and where full or partial failures can lead to data loss or corruption. This is typical of applications in the finance industry, where logical data loss can lead to physical money loss. The question of Web service reliability and related nonfunctional requirements such as security, performance, reliability, integrity, accessibility, and availability have not been sufficiently addressed in the standards developed so far; it is necessary to build your own services to monitor system state and quality of service, especially in a heterogeneous environment.

While the heartbeat exercise is a useful first step to ensuring quality of service, I don't mean to imply that just because the client and server can communicate, sufficient quality of service has been established. Because Web services are very verbose and are likely to be considerably more CPU-intensive than other technologies such as EDI, further strategies will be required to ensure adequate if not optimal performance with Web services. Even though we might have a heartbeat, we have no assurance of reliability that messages are not lost or corrupted.

CHAPTER 10

■■■

Conversations, Workflows, and Transactions

As discussed in Chapter 1, a large number of immature Web services protocols build upon the basic but mature protocols that have been the major focus of this book. Yet the immaturity of these services does not make them any less important; if Web services are to move beyond single invocations of simple stateless services to providing solutions to real business problems, these advanced protocols must be further enhanced and refined, especially where state management is concerned. Development tools must also be created to make these protocols easy to work. In this chapter, I focus on exploring the linking together of multiple services, potentially from different service providers, and the issues that this raises, including operation ordering and failure semantics. Once multiple operations are invoked, then these will typically require transactional properties, such as atomicity, meaning that all operations must either succeed or fail together, as a whole. Finally, I examine how to implement business workflows that consist of these transactions, and how Web services can assist with solving interoperability problems between different workflow products.

Conversations

As you've seen in previous chapters, WSDL is responsible for describing the static aspects of a Web service interface. Although a single WSDL file can contain many different interfaces to different services, nowhere does it actually specify the order of operations required to link these services to perform a complete set of related operations. For example, to buy stocks through an on-line brokering service, you would have services for authentication, quotes, orders, settlement, etc. It may seem obvious to you and I, as developers, the order in which these services can be invoked. However, WSDL does not specify the ordering, so you can literally invoke any service you like, irrespective of what the correct ordering should be, according to the business process. For example, before placing an order, a client's cash management account may need to be checked for sufficient cleared funds to proceed with the order (otherwise, abort the order and alert the customer). Omitting this step could have disastrous consequences, because clients could inadvertently overcommit themselves.

By not including ordering of operations in WSDL, the correct implementation of business logic is left solely in the hands of developers. This is not necessarily a bad thing for services deployed locally, but it does not enforce consistent usage of services by external clients, which raises trust questions. It also does not permit the automatic binding of clients to new services created later, meaning that all future changes to application behavior must be hand-coded. For example, if a stock ordering service moved from manual to straight-through processing, it would be inefficient to require every client to change its WSDL. If the interface were self-describing, then the client would know whether a new service was compatible and appropriate.

While the (very difficult) self-description problem is being tackled as part of the Semantic Web effort, where ontologies of just about everything are being created to allow for more accurate service discovery, the Web Services Conversation Language (WSCL) has been created to describe the pattern of ordering required to perform complex service invocations. This allows us to move beyond simple, single-service invocations to complex sets of applications based on very dynamic patterns of invocation, which lets us implement very different types of use cases, including alternative flows, special requirements, preconditions, and postconditions. WS-SecureConversation from Microsoft also covers important conversational issues.

In previous chapters, we've examined simple Web services based on a stateless single-client request, single-client response model. But in reality, most services need to be far more complicated than this to be useful. Complex services will almost certainly consist of multiple request-response cycles, known as conversations, where the ordering of operations is critical. Because the success of any operation depends on the completion status of all previous operations, failure semantics must be very well defined when services are logically linked. A WSDL file can specify multiple services, but the interface requires no explicit ordering of operation invocation.

Linking Services

Let's examine a simple example from the operations required to emulate a cash balance request from an ATM acting as a client to a central bank server.

```
<s:element name="ValidateCard">
  <s:complexType>
    <s:sequence>
      <s:element minOccurs="0" maxOccurs="1" name="cardNumber" type="s:string" />
    </s:sequence>
    </s:complexType>
</s:element>
```

```
  <s:element name="VerifyPIN">
    <s:complexType>
      <s:sequence>
        <s:element minOccurs="0" maxOccurs="1" name="PIN" type="s:string" />
      </s:sequence>
    </s:complexType>
</s:element>
<s:element name="ReturnBalance">
  <s:complexType />
</s:element>
```

Here, we have three operations—ValidateCard, VerifyPIN, and ReturnBalance—that compose the set of operations required to return a bank balance, as shown in Figure 10-1. ValidateCard would run a check on the number supplied to determine its validity. If the card were valid, then the VerifyPIN operation would check that the PIN supplied matched that which was stored in the central computer, completing the authentication sequence. If the card was invalid or the PIN was incorrect, then the operation concerned would need to be repeated before the balance was returned using the ReturnBalance method. You could implement this set of service in C# like this:

```
[WebMethod]
public string ValidateCard(String cardNumber)
{
    …
}


[WebMethod]
public string VerifyPIN(String PIN)
{
    …
}


[WebMethod]
public string ReturnBalance()
{
    …
}
```

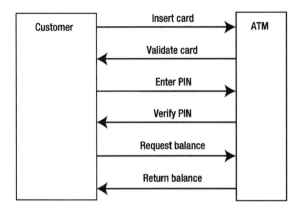

Figure 10-1. *ATM example*

While the sequence of operations seems obvious to us (identification, authentication, business method implementation), nothing in the WSDL prevents ReturnBalance being invoked without a positive response from the ValidateCard and VerifyPIN methods. We could invoke one method, two methods, or three methods, all in different sequences, using this interface, and a service consumer would have to guess which combination to use, and it would have no way to verify that it had actually guessed the right combination.

If the developer of the client is trustworthy, you might argue that this is not necessary. However, since the client's identity is not known at design or run time, it is necessary to ensure sequence integrity—especially in the finance industry.

Structuring Conversations

This is where WSCL comes into play. If a Web services conversation always follows a certain structure, this can be specified using WSCL, since we can't assume that a computer will understand the service context at all unless it has access to a Semantic Web of some kind. Given the large variation in potential responses to a service invocation, and the many possible error conditions, the computer can't always anticipate what service a particular client requires. Thus, the ad hoc organization of simple services needs to be tightened based on the anticipated semantics of conversations. Not every error condition can be anticipated either, so the framework for specifying sequences must be flexible.

As mentioned previously, for internal service provision scenarios, the coding of sequence logic can be left to the development team. But external integration of Web services in the B2B sphere is its great driver, so most significant B2B business processes involve conversations based on controlled, multiphase service invocations. In these interactions, which may involve multiple participants, each actor must know when to send requests, process requests, and send responses, and in what format these should be. These interactions must be transparent to ensure that both humans and systems can manage and discover services, respectively.

Stateless Web services are now available everywhere on the Web. They are easy to implement and support, but are not particularly useful for B2B e-commerce or for banking. Conversations, and the applications that use them, require sophisticated state management that is fault-tolerant and transparent. Returning to the ATM example, once a card has been identified and authenticated, there is no business need to reauthenticate when performing other privileged operations, such as withdrawing or depositing cash. Yet as you saw in Chapter 8, protocols for providing single sign-on are difficult to implement because of state management.

As B2B interactions grow more complex, the number of possible n-way interactions increases with the number of available services and the number of participants. WSCL was developed to manage this complexity, and to provide discoverable characterizations of B2B service interactions. WSCL allows temporal aspects of service consumption to be defined and honored, with the orchestration of operations assured with respect to the set of acceptable messages and message types. Different message types can be defined to only be eligible to participate in certain kinds of interactions, and the conditions under which each part of a conversation is understood to have succeeded or failed can also be specified.

WSCL and WSDL

WSCL is certainly not a replacement for WSDL, but it does provide significant enhancements. While WSDL is still responsible for the formatting of messages and associated operations, WSCL provides a state machine for managing conversations. Rather than requiring hand coding, WSCL is supported by a number of toolkits that allow some of the sequencing issues to be handled automatically. For example, Java toolkits use exceptions to handle alternative flows. In the ATM example, you would simply throw an InvalidCardException() if the card was not valid, or an IncorrectPINException() if the PIN was incorrect. The client would then be required to honor these exceptions and would be prevented from proceeding to the returnBalance() method. The following examples show how this might be done:

```
public string ValidateCard(String cardNumber) throws InvalidCardException
{
            if (cardNumber.length<16)
                throw new InvalidCardException();
}

public string VerifyPIN(String PIN) throws IncorrectPINException
{
```

```
        //Retrieve PIN from database for cardNumber retrieved from cookie
        if (!_PIN.equalsIgnoreCase(PIN))
            throw new IncorrectPINException();
}
```

Using these exceptions, the toolkit-generated proxy from the WSCL specification can handle the errors in a standard way at each stage of the process. Other toolkits and languages (such as C#) use equivalent constructs to manage the conversational flow.

WSCL Patterns

WSCL conversations consist of a number of conversational patterns for message exchange similar to those defined for WSDL. All are based on request-only or request-response cycles initiated by either the client or the server. The conversations are then built up from a combination of these message exchange patterns. The patterns are

- Send: The server sends a request-only message to the client. No response is expected or able to be processed.

- Receive: The client sends a request-only message to the server. Again, no response is expected or able to be processed.

- SendReceive: The server sends a request message to the client and waits for a response.

- ReceiveSend: The client sends a request message to the server and waits for a response.

Like One Way, Notification, etc., from WSDL, these patterns fit most business interaction types for client-server systems with 1-1 interactions. Note that there is no extension of the concepts to 1-many (publish/subscribe) or many-many (peer-to-peer) systems, although this is an active area of research.

Returning to the ATM example, you can see that the three operations defined—ValidateCard, VerifyPIN, and ReturnBalance—are all ReceiveSend operations, because the client sends a request, and waits for the server to issue a response. However, there may be other operations where a Receive alone would be appropriate. For example, when a user's card is removed from the ATM, only a Receive message is required to terminate the session, because the session is terminated at the client side by the ATM hardware. The server is not required to send a response.

Similarly, there may be situations where the server may issue a SendReceive message after the completion of a ReceiveSend. For example, when a customer checks an account balance, the ATM sends the request to the server, and the response is displayed on the screen. However, a second message typically follows, asking if the customer wishes to use another operation, such as cash withdrawal. A Send might be appropriate to send to the client when the server is down for maintenance, and a second Send might be sent when the connection is open once again for transactions.

Data Structures

So far, we've focused on simple data structures to pass balances and other data items between the client and server. However, in a real Web service, these are more likely to be objects or other complex structures with multiple fields and lists of items, as per XML Schema. Indeed, many such standard structures are being developed in the finance industry to permit the open exchange of data items between financial institutions. This type of activity is occurring across many vertical industries, but as yet, few standards are being utilized.

As an example of how such data structures might be developed, it's useful to look at the real-world objects that they model. For example, all credit cards have a standard set of elements, such as the card number, customer name, expiry date, issuing bank, credit limit, and so on. These can be encapsulated into a simple XML schema as follows:

```
<?xml version="1.0" encoding="UTF-8"?>
<xsd:schema xmlns:xsd="http://www.w3.org/2001/XMLSchema">
    <xsd:element name="CreditCard">
      <xsd:complexType>
        <xsd:sequence>
          <xsd:element name="customerName" type="xsd:string" />
          <xsd:element name="cardNumber" type="xsd:int" />
          <xsd:element name="expiryDate" type="xsd:string" />
          <xsd:element name="issuingBank" type="xsd:string" />
          <xsd:element name="creditLimit" type="xsd:double" />
        </xsd:sequence>
      </xsd:complexType>
    </xsd:element>
</xsd:schema>
```

As the data structures we developed become more complex, so does the exception handling required to manage conversational flow. For example, for the CreditCard schema, exceptions would have to be defined for valid customer names, valid card number of digits, valid range of digits, valid checksum, valid expiry date, valid bank issuing code, and so on. There may also be further interactions between the validations of each element, such as cross-checking the issuing bank code with the card number. With respect to WSCL, the question is whether these interactions, for large schema, make exception handling at this level impractical, or just an essential but time-consuming aspect of creating Web services.

For each of the schemas we create, we need to define the XML schemas for the specific interactions associated with the data elements. For the credit card example, we need to associate the `CreditCard` schema with each of the operations that use it, as shown here.

```xml
<?xml version="1.0" encoding="UTF-8"?>
  <xs:schema targetNamespace=http://somebank.com/ValidateCard
xmlns:xs=http://www.w3.org/2001/XMLSchema
    elementFormDefault="qualified"
    attributeFormDefault="unqualified">
    <xs:element name="ValidateCard" type="c:CreditCard"/>
</xsd:schema>
```

```xml
<?xml version="1.0" encoding="UTF-8"?>
  <xs:schema targetNamespace=http://somebank.com/VerifyPIN
xmlns:xs=http://www.w3.org/2001/XMLSchema
    elementFormDefault="qualified"
    attributeFormDefault="unqualified">
    <xs:element name="ValidateCard" type="c:CreditCard"/>
</xsd:schema>
```

```xml
<?xml version="1.0" encoding="UTF-8"?>
  <xs:schema targetNamespace=http://somebank.com/ReturnBalance
xmlns:xs=http://www.w3.org/2001/XMLSchema
    elementFormDefault="qualified"
    attributeFormDefault="unqualified">
    <xs:element name="ValidateCard" type="c:CreditCard"/>
</xsd:schema>
```

Grouping Interactions

A conversation is created when the interactions between multiple message exchanges are grouped together. The procedure for creating a conversation in this way involves working out all the exchanges potentially required to complete all the specified tasks, and then to specify a set of message exchanges that compose valid conversations. The interactions are defined by an `Interaction` element, with its associated `interactionType`; and Send, Receive, SendReceive, ReceiveSend are all supported. Every element is identified by a unique identifier and has an `hrefSchema` to specify the schema it is associated with (i.e., its public, not private, URI).

All message exchanges are associated with one of two embedded document elements, known as `InboundXMLDocument` and `OutboundXMLDocument`, and each is associated with each request-only WSCL message exchange type.

- `Receive`: `InboundXMLDocument` only

- `Send`: `OutboundXMLDocument` only

For the Request-Response message exchange types, the arrangement is more complicated.

- `ReceiveSend`: one `InboundXMLDocument` plus at least one and possibly multiple `OutboundXMLDocuments`

- `SendReceive`: one `OutboundXMLDocument` plus at least one and possibly multiple `InboundXMLDocuments`

As an example, consider the interaction for the `ValidateCard` operation. On the client side, the `Request` operation might be characterized as "Send credit card number 4587665433214453 for validation." On the server side, either an `isValid` or `isNotValid` status will be returned. The following `Interaction` shows how to tie together the `InboundXMLDocuments` and `OutboundXMLDocuments`:

```
<Interaction interactionType="ReceiveSend" id="ValidateCard">
    <InboundXMLDocument hrefSchema="http://somebank.net/SendCardNumberMsg"
    id="SendCardNumber"/>
    <OutboundXMLDocument hrefSchema="http://somebank.net/CardValidateMsg"
    id="CardValidateMsg"/>
</Interaction>
```

Transitions

After all messages and interactions for the conversation have been defined, the ordering of operations must be defined. This process often is initiated by identifying the conversational starting and ending points. All relevant constraints and error conditions must be identified during the conversation definition process, ensuring that the sequence proceeds from one interaction to the next only if all of the relevant conditions have been met, and if there have been no exceptions. One problem here is that all error conditions must be anticipated in advance, and in practice this may be impossible, given the number of higher-order interactions between elements that may cause an exception.

Developing a regression test suite covering all boundary conditions is a tedious but necessary activity during the design of the system.

An example transition condition is shown here.

```
<Transition>
  <SourceInteraction href="ValidateCard"/>
  <DestinationInteraction href="VerifyPIN"/>
  <SourceInteractionCondition href="CardIsValid"/>
</Transition>
```

Here, we specify that VerifyPIN must always be preceded by a successful ValidateCard interaction, subject to the condition that the CardIsValid. A SourceInteraction always precedes its DestinationInteraction in the <Transition>, and SourceInteractionCondition refers to an OutboundXMLDocument of the SourceInteraction when it is a ReceiveSend interaction and vice-versa with SendReceive. The SourceInteractionCondition is required when a SourceInteraction allows multiple document exchanges and the document affects subsequent interactions.

The conversation can proceed only if the referenced message was the last document sent. In the ATM example, if the CardIsValid condition is met from the ValidateCard interaction, then the VerifyPIN operation can proceed; otherwise, it cannot. It's worthwhile noting that a <Transition> can have multiple SourceInteractions associated with it, allowing for complex business logic.

Conversations

The final link in the chain is the <Conversation>, which specifies the starting and ending points of a conversation, and all of the transitions therein. It uses interactions, transactions, and messages to specify the dialogue sequences at each level. The following example shows how all of the elements in the ATM example can be bound together to define the conversational sequence:

```
<Conversation name="ATM" version="1"
  xmlns="http://www.w3.org/2002/02/wscl10"
  initialInteraction="ValidateCard"    finalInteraction="ReturnBalance"
  targetNamespace="http://somebank.net/conversations/ATM"
  hrefSchema="http://somebank.net/schema_files/ATM.wscl"
  description="ATM Banking">
  <ConversationInteractions>
...
  </ConversationInteractions>
  <ConversationTransitions>
...
  </ConversationTransitions>
</Conversation>
```

Business Process Execution

Businesses currently have many operations supported by information systems. Yet the management of these operations and their dependencies is often ad hoc, unless a workflow system is used to automate business process management. The goal of using such systems is to engineer business process implementation in such a way that processes can be readily modified without requiring extensive code rewrites. For example, if the government requires a new tax to be collected at point-of-sale, then this is simply a new step in an existing process that needs to be defined. If a workflow tool is used, then the change is easy; if not, then all occurrences of references to the point-of-sale module may need to be manually updated.

Virtual Enterprises

While workflow systems have important applications within a single business, they deliver on their promise of making integration easy when they are used to integrate multiple businesses. Quite often, different services offered by a number of cooperating organizations is described as a *virtual enterprise*. The *virtual* can refer to the e-commerce aspect of the enterprise, since virtual means "created, simulated, or carried on by means of a computer or computer network."[1] Virtual enterprises can be formed to service B2C markets, but more commonly are created to provide aggregated services in the B2B space.

Many existing systems allow the physical interchange of business data. Workflow systems can be used with these systems to automate and virtualize business process execution—moving from paper forms to electronic forms being a simple example. Particularly in the area of supply chain management, a high level of automation and inter-business integration can achieve great economies of scale and cost savings. By being a virtual business, companies can sell to a global rather than a local audience. By integrating many services from different companies into a single marketplace or portal, significant reductions in staff training, credential management, and hardware investment can be achieved.

Forming a virtual enterprise is very common in manufacturing, where specialized goods manufacturers combine forces to produce a composite product. Traditionally, all work was done in-house to reduce the risk of partner failure, but high capital costs and the push toward specialization and high quality in most vertical industries has changed this. Suppliers and manufacturers now form virtual enterprises, and they require the integration of internal and external business processes to achieve this. The benefits of virtual enterprises include rapid time to market and a focus on what each business does best. The disadvantages include the coordination of process execution between organizations, especially when synchronization of operations executed in parallel is required. The key issue to be solved is how to create a flexible infrastructure.

---

1. *The American Heritage Dictionary of the English Language*, 4th ed., s.v. "virtual."

For example, car manufacturers rely on a large number of component manufacturers for each vehicle built. But the notion of binding together services in real time to form a virtual enterprise based solely on the exchange of information is relatively new. Particularly in financial markets, where data often represents intangibles anyway, building composite services that are conversational in nature is exciting—especially where multiple participants are involved, and when they can be bound together in real time. By providing services over the Internet through a virtual enterprise, the term *virtual* (relating to the Middle English root *virtuall*, meaning "to be effective")[2] is the most accurate description. Workflow systems can be used to bind together these services, with the underlying integration being performed by Web services.

Web Services and Virtual Enterprises

Why is it advantageous to "Web service-enable" workflow systems? To demonstrate its importance, let's look at an example of a financial transaction that is primarily based on the exchange of paper documents. In the purchase and sale of real estate, a large number of actors must exchange information before the sale can be completed. The actors can include the following:

- The vendor

- The buyer

- The vendor's bank

- The buyer's bank

- Real estate agents acting for the vendor

- Real estate agents acting for the buyer

- Lawyers acting for the vendor

- Lawyers acting for the buyer

- Lawyers acting for the vendor's bank

- Lawyers acting for the buyer's bank

- The government

- Pest and building inspectors

---

2. *The American Heritage Dictionary of the English Language*, 4th ed., s.v. "virtual."

- Insurance companies

- Valuers

This list is not exclusive, and it changes with local custom. What remains the same is that each actor needs information, and time is usually of the essence. The process usually follows a workflow like this:

- Vendor places a house for sale
    - Buyer decides to purchase the house
    - Buyer makes an offer
        - Vendor accepts the offer or
        - Vendor rejects the offer
            - Buyer submits a second offer
                - Vendor accepts the offer or
                - Vendor rejects the offer

- Contracts are exchanged
    - Buyer pays deposit
    - Buyer organizes finance
        - Bank obtains valuation
        - If valuation less than price offered
            - Bank rejects mortgage application
            - Buyer applies to the next bank
    - Buyer gets pest and building reports

- Five-day cooling-off period
    - Buyer can rescind contract if unhappy or
    - Buyer proceeds

- Prior to settlement (six weeks later)

    ° Title searches are performed

    ° Mortgages are prepared for registration (buyer) and deregistration (vendor)

    ° Mortgage tranches must be organized for new mortgage

- Settlement

    ° Seller paid by buyer's bank

    ° Seller's bank deposits check

    ° Bank receives fees

    ° Solicitors receive fees

    ° Title changed

With each of these nested activities, numerous exceptions must be handled, and a workflow system provides many facilities for specifying alternative behaviors in such situations. A workflow language like Business Process Execution Language (BPEL) could be used to represent this concrete process.

Automation

Today, most of these activities are undertaken by pen and paper, which is why settlement takes around six weeks. Obviously, vendors are keen to get their money earlier, and buyers want to move into their house more quickly. If the system was automated, and all of the different parties could exchange information and invoke each other's services as required, the processing time could be substantially reduced. The only bottlenecks would be the physical inspections of the house for pests. Computers can do almost every other operation, including title searches and loan approvals.

The major characteristic of a workflow like the real estate purchase scenario is a linear progression through a series of well-defined stages, where an exception at one stage may abort the transaction or require manual rectification. There are dependencies between many tasks, and their sequencing is critical. For example, the title to the house should only be changed concurrently with the transfer or mortgage funds. Often, serialized execution is required, so we need to engineer the underlying business processes to be as parallel as possible. For efficiency, we must be able to outsource key tasks while maintaining the internal consistency of each actor's business processes.

What is the biggest stumbling block to allowing this type of automation? You guessed it: the mechanics of integrating so many different services from so many different actors into a single system. While workflow systems can provide the coordination of many different operations, the sad fact is that most workflow systems are not interoperable. That's where Web services become important, through the specification of business process execution languages, as discussed next.

Workflow Management Systems

To build an automated real estate virtual enterprise, developers would need to be able to implement flexible and agile internal business processes, and be provided with a consistent view of internal and external interactions. When working with representations of external processes, they should be as easy to work with as if all services were local. The business analyst should have a comprehensive perspective of all interactions, including external interactions.

Workflow management systems provide exactly this functionality. They contain tools for process specification and process management and make it easy to change the form or function of existing processes. They can be implemented using any reliable distributed computing system. Workflow management systems have existed for some time, but have not been highly successful in building new virtual enterprises. Failures have been largely caused by the inability to handle exceptions interoperably between platforms, and by the inability to scale-up problems for inter-enterprise tasks. The question is, will XML Web services provide a successful framework for enabling workflow interoperability?

Without a workflow tool, all interactions between services must be built and maintained manually. The developer must hard code all interactions and exceptions. Once written, we can expect that the code will execute reliably for the scenarios envisaged at design time. However, because business processes change frequently, the resulting implementation would be inflexible and prone to error. With each change, a regression test would need to be performed for the entire system, which would be time consuming and slow.

Workflow management systems allow the high-level design of business processes without lots of manual coding for each change. Workflows are logical representations of business processes that accurately represent physical processes, and are based on a generalization of matrix management philosophy, since tasks are matched to resources that are then matched to their implementing IT systems. A workflow may involve hundreds and thousands of tasks and resources. All current workflow management systems use their own internal (often proprietary) representation of data in the workflow, just like current messaging systems and formats.

XML Web Services are currently being touted as the basis for new standards of workflow interoperability. This view sees external workflows being seamlessly integrated with internal systems—but how realistic is this goal? BPEL is currently the main contender for a standard to capture workflow activities and external interactions in XML.

Existing stateless WSDL interfaces contain message-correlating features to emulate state management, just like WSCL does for conversation management. BPEL is not the only proposed standard for choreographing Web services: Business Process Modeling Language (BPML), Web Services Choreography Interface (WSCI), Web Services Flow Language (WSFL), and Microsoft XLang are all competing, although XLang and WSFL combined to form the current BPEL specification. As noted earlier, it is also possible to use WSCL to correlate messages and conversations for one-one interactions, and rather than creating more and more standards, it may be more fruitful to generalize this approach to the many-many interactions required for virtual enterprises.

Like WSCL, BPEL is based on a stack designed to capture interactions between partners and services; XML message properties form the base horizontal layer, and all layers are linked by a vertical state-management system. These layers include message correlation, above which sit scopes (with structured and basic embedded activities) and then partners (with service links and references). Scopes comprise activities that represent the building blocks of workflows, and partners are associated with service providers and consumers. Like WSCL, the various stages of the workflow can be tracked by using message correlation, which can extend to multiple parties and activities. Within stages, activities are composed into workflows and implemented using a workflow engine. BPEL-supported engines are available from vendors like Collaxa, Microsoft, and IBM.

BPEL has a number of fundamental activity types, which are classified as either structured or basic. Basic activities are responsible for fundamental processes like exception handling and state management, while structured activities deal with actual flows and their dependencies. Communication activities are responsible for sending and receiving messages between Web services and different instances of workflow processes. There are also specific exception-handling activities, allowing for compensator's post-transactional commit, and miscellaneous activities for copying data, etc.

Further discussion of BPEL is beyond the scope of this book (it could take an entire book to describe in any detail), but the development of interoperability standards for workflow systems is an ongoing area of activity necessary for the realization of service-providing virtual enterprises in finance.

Transactions

Transactions are the basis for reliable computing in enterprise systems, whether in finance or other vertical industries. Transactions ensure data integrity to a very high degree, because they allow related operations to be bundled atomically; if one operation fails, even if it is the last of a long sequence, then all operations in that sequence are rolled back as if the transaction had never begun. This allows information systems and databases to preserve the consistency of data and its logical mapping onto the physical world.

Returning to the ATM example, imagine if Arwen and Bounty are sisters who share a joint bank account. They have a $100 balance. After studying computer science, they realize that a race condition exists because one physical account can be accessed by two users simultaneously. Since ATMs operate on asynchronous messaging, they know that if they both withdraw $100 at the same time, then both will be issued with a $100 bill, even though there is only $100 in the account. Transactions do not protect against this kind of fraud, although the -$100 balance would certainly be reconciled with the account holders in due course.

Transactions are more useful in the following situation: Arwen decides to transfer $100 to her mother's bank account as a birthday gift. Halfway through the transfer, after the bank has withdrawn the money from the account but has yet to transfer it, Arwen hits the cancel button. With a transactional system, the $100 is returned to Arwen's account. Without a transaction atomically protecting the set of operations, Arwen would be down $100, Arwen's mom would have nothing, and the bank would have $100 extra.

There are many excellent database textbooks that explain the core ACID transaction properties, so I assume that you are familiar with them. You may also be aware of distributed transaction processing systems, like CICS and Tuxedo, where protocols like two-phase commit (2PC) have been created to ensure that distributed transactions maintain the same set of core properties as transactions executed locally. This is not always possible. For example, once a transaction has been committed, it can't be rolled back. Instead, a compensating action is initiated. For example, if Arwen decided she wanted her $100 back after it was committed to her mom's account, she could request the bank to initiate a second, compensating transaction to return the money to her account. For a system within a single bank, this is relatively simple, but could you rely on an external bank to honor a request to compensate a committed distributed transaction?

Other problems arise when extending transactions into the sphere of distributed computing. Transactions rely on locking database items of all entities involved in the transactions, which, depending on the granularity level, may include rows, pages, or tables. Given the problems associated with latency in distributed systems, is it wise to allow an external partner to lock records in your database, especially if the locking is done over the Internet? Not only does locking present a potential denial-of-service entry point, but it also presents scalability problems, particularly if a high transaction isolation level is chosen.

None of these technical issues removes the need for transactional systems to support real business process implementations. Therefore, the designers of transactional protocols that operate using Web services, like the OASIS Business Transaction Protocol (BTP), have decided that it is necessary to relax some of the cornerstone properties of transactions in this environment, to ensure that they are secure and scalable. For example, consistency can never be guaranteed, because external data/service opacity/control is lacking, and the focus has moved to accepting that transaction outcomes will be consistent, and that subsets of Web services will be consistent, rather than insisting on end-to-end consistency. On the other hand, atomicity is always preserved, since this is the most basic property of a transaction and must be preserved at all costs. As long as transactional outcomes are consistent, in a distributed system we have to accept that there may be run-time inconsistencies along the way.

Recall that locking usually provides isolation levels. However, as mentioned earlier, since Web service consumers are unknown at run time and are potentially untrusted, we can't allow these users to directly lock local database tables. This could lead to denial of service and unacceptable delays in processing concurrent requests, resulting in exceptions and timeouts of other legitimate operations. Thus, isolation levels may not be a realistic property to aspire to in transactional Web services. However, durability is quite necessary, since recoverability is critical to the integrity of the system. This could be provided by the equivalent of a distributed transaction coordinator or similar. At present, there are no system-level guarantees of recoverability in Web services.

The OASIS BTP is a protocol for the coordination of loosely coupled but transactional systems. It retains many properties of distributed 2PC systems and features many of the relaxed ACID properties discussed previously. BTP is restricted in the sense that it only deals with how messages should be exchanged to enable transactional interactions and how the senders and recipients of those messages should behave. It is quite general, so no specific architecture or general implementation is available (but several vendors do provide toolkits). However, BTP does provide a useful starting point for considering how to structure transactional Web service interactions in the future. For example, it introduces two new transactional types, atoms and cohesion, that work in two phases, but do not provide 2PC. In BTP, the party coordinating the transactions doesn't have complete control over the interactions between participants, who are free to specify the criteria under which they join and leave a transaction. Since there is no central point of authority or trust, or assumptions made about failure semantics or back-end infrastructures, is BTP currently useless for real business systems? Perhaps, but it does provide some useful activities, such as ensuring successful message transfers, and assuring consistent outcomes, even if transactional consistency cannot be guaranteed in loosely coupled systems. Participants using the same atom see the same outcome all the time, while cohesion allows participant subsets to be included while others can be excluded.

Summary

OASIS BTP's dynamic focus on the formation of temporary alliances created and disbanded in real time strongly resembles the character of the virtual enterprises of services discussed earlier. While the technology infrastructure in these areas is the least mature of any Web services standard, real business systems could be further automated today if these standards do mature with time. There are also emerging standards for advanced Web services protocols such as Interoperability, Reliable Messaging, Context, and Business Integration (Collaboration/Choreography) that are beyond the scope of this book, but which are nonetheless significant. Web services Choreography is more recent than

WSCL (http://www.w3.org/TR/2004/WD-ws-chor-model-20040324/). A good description of workflow issues and BPEL4WS appears at http://www-106.ibm.com/developerworks/library/ws-bpel/. Other useful specifications such as WS-Transaction (http://www-106.ibm.com/developerworks/webservices/library/ws-transpec/) and WS-Coordination (http://www-106.ibm.com/developerworks/webservices/library/ws-autobp/) provide different perspectives on these important issues.

Index

forums.apress.com

JOIN THE APRESS FORUMS AND BE PART OF OUR COMMUNITY. You'll find discussions that cover topics of interest to IT professionals, programmers, and enthusiasts just like you. If you post a query to one of our forums, you can expect that some of the best minds in the business—especially Apress authors, who all write with *The Expert's Voice™*—will chime in to help you. Why not aim to become one of our most valuable participants (MVPs) and win cool stuff? Here's a sampling of what you'll find:

DATABASES
Data drives everything.

Share information, exchange ideas, and discuss any database programming or administration issues.

PROGRAMMING/BUSINESS
Unfortunately, it is.

Talk about the Apress line of books that cover software methodology, best practices, and how programmers interact with the "suits."

INTERNET TECHNOLOGIES AND NETWORKING
Try living without plumbing (and eventually IPv6).

Talk about networking topics including protocols, design, administration, wireless, wired, storage, backup, certifications, trends, and new technologies.

WEB DEVELOPMENT/DESIGN
Ugly doesn't cut it anymore, and CGI is absurd.

Help is in sight for your site. Find design solutions for your projects and get ideas for building an interactive Web site.

JAVA
We've come a long way from the old Oak tree.

Hang out and discuss Java in whatever flavor you choose: J2SE, J2EE, J2ME, Jakarta, and so on.

SECURITY
Lots of bad guys out there—the good guys need help.

Discuss computer and network security issues here. Just don't let anyone else know the answers!

MAC OS X
All about the Zen of OS X.

OS X is both the present and the future for Mac apps. Make suggestions, offer up ideas, or boast about your new hardware.

TECHNOLOGY IN ACTION
Cool things. Fun things.

It's after hours. It's time to play. Whether you're into LEGO® MINDSTORMS™ or turning an old PC into a DVR, this is where technology turns into fun.

OPEN SOURCE
Source code is good; understanding (open) source is better.

Discuss open source technologies and related topics such as PHP, MySQL, Linux, Perl, Apache, Python, and more.

WINDOWS
No defenestration here.

Ask questions about all aspects of Windows programming, get help on Microsoft technologies covered in Apress books, or provide feedback on any Apress Windows book.

HOW TO PARTICIPATE:
Go to the Apress Forums site at **http://forums.apress.com/**.
Click the New User link.